**The Housing Design Han**

# THE HOUSING DESIGN HANDBOOK

## A guide to good practice

**David Levitt**

Levitt Bernstein

Routledge
Taylor & Francis Group

LONDON AND NEW YORK

First published 2010 by Routledge
2 Park Square, Milton Park, Abingdon, Oxon,
OX14 4RN

Simultaneously published in the USA and
Canada by Routledge
270 Madison Avenue, New York, NY10016

Routledge is an imprint of the Taylor &
Francis Group, an informa business

© 2010 David Levitt

Designed by Claudia Schenk
Drawings by Laura Weafer
Edited by Tom Neville

Printed and bound by Replika Press Pvt Ltd,
Sonipat, India

British Library Cataloguing in Publication
Data
A catalogue record for this book is available
from the British Library
Library of Congress Cataloging-in-
Publication Data
A catalogue record for this book has been
requested

ISBN10 0-415-49150-9 (pbk)

ISBN13 978-0-415-49150-1 (pbk)

**Picture credits**
The author and publisher gratefully
acknowledge the following individuals
and institutions for giving permission to
reproduce illustrations. Every effort has been
made to contact copyright holders, but if any
errors have been made we would be happy
to correct them in a later printing.

Tim Crocker: pages 18, 19, 33, 35 (top right,
bottom centre and right), 36, 37, 38, 47
(top), 51 (top, right centre), 53, 55, 57, 64,
65 (centre left, right), 67, 69, 71 (bottom), 81
(top), 99 (top), 105, 109, 111, 112, 113, 114,
115, 117 (bottom left and right),119, 122 (top),
123, 137 (top left), 138, 139, 143, 145, 150,
200, 201, 206, 207, 209, 211 (bottom), 233,
235, 259 (top, left), 263 (bottom)
David Churchill: page 135
Peter Cook: pages 13 (bottom right), 25
(bottom right), 31 (top, left, bottom right), 101,
103 (centre right)
John Davies: page 65 (top)
Peter Durant: pages 9 (bottom), 98 (top), 181
Richard Einzig – Arcaid: page 177
Envac: pages 269 (bottom), 270, 271
Dennis Gilbert: pages 9 (centre left), 162
David Grandorge: page 65 (bottom left)
Richard Hanson: page 103 (left)
Hawkins\Brown: pages 221 (top), 223
HHP: page 272
HHP/Bill Bolton: page 273
Hufton and Crow: pages 185 (bottom left),
197, 199, 249, 251
Roger Holdsworth: pages 167, 169
Katsuhisa Kida: pages 257, 259 (right)
David Levitt: pages 4, 5, 13 (top), 17, 25
(bottom centre), 70, 88, 96, 99 (centre and
bottom centre), 126, 137 (right), 149 (bottom
right), 155, 230, 236
Benedict Luxmore: pages 255, 257
John MacLean: page 159 (top and bottom
right)
Metropolitan Workshop: pages 39, 72
Killian O'Sullivan: page 125
Peter Barber Architects: page 176
Pollard Thomas Edwards: pages 8. 159
(bottom left)
PRP: page 269 (top)
Rolf Disch SolarArchitektur: pages 238, 243,
246, 247
Tom Scott: pages 31 (centre), 228
Galit Seligmann: pages 25 (top), 47 (bottom),
51 (bottom left)

Joanna Shaw: pages 253, 255
ShedKM: page 256 (bottom left)
Morley von Sternberg: pages 7, 9 (top), 11,
13 (centre left), 15, 35 (top and bottom left),
71 (top), 98 (bottom), 110, 131, 133 (top and
centre),147, 149 (all except bottom right),
187, 189, 261, 263 (top three)
Edmund Sumner: page 117 (top)
Sylvie Turner: page 229
Charlotte Wood: pages 210, 211 (top)
Nick Wood: pages 23, 25 (centre left), 29
www.ruralzed.com: pages 213, 214, 215

Other images Levitt Bernstein Associates

# Contents

# Foreword

In this book, David Levitt does what all good
architects should do. He takes a lifetime of
experience in housing, selects the best work
of Levitt Bernstein and others in the same
field, and distils all this accumulated wisdom
into a book that students and architects and
those both commissioning and regulating
housing will find invaluable.

David is concerned not only with the
practicalities of designing housing of all
types, in all kinds of different environments
from the urban to the rural, but also with
social, economic and sustainability issues.
Presented in a clear, logical fashion that
combines historical retrospective with an
up-to-the-minute knowledge of the rules,
regulations and attitudes that inform housing
design, this book demonstrates the value
of good architecture in this most vital of all
building types. It is a thoughtful, generous
and essential guide.

**Hugh Pearman**
Architecture critic, *The Sunday Times*
Editor, *RIBA Journal*

The book contains a number of references
to Regulations, Codes and Standards
applicable to Housing Design. The
references were current at the time of going
to press.

Where Regulations, Codes or Standards have
changed or been updated since publication,
the latest versions are listed on the web page:
**www.levittbernstein.co.uk/
housingdesignhandbook_updates**

# Introduction

'If only I had known then what I know now.' How many times have we all wished for the benefit of hindsight in the design and commissioning of new buildings – as in so much else?

*The Housing Design Handbook* is a design primer. It does not tell you how to be a creative designer but it will help to unravel the complexities of housing design. In essence the creative skills involved in the design of good housing are much the same as those involved in the design of anything else, and there is no substitute for them. Architects feed their creativity as they gain experience until they build an intuitive base, a kind of platform from which to develop their own innovations.

Housing is the most significant built form in the urban landscape and its success in achieving a sense of place is one of the bedrocks of social continuity. As a primer, this book is intended to build up a firm foundation of practical knowledge, as an aid not only to architects but to everyone involved in commissioning architects, placing on record accumulated knowledge about the practicalities of design and construction. It does not attempt to address any of the categories of special-needs housing, particularly the needs of the elderly or people with any kind of physical disability beyond the provisions of Lifetime Homes. Neither does it attempt to tackle the implications of climate change for the existing housing stock. These major subjects all need constant detailed study and are worthy of separate publications altogether.

The book is divided into three parts: built form, social issues and technical issues. Included in each chapter is a range of case studies used to illustrate the way that different topics in the design of housing have been approached, and with what degree of success. The examples interleave the work of Levitt Bernstein with that of many other UK and European practitioners to illustrate good practice.

As an aid for the future, the case studies deal with schemes spanning from the 1980s up to current practice, including several not completed at the time of writing. The book also uses examples from a variety of different sources, and revisits examples of the past 40 years to see whether the ideas that lay behind their designs have proved sustainable in practice, and what fundamental changes are needed if the objectives for environmentally sustainable housing, as well as the challenges posed by increased densities, are to be met.

With only two exceptions there are no examples in this book from the heroic post-war period of UK and European housing. This is partly because the best-known of them have been well-documented already and partly because they represent a 'top-down' period of architecture, while this book is devoted to a 'bottom-up' approach. The best-known works of the period from 1945 to 1968 (when the collapse of Ronan Point effectively put an end to the construction of large-panel system-built tower blocks), hugely influenced by Le Corbusier and the Brutalist movement, put out an enormous number of ideas, many of which are still only partly digested by the public at large. Much of the housing built during this period fuelled a healthy dialogue between all the leading architects of the day, but this passed completely over the heads of the people it was built for – mostly tenants of local authorities. That dialogue, part of the feverish post-war architectural debate about every building type that continues to this day, largely overlooked the domestic sensitivities that are so crucial to successful housing and which this book attempts to address.

While some of the schemes that represent these ideas have not survived at all – James Stirling at Runcorn – or have been altered beyond recognition – Darbourne & Darke's Marquess Road – while others such as the Smithsons' Robin Hood Gardens are under constant threat, Neave Brown's Alexandra Road in Camden and Patrick Hodgkinson's Brunswick Centre in Bloomsbury are both listed, respected and influential. Without doubt many of these schemes and those by other UK architects such as Benson & Forsyth, and much of the early work in the New Towns, hugely influential among architects at the time, are now increasingly appreciated by some sections of the public as well. Architectural tastes outside the cities may still be inherently conservative, but the same can no longer be said of those whose choice is to embrace higher-density urban lifestyles. And whereas most experimentation in housing during the post-war period up to 1970 was apparently imposed on those who had no choice, it is now those who can afford to choose who are leading a change of taste and, in the process, carrying those who still have little or no choice along with them.

The second part of the book uses recent examples to explore why certain social groupings are more resistant to design innovation than others, and why there has been such an architectural breakthrough in market-led higher-density urban living while the volume housebuilders, providing essentially for families outside the urban areas, seem unable to capture the public imagination with well-designed, energy-efficient modern homes.

The final part looks at as many aspects of the 'S' word as broadly as possible. Sustainability, combating climate change, call it what you will, is too urgent to permit any more failed experiments in housing generating yet another round of wholesale demolition and replacement. This is the last chance to get the design fundamentals of new housing right. What is built now has to be sustainable in the broadest sense. True sustainability means getting the whole balanced package right, not just tacking on a list of technical wizardry to an otherwise outdated concept.

Unlike many other components of the built environment, housing cannot be completely recycled every few generations. Communities do not flourish in decaying neighbourhoods and complete rebuilding every 60 years or so is not affordable. What we build now has to adjust not only to climate change in all its aspects, including weathering, but to changes in building technology and housing need as well.

**Part 1_Built form_**A sense of place exists when residents have a permanent sense of belonging to somewhere of value. This value can be identified with a neighbourhood or even with a component of a neighbourhood that works and, most importantly, is esteemed by residents.

# Places that get better over time

A sense of place exists when residents have a permanent sense of belonging to somewhere of value. This value can be identified with a neighbourhood or even with a component of a neighbourhood that works and, most importantly, is esteemed by residents. If we accept that a sense of place has importance, obvious questions are: how large or small must a scheme be if it is to create a sense of place, what components or characteristics are essential, and what can new buildings contribute to an existing place, either to reinforce what is there already, or to provide the vital ingredient that cements together a neighbourhood for the first time?

Part of the answer is longevity. Subsidised new housing used to have an official design life of 60 years and refurbished housing a design life of 30 years. Around 1965, after the government-funded local-authority building spree of the early post-war years, many social-housing programmes switched from new-build to refurbishing nineteenth-century terraces. On the basis of funding for a 30-year life, by 1995 they would have been due for demolition, but of course they have not been demolished. Bits of them – roofs, windows, services, fragile internal components – need replacing, which is hardly surprising as the structures were already a century old when investment for a further 30 years of life took place. And the reason these nineteenth-century structures are still worth far more than their intrinsic value in bricks and mortar is that they form part of the backdrop to a square or a street that has itself acquired a sense of place almost beyond price.

Several schemes built from the 1950s to the 1980s exclusively as social housing can now safely be judged as successes or failures in place-making terms, while other more recent mixed-tenure examples can usefully be revisited although they have only been inhabited for a few years. Architects tend to build reputations on what they have achieved most recently, recording their latest built schemes for publication. However, in terms of creating a lasting sense of place there is much to be learned from a close and often painful scrutiny of what has been subjected to the test of time.
Not all cultures thrive on a desire for

continuity – much of the USA, Japan and now China seem to value innovation before rootedness – and it is not just age that can create the elusive feeling of permanence that is so highly valued. But longevity is important in creating stable communities and neighbourhoods. New places need to settle into the topography of an area, and the use of indigenous materials and planting help a scheme to appear rooted.

The well-documented failures, often ending in demolition, of large housing projects are uniquely confined to social housing, mostly put up by local authorities. The success of new private housing is usually measured by what happens to its market values relative to average local values once the initial gloss has worn off; but this is a difficult measure to use for social-housing schemes unless a widespread 'right to buy' makes market testing possible. Until the recent acceptance of modern, mostly flatted developments in the inner city, developers built what they knew they could sell and commissioned their designers accordingly. No such constraint applied to the designers of social housing and even the best talents in the post-war world sometimes used these programmes as experiments in architecture, urban design, construction and social engineering. Every flat and house would have been let, invariably to someone who had moved out of old and unsatisfactory accommodation. Even if it was in a form that was entirely strange, the new accommodation – with central heating, fitted kitchen and bathroom – must have seemed like heaven. But by the time these homes proved to have serious problems, their creators were far away and on to something else, or were riding it out, complaining that 'it wasn't their designs at fault; it was the people who lived in them'. So while the creators of private housing needed to satisfy their punters from the start, no such check was available to their public-sector equivalents; they could engage in bold experiments without market-testing their ideas on the communities in whose name they were working.

As well as tenure, location undeniably plays an important part in the success of any housing project, and if such schemes as

Resident members of Wick Village Tenant Management Cooperative outside the new homes for which they acted as client.

The Brunswick Centre, Bloomsbury, London. A stunning concept, never properly completed until a makeover, 35 years after completion, after which Patrick Hodgkinson's idea of a centre for Bloomsbury came to be appreciated for the first time.

# Places that get better over time

the Barbican in the City of London or the Brunswick Centre in the London University quarter, had found themselves in one of the less salubrious London suburbs they might both by now be candidates for the wrecker's ball. Interestingly, while other very similar projects have failed, several Modernist schemes in London have survived a period of intense unpopularity and are now highly valued by their residents simply because of the resources that have been poured into keeping them in good order.

The ability to capture the imagination of residents, though nebulous, can combine with other essential factors to make the long-term difference between success and failure. These factors can be defined as:
• creating a sense of enclosed external space, outside rooms balanced by buildings of the right height, scale, proportion and able to trap sunlight. Baroque architects studied the cross-sections of streets and squares to achieve this; the contemporary design of external spaces is often determined by more mundane issues of privacy distances, road widths and parking-bay sizes;
• designing routes from individual dwellings to the public realm that are secure and friendly and feel connected. Shared circulation is dealt with in detail elsewhere; here let us just note that the way entrances connect with outside spaces sets the tone for what can be expected inside and needs to have a positive impact;
• eliminating the dominance of cars where they share space with residents: speeds should be restricted to levels compatible with children playing;
• making sure that all outside spaces are useful and well overlooked. These areas are not specifically covered by what is generally known as 'defensible space', a term that tends to be applied more to the private than the public realm. However, providing a feeling of security is vital for their success;
• devising ways of encouraging street life, making people want to linger and to make connections with neighbours. Architects are notoriously over-ambitious when they plan for the creation of a critical mass of pedestrians in a space. Perspectives of unbuilt schemes invariably feature much larger numbers of people – adults using and children playing

– than are ever seen in the completed space;
• taking care over the design of lighting. The method of lighting is important quite apart from its role in providing security, and can contribute hugely to the night-time impact of a public space. Lighting building fronts is almost always effective but often leads to complaints about glare from occupants. Going beyond the basics of street lighting is not worth doing if lamps are difficult to replace, and may be impossible if the public realm is to be adopted by the local authority;
• choosing a palette of materials and components, including planting, that wears well and is easy to maintain. While it is common sense to avoid obviously vulnerable details, the temptation to produce 'vandal-proof' details should be resisted. Oversizing details in the hope that they will resist abuse often just poses a challenge to see if they can be destroyed. Trees are important components of the public realm but they should be semi-mature when planted, well protected and irrigated in their early years;
• devising an architectural style that has a broad appeal to its client group. This does not imply opting for some hopelessly unconvincing and derivative style, which will date as quickly as much of the Postmodernism of the 1980s. However striking the initial impact of a good design, it has also to be strong enough to allow for some of the crispness to wear off after a few years. A sense of place grows out of continuity and the ability of buildings to weather gracefully.

Apart from the built form itself, the ability to provide continuity is likely to be particularly evident in the quality of soft and hard landscape. Developers tend to plunder the landscape budget and to delegate responsibility for maintenance. Similarly, they seem unable to see the importance of keeping funding available to replace damaged brickwork, paving, metalwork, fencing, grass and trampled planting in the early years, the most important period in the life of a housing scheme. Whoever holds the freehold needs to be sure of the resources needed to demonstrate their on-going commitment, until the landscape matures and captures the imagination; a process that can take several decades.

A resident of Ferry Street, Isle of Dogs, enjoying her garden in August 2008, 25 years after first moving in.

A child's birthday party in Old Royal Free Square in Islington in August 2008. The project was completed in 1994.

# Old Royal Free Square, Islington, London N1

A collaboration between two housing associations and two firms of architects had the goal of creating nearly 200 flats and houses, all for affordable rent, on the site and from the shell of a redundant maternity hospital in the heart of fashionable Islington. How did such a thing come about when, at the height of a property boom towards the end of the 1980s, it was almost as difficult to provide affordable housing in high-value parts of London as it was 20 years later?

The London Borough of Islington had acquired the old Royal Free Hospital site some years earlier, but was unable to develop it due to the embargo on new council housing imposed by the Conservative government then in power. The council's solution was to transfer the whole property to two housing associations that would do the job instead, the amount of public subsidy involved being too much for one association on its own.

When the scheme was funded a much larger proportion of the total cost of housing for affordable rent was eligible for public subsidy than is the case now. At the same time, although the idea of mixing types of tenure in a project was unheard of, there was an interesting mixture of housing types for rent to tenants who included ex-psychiatric patients, young ex-offenders, nurses, the elderly and the disabled. Objections from neighbours to some of these categories would normally have been inevitable, but the authority chose to avoid this by the simple expedient of not telling anyone beforehand; local people had no subsequent cause for complaint.

The two architectural practices involved adopted three over-riding principles:
• to avoid wildly different architectural languages between the two halves;
• to avoid designs that looked obviously like social housing;
• to avoid cul-de-sacs, especially any that consisted entirely of social housing.

The existing hospital buildings more or less covered a site stretching between two busy streets, Upper Street to the east and Liverpool Road to the west. It was decided early on to make a public right of way straight through the central axis to encourage the worthy burghers of Barnsbury to use it as a shortcut on their way to and from the shops, and thus to reinforce the 'sense of place' and a feeling of 'connectedness'.

Using the best of the existing Grade 2-listed hospital buildings as a template, it was decided to form a central courtyard the size of a traditional London square, surrounded by a mixture of terraced three-bedroom family houses and one-bedroom flats in small blocks of not more than eight per common stairway. The architectural language aimed at removing any implication of social housing, picking up references to mews housing and the remaining hospital buildings themselves. Buildings in the central square are faced in second-hand London stock bricks and their details are deliberately not in contrast to those of the retained hospital buildings.

This is an area of very high property values. Every centimetre of space counts for something. It was not designing out of character when – to achieve the target density of around 80 dwellings per hectare, with 70 per cent car parking – all the ground-floor houses and flats were given small rear gardens, and the scale of the spaces between buildings was reduced. In the most extreme case this involved creating a street with houses on both sides that was just 7 metres across, one third of the normally accepted minimum (see Chapter 9). The contrast between small-scale mews-like spaces and the central square adds to the emphasis on the square itself.

This scheme – winner of Civic Trust and Europa Nostra awards – was popular with residents from the outset. Fifteen years on, Old Royal Free Square is triumphantly reaching a handsome maturity, and its public spaces more than justify the higher than average expenditure on materials and tree planting.

The central courtyard, which is the only open space available for children, was originally turfed but turned into a muddy patch after just a few months. Unusually, funds were found to replace the grass with AstroTurf, with the addition of much-needed play equipment.

**Architects** Levitt Bernstein Associates and Pollard Thomas Edwards Architects
**Developers** Family Mosaic Housing Association and Circle 33 Housing Trust
**Site area** 1.557 hectares
**Number of dwellings** 182
**Density** 117 dwellings/hectare
**Mix** 109 x 1B + 26 x 2B + 40 x 3B + 7 x 4B
**Affordable** 100 per cent
**Parking spaces per dwelling** 0.5
**Non-housing uses** psychiatric day centre

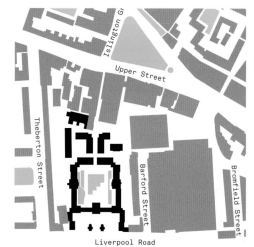

Site plan.

**Right** New terrace houses and flats on the site of the Old Royal Free Hospital in Islington, photographed in 2009 after the first 15 years of their life.

This underlines the importance of funding for adjustments once a building has had time to settle down.

In many ways this was planned as a 'home zone' (paved streets, without separate pavements, that can be shared by slow-moving traffic, pedestrians and children) before the concept was imported from Holland. The sense of intimacy in the small-scale streets and squares is clearly popular even if – as with the scheme in Ferry Street on the Isle of Dogs – insensitive maintenance has coarsened some of the details and the choice of buff facing brick for the mews houses would not be repeated.

Surprisingly, no community facilities were planned into the original scheme. Although at the time of completion there was much pressure to provide at least a modest hall and a site was located, funds have clearly not been forthcoming.

**Above** Aerial view.
**Right** Layout plan with existing buildings shaded. A combination of terrace houses and small blocks of flats, about a third fitted into existing buildings, form a new square with a public pedestrian right of way through the centre, linking two major streets. The scheme incorporates a psychiatric day centre and accommodates various groups of residents with special needs.

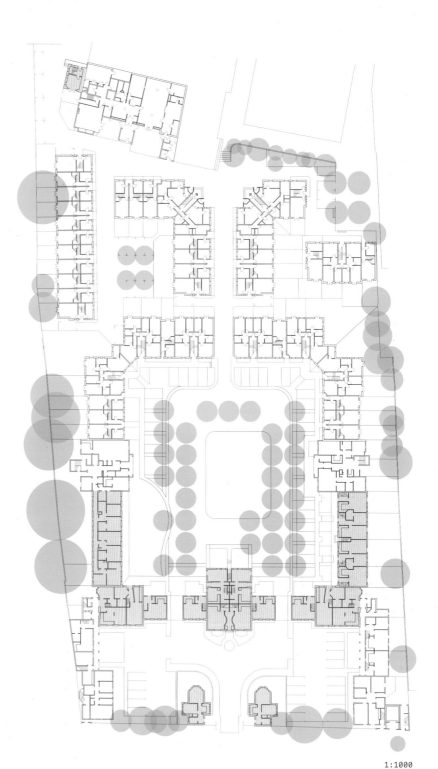

1:1000

**Top** A view of the main square in 2009.
**Above** Shared garden for sheltered-housing tenants (1992).
**Right** One of two symmetrical archways formed in the existing buildings to give access to the new square.

# Wick Village, Hackney Wick, London E9

Conceived around 1990 and completed in 1995, this is one of very few entirely resident-inspired regeneration schemes in London. The architecture may now look quaint, but its history explains a great deal about the design of new homes that is genuinely client-led.

The Trowbridge Estate was built by the GLC in the 1970s. It followed a familiar pattern with its 22-storey system-built tower blocks consisting entirely of one- and two-bedroom flats, and a collection of austere terraces, up to three storeys high, of larger homes occupying the rest of the site. These were arranged in a Radburn layout of completely separate vehicle and pedestrian access. While this principle, widely used throughout the 1970s, was intended to provide more usable green open space than traditional street-based housing, in practice it was a sophisticated concept that allowed the anti-social activities of a small minority, mostly teenagers, to disrupt the lives of almost everybody.

Within ten years of completion the first two precast-concrete-panel towers, suffering from an alarming collection of serious defects, were blown up. Even their ignominious departure was marked by a botched demolition that left one tower reduced to half its height protruding at a drunken angle from a pile of rubble.

Some years elapsed before a group of residents, their lives in the remaining towers now intolerable, made contact with a government-funded advice agency and approached Hackney Council demanding that they be moved out and rehoused. After much negotiation over whether there was sufficient space, the council agreed to make the site of the demolished towers available for new homes. That a site previously occupied by two 22-storey towers could be considered large enough to accommodate the residents of two similar towers in new homes of not more than three storeys was partially explained by the fact that not only were half the occupants of the remaining towers found to be there illegally, but also by the rediscovery that streets and squares are an efficient way to achieve higher densities than the GLC's Radburn layouts.

Funding was obtained through a central-government programme called Estate Action, which meant that the London Borough of Hackney could retain the freehold of the new scheme while passing day-to-day management over to a tenant management cooperative.

So it was that the tenants, ably assisted by their advisors, became the very real client. This determined much of the eventual outcome, influencing everything from the layout, the materials used, the external details and, most importantly, the bespoke features inside the new homes, some of which the tenants paid for themselves. Having actual future residents acting as a steering group is a formidable check on the architect at design stage, ensuring that what is built will fulfil the hopes and dreams of people who have never previously had the opportunity of choice. In this case it resulted in some of the more obvious features, such as Victorian lamp posts and porches with red-tiled roofs.

As always in a rough neighbourhood, security was of paramount importance and the distinction between private open space and communal areas was a strong determinant from the outset. The designers had to resist pressure on two main fronts, one from residents who, after their recent experiences, would have chosen a 'walled camp' with only one way in and one way out, and another from the police who thought that having the back gardens of houses running down to a 3-metre-high metal fence right along the river frontage was the only way to make sure that children would not fall in and drown. By choosing two linked courtyards with street access at either end and a pedestrian way through in the centre, and with all three access points protected by gates that could be closed if intruders became a problem, the scheme is neither a cul-de-sac nor a thoroughfare, and a compromise was thus achieved between permeability and security.

On the question of safety and the river frontage, the police met their match and had to compromise. Residents wanted a riverside walk with houses on one side that fronted on to the river. When it became clear that one of these houses was to be occupied by a

**Architect** Levitt Bernstein Associates
**Developer** Wick Village Tenant Management Cooperative
**Site area** 1.6 hectares
**Number of dwellings** 119
**Density** 75 dwellings/hectare (240 HR/hectare)
**Mix** 28 x 1B + 47 x 2B + 38 x 3B + 6 x 4B
**Affordable** 100 per cent
**Parking spaces per dwelling** 0.8

Site plan.

View from the River Lea. Terrace
houses and non-family flats in small
blocks — not more than eight to
ten flats in a block — replacing a
former tower-block estate in an area
of East London with a high crime
rate. Although the site is council-
owned, the existing residents formed
themselves into a tenant management
cooperative; this acted as client
throughout and determined what style
of building they wanted, including
the 'Victorian' lamp posts and red-
tiled porches.

tenant who had become a senior paramedic in the London Ambulance Service, and who maintained that there is less likelihood of a child falling in and drowning when the eyes and ears of 30 or so households are on watch, the police backed off.

Returning after ten years, it is apparent that the initial consultations have proved triumphantly fruitful. The public realm is tidy and the external environment is obviously appreciated, with no evidence of vandalism or graffiti. So much for resident control.

At Wick Village, as the 'estate' is still owned by the council, the residents kept the right to buy their homes, and a small number have. Inevitably, many of the new owner-occupiers are the same people who participated actively in the early development stages and this maintains continuity. Had there been no right to buy, these people would probably have bought elsewhere and moved away.

What can be seen suggests that tenant management is less effective at controlling the quality of landscape management, the pruning of trees, etc., and that ten years on there is little sign that the few broken fences and dilapidated children's play equipment are likely to be replaced any time soon.

Wick Village is largely home to tenants at the lower end of the economic scale. Even with a minority of owner-occupiers who have exercised their right to buy, service charges, whether levied through a TMC or a larger absentee landlord, are a major issue that needs to be addressed if the success of the scheme is to be maintained.

While tenant management does not mean that residents can be expected to roll up their sleeves and get down to physical work to make up for the shallowness of their pockets, it does clearly mean they feel more of a sense of ownership of their homes and the spaces roundabout. This is a fragile success story, much in need of encouragement.

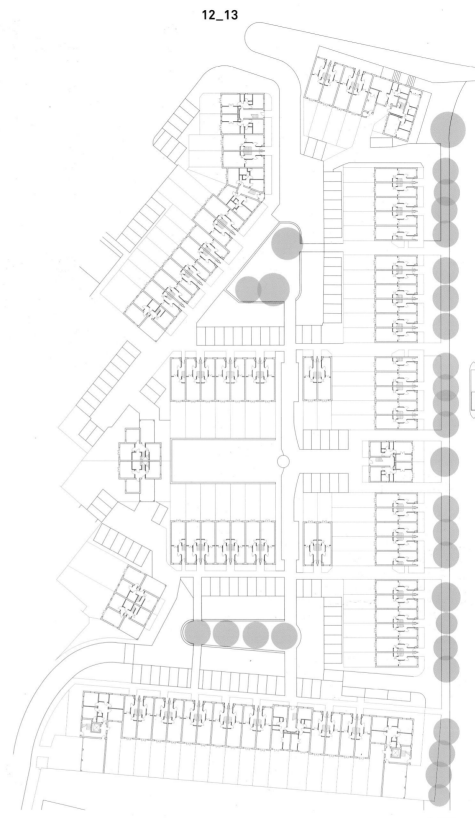

River Lea

1:1000

Layout plan. The layout is dominated by the need to make residents feel secure in their new environment, a contrast to the brutality of the former tower-block estate. Some terrace houses face on to a new riverside walkway. The rest are grouped around two squares that only have a pedestrian link. Car parking is visible from residents' homes. The 'estate' has only two entrances and can be 'gated' if threatened by vandalism from outsiders: however, this has not yet happened. At the centre is an equipped play area for small children, overlooked by the largest family houses.

**Above** One of the two central squares.
**Left** The small children's play area is overlooked by surrounding houses and flats – in this case a block containing just six flats.
**Below left** Pedestrian walkways are secured as there are only two points of entry into the whole development.
**Below right** Terrace houses with small front gardens face on to the riverside walk and the river.

# Ferry Street, Isle of Dogs, London E14

Ferry Street is a small scheme of 46 rented houses and flats, completed in the early 1980s on the southernmost tip of the Isle of Dogs. One of the most strategic sites in the whole of London Docklands, its acquisition for affordable rented housing by a housing association was only possible because of one of the periodic dips in the property market – this one in 1974. It was built before the explosion of development started by the London Docklands Development Corporation that produced Canary Wharf and enormous amounts of almost exclusively private housing along the river frontages.

This is a design that needs to be seen in context. The collapse of the Ronan Point tower block in May 1968 initiated a popular reaction against Modernism as it had been applied to the design of social housing, and along with it buildings faced with concrete and with any form of flat roof. And although this was a rare opportunity to maximise the potential of a south-facing riverside site, the Ferry Street scheme was limited by a maximum allowable density of only 250 habitable rooms per acre (approximately 60 per hectare) and a restriction, introduced in 1976, limiting access to socially rented family homes to not more than two storeys above ground level.

Given a superb site looking south over the Thames to Greenwich, the objective was to give every flat and house its own view of the river, its own south-facing private open space, minimal common circulation, and public access to what the local authority originally intended to be a continuous riverside walk right around the Isle of Dogs. However, the project was also something of an experiment in terms of form and external materials, having stock brick and timber cladding with pitched roofs, chosen as an antidote to the severity of the social housing of the previous 25 years.

The solution to the density problem was to avoid a simple multi-storey wall of flats facing south across the river and, instead, to use the full depth of the site to satisfy the need for family accommodation in houses.

This presented a design challenge: how to give every household a clear view of the river. It was answered by placing the single-storey dwellings closest to the river and planning the family houses behind them; their living rooms were at first-floor level, allowing views over the roofs of the single-storey flats in front. It was therefore essential to avoid steep-pitched roofs and the solution was to use coated corrugated aluminium at a shallow pitch in long sheets with no lapped joints. The single-storey flats for the elderly have their own riverfront patios, while the houses behind them have ground-level gardens tucked in at the rear. In this way the whole depth of the site has been used to its maximum and there are well-overlooked pathways to and from dwellings sandwiched between the two rows of housing.

Also groundbreaking was the use of timber cladding for external walls, the upper floors on the exposed river-facing elevations being clad in feather-edged pressure-treated softwood with lapped joints, laid horizontally.

Twenty-five years on, it is apparent that this is successful housing, and obviously much cherished by residents, some of whom have lived here since it was built, even if by current standards in Docklands it represents an extravagant use of land. All residents enjoy a combination of living at a domestic scale with generous private gardens and direct entrance to the street from every dwelling, as well as the best-possible orientation and a stunning view. Both the aluminium roofs and the timber cladding remain in good condition and the common areas, with much of their original planting intact, have reached a maturity seldom achieved in affordable rented housing.

Less successful are some of the maintenance decisions made by the managing housing association, allowing the replacement of windows with uPVC, an incongruous variety of cheap uPVC front entrance doors, and an unsuitable choice of white paintwork insensitively applied without regard to the original design intentions.

**Architect** Levitt Bernstein Associates
**Developer** Circle 33 Housing Trust
**Site** 0.6 hectares
**Number of dwellings** 46
**Density** 76 dwellings/hectare
**Mix** 10 x 1B + 24 x 2B + 12 x 3B
**Affordable** 100 per cent
**Parking spaces per dwelling** 0.5

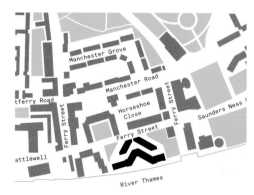

Site plan.

**Right** A collection of 46 houses and flats completed around 1980 on the southern tip of the Isle of Dogs facing the River Thames, laid out on the principle of giving every house and flat the spectacular view and south-facing orientation. A passageway separates the elderly people's single-storey houses on the river from the three-bedroom terrace houses behind them. The houses are planned with their living rooms at first-floor level so that each has a view to the south and the river, over the roofs of the single-storey houses in front of them.

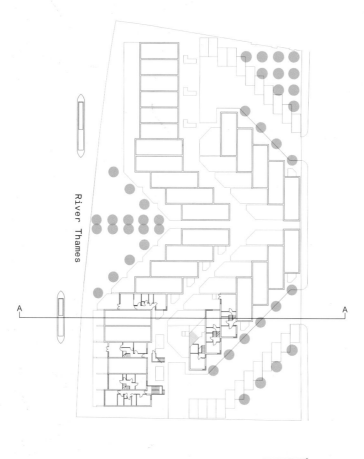

River Thames

A ———————————————————————— A

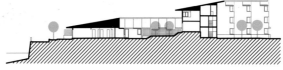

Layout plan and section A-A.                    1:1000

**Top** Single-storey houses for elderly people overlook the river and a public-access riverside walk.

**Above left** The three-storey houses are arranged in a staggered 'V' formation. This allows all their living rooms to have an uninterrupted view of the river. The windows facing the street have a good view of the two triangular parking areas.

**Above right** Between the backs of the single-storey houses and the gardens of the three-storey terrace houses is a walkway.

**Right** All gardens face due south.

# Mixing housing with other uses

Combined facilities for the Chalkhill estate regeneration in Brent, north-west London, by Levitt Bernstein Associates. These consist of 42 flats for shared ownership, a community centre, regional offices for the Metropolitan Housing Trust, two GP surgeries and a health centre.

There was a time when every new housing estate came with a central parade of small single-storey shops and a stand-alone community hall. All subject to periodic bouts of vandalism, they were, in any case, a bad use of land. When the parade of shops was located under three or four storeys of flats there was some protection from vandals but, as their viability reduced, the obvious lack of commercial success blighted the whole neighbourhood.

Changes in the patterns of shopping and the tendency of these small neighbourhood centres to become targets for anti-social behaviour have left many of them sad and neglected places and forced a rethink of the needs of 'out-of-town' communities. Although local food outlets may no longer be viable propositions for every neighbourhood, ways have been found to incorporate a newsagent/convenience store in a position that means it can flourish from passing as well as local trade. Research into the viability of convenience stores shows that they need a surprisingly large catchment area in order to succeed, and for this reason have to be located on a local distributor road along

which there is plenty of passing car traffic. Ideally, in suburban locations they need a small amount of short-term parking. The latest examples of community facilities avoid the kind of institutional architecture that seems to invite vandalism.

Now that most regeneration schemes involve increasing densities, and faced with the need to intensify the use of urban land and reduce the amount of private-car use, architects have successfully demonstrated their ability to 'think outside the box', providing various combinations of living, working, trading and leisure activities on the same sites. They have also been able to show how the housing component can benefit financially from these combinations.

Land shortages mean that developing sites classified as brownfield for housing alone is not enough in the areas of highest value and greatest need. Here, radical solutions have to be found where housing – that is, flats – needs to be combined with other uses that have previously always kept themselves to themselves. Aside from the obvious economic sense of sticking flats on top of

## Mixing housing with other uses

other street-level uses, especially when the street is unsuitable for housing, there are now numerous successful examples of flats and maisonettes located over modern large-volume retail outlets, notably supermarkets, and other non-housing uses. Apart from the obvious financial advantages of the dual use of sites, housing can very successfully help to overcome the urban-design dilemma posed by the economic need to have supermarkets or other major retail outlets in town and city centres while also wanting to avoid large amorphous sheds with no windows and no presence on the street apart from their entrances.

The reason for concentrating here on housing over major retail is that this combination is one of the most challenging types of mixed use to achieve satisfactorily. There are, however, dozens of other built combinations, of which primary healthcare, primary schools, nurseries, offices, small business units and small shops are just a few. Offices usually have very defined bay requirements, while education, leisure and community facilities need a wide range of spaces that can be difficult to fit into the residential grid – so a transfer structure is usually inevitable. These building types sometimes include large structures such as sports halls, performance spaces and sometimes even pools, which must be column-free and need a range of ceiling heights, making it difficult to establish a consistent podium level for the housing above without wasting space in some areas.

The transfer structure is primarily selected for the upper levels of flats and the services for the flats also need to pass through the lower levels with the minimum of diversion or complications to the layout of the ground floor. A particular opportunity sometimes provided in mixed housing above a supermarket stems from the fact that retailers prefer not to have either natural daylight or window displays at street level. If the surroundings are suitably residential this allows for single-aspect flats or maisonettes to provide a live street frontage with their own direct entrances from the street. Providing the orientation is suitable for single-aspect dwellings and allowance is made for large

balconies to replace private space at the rear, this kind of accommodation is popular in high-density locations. Given that the average fully fledged supermarket needs an area in excess of 3700 square metres (40,000 square feet), there is considerable scope for establishing a secure podium above the main retail floor. To achieve adequate security the number of access points to this kind of residential podium may be restricted to a single core, an ideal location for concierge control, but only if the scheme is large enough.

Whatever the ground-floor use is to be, the housing above needs more space at street level than just an entrance lobby if it is to cater successfully for the needs of today's residents. Recycling facilities, secure cycle stores and general storage all need to be provided.

Open courtyards above a ground-floor use such as a supermarket form useful amenity spaces for residents: they are also ideal locations for transferring access to the flats themselves from a single point of entry at street level to a number of separate lift and stair cores at courtyard level. Groups of preferably not more than 25–30 flats can be served from each core. Using a courtyard as the point of transfer also guarantees that it will function as a lively meeting place.

Such schemes inevitably involve elaborate vehicle-servicing and storage arrangements, usually combined with car parking for the supermarket as well as residents. Successful though the idea may be, by revisiting several examples after some years of use it is possible to get some idea of the complexities that inevitably arise when entirely different uses are sandwiched one above the other. If housing management and maintenance are complicated enough when large numbers of homes of different sizes and tenures are squeezed together on one site, the problems become vastly magnified when that housing sits on top of other uses. Foremost among these problems, apart from the occasional need for a transfer structure to carry the housing loads through the retail levels, is the untangling of responsibility for the various services that thread their way through the

Chalkhill: entrance foyer to the community centre, housing association offices and GP surgeries.

different layers of the building, establishing who is responsible for what and how access is provided when something ceases to work. Services and security systems, etc., for the different uses should be kept as separate as possible.

Clients with experience of this type of development believe that the key is to devise and sign up to a joint management plan before handover. And from the outset the architect needs to play a key role towards this end in order to ensure that future maintenance and management regimes can operate efficiently.

Mixed use, Bermondsey, south-east London. The diagrams on these pages show the three lowest floors (left, street level; top right, first-floor level; below right, second-floor level) of a nine-storey block of flats (in blue), which have a two-storey primary health-care centre below them (in white). They give some idea of the complexity of planning different uses above each other and of getting the circulation and service cores and access for the flats above to work efficiently.

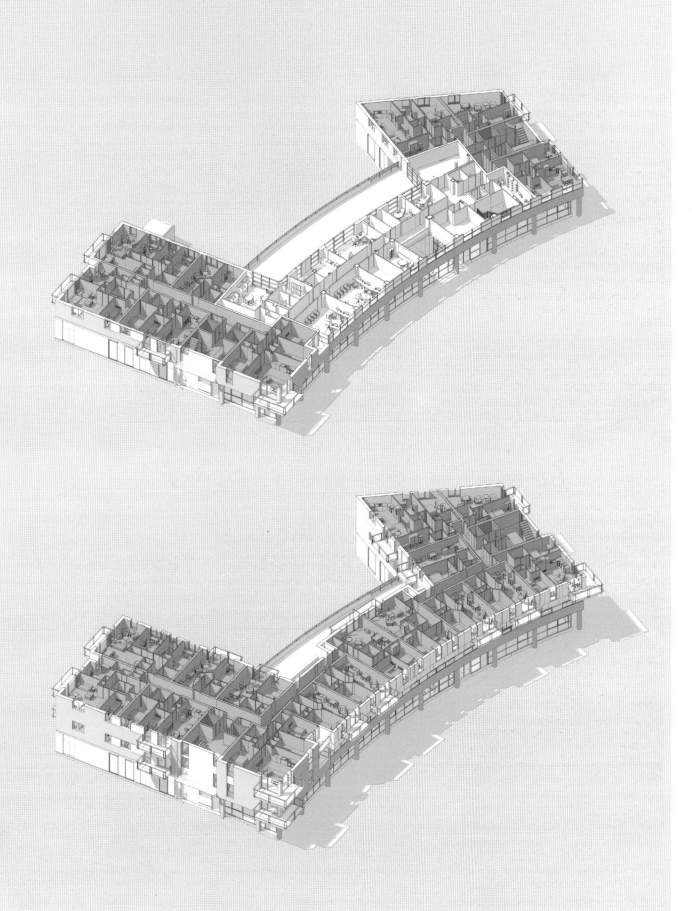

# Brunswick Centre, Bloomsbury, London WC1

Much has been written about Patrick Hodgkinson's design for what is now called the Brunswick Centre but which started life around 1959 as a replacement for the Foundling Estate, a portfolio of eighteenth-century residential street properties whose revenues provided the income for the nearby charitable Foundling Hospital. Radical redevelopments were not unusual at the time: Denys Lasdun's London University buildings cut another great swathe through Bloomsbury, while Sir Leslie Martin proposed to demolish half of Whitehall and all the streets south of the British Museum down as far as New Oxford Street to make way for the new British Library.

The Brunswick took twelve years from the architect's inception to completion. During the final few years Hodgkinson was excluded from the project, his commission having been terminated as the result of a belt-tightening exercise by the contractor, who purchased the building from the original developer in 1967. The gestation was therefore turbulent and the completion far from what had been conceived and hoped for.

In mid-1950s' London most new housing development concentrated on replacing what had been lost in World War 2. It was mainly for the benefit of those who could not afford to house or rehouse themselves, the middle classes who had been bombed out of London having largely removed themselves to the wealthier suburbs. What Hodgkinson was asked to do – a brief to which he enthusiastically responded – was to explore new urban housing for the middle classes and to provide a new centre for Bloomsbury, which, although immortalised for its literary and university associations, had become a faded shadow of its confident pre-war self.

The original scheme proposed expensive shops, lots of underground parking (the Buchanan report of 1963, *Traffic in Towns*, had encouraged the opening up of London to hitherto unimaginable levels of traffic), and generous flats for the middle classes, built to the highest density permitted anywhere in London (200 people per acre – approximately 500 per hectare – was the highest density permitted from 1945 to

the establishment of the Greater London Authority after 1997), all in one building of not more than eight storeys. However, a reverse in the developer's fortunes resulted not only in the sale of the project to the contractor and to the mass exodus of potential high-end retailers, but also to a wholesale redesign of the accommodation to fit government standards for social housing.

For almost 20 years after completion in 1972 the Brunswick staggered on, the housing leased to the London Borough of Camden, while a succession of freeholders struggled to keep the shopping street economically active, until in 1998 Allied London Properties saw the potential that could be realised by massive reinvestment.

Although David Bernstein and David Levitt had both worked on the original design programme in the 1960s, Levitt Bernstein's involvement only began after Allied London became the owner. By the end of the 1990s it was possible to take stock of what priorities had changed in terms of the design. Inevitably the scene had shifted, both for shopping and social housing, since this outstanding and unique building was first conceived by an architect who had been schooled in the very latest thinking about social housing some 50 years earlier.

Specifically:
• only two-thirds was built owing to difficulties in assembling the land north of Handel Street. This ragged and unresolved northern elevation had been left by the original team in the vain hope that somehow the remaining third up to Tavistock Place would be added to complete the whole grand design;
• the idea of security, now on the lips of anyone involved with urban design, was scarcely thought about when the building was conceived. By the time Camden Council had erected crude barricades to all the housing entrances in the 1980s, five of the grand staircases and two ramps leading from street level to the residents' terrace had been demolished;
• since the shopping level had been so unsuccessful commercially, it was time to take stock and to discover what needed to

**Architects** Levitt Bernstein Associates with Patrick Hodgkinson
**Developer** Allied London Properties
**Site** 2.6 hectares
**Number of dwellings** 385
**Density** 151 dwellings/hectare
**Mix** 201 x 2B + 140 x 1B + 44 x 1B studios
**Affordable** 75 per cent
**Parking spaces per dwelling** 1
**Non-housing uses** retail and cinemas, 1.3 hectares

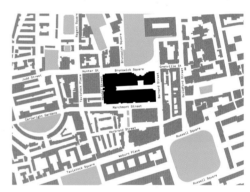

Site plan.

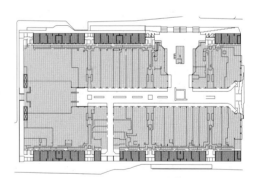

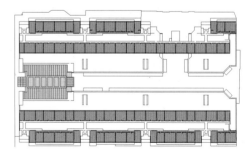

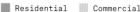

Usage diagrams.  ▮ Residential  ▯ Commercial

Brunswick Centre refurbished. One of the most heroic examples of mixed use from the 1960s, once written off as a failed council estate before being completely remodelled as a thriving retail centre for Bloomsbury. Although the housing itself remains unaltered, external cleaning and painting alone have given it a completely new lease of life.

be done for twenty-first-century retailers and shoppers.

The new owner's analysis was that:
• the emphasis on security was irreversible and the architecture needed to be sensitively modified to accommodate these changes;
• the central street was too wide and not legible from the surrounding streets, particularly from Bernard Street at the southern end;
• shop fronts set at the back of an arcade of robust circular columns down each side of the street were too hidden;
• the only supermarket was much too small;
• as freeholders they had inherited responsibility for repairing the fabric of the entire building, but the revenue from the shopping centre was totally insufficient to meet all the costs of long-outstanding repairs.

By the time the building had been listed Grade 2 in 2001 it proved difficult to convince the conservation lobby that any radical change was needed, especially the idea of closing off the northern end to the street, even though it had not been built as designed. Nevertheless, eventually planning consent did allow the formation of a large supermarket right across this end, leading to a resolution not unlike Hodgkinson's original design for a central covered shopping hall. This was a clear improvement to the by-now-permanent end to the building at Handel Street. An overwhelming advantage of this approach has been to disguise almost completely what would elsewhere have been a large ugly metal shed: surrounded with housing, only the supermarket entrances are visible.

The 'illegibility' of the shops was addressed by bringing the line of all shop fronts forward and providing lightweight fabric canopies for weather protection instead of the arcades. This had the double benefit of increasing the area of each shop and reducing the width of the street.

At the southern end, a ramp leading up to the residents' terrace on each side had been long since barricaded off when security first became an issue. Two large units, one a café restaurant, now replace those ramps and have shop windows right down their frontage on to Bernard Street. Combined with new, shallower steps and diagonal wheelchair ramps, this opens up the new shopping street to the outside world.

Developing housing regardless of tenure above shopping clearly has many advantages and very few disadvantages. Land devoted solely to modern retail has a deadening effect on the urban landscape but, conversely, towns and cities that have seen their principal retailers move camp to the periphery are experiencing an inevitable decline at the centre. Even without a complete level of shopping the Brunswick would be a high-density housing development in its own right. However, by combining a number of uses on one central site residents enjoy many advantages from the location, particularly those of good public transport and access to facilities. At these densities flats take the place of houses, but even when it comes to private open space, at the Brunswick sunny private balconies replace the small rear yards of the traditional houses, many of them north-facing, that were on the site before.

While the retail revenues have exceeded all expectations and have been sufficient to cover all the freeholder's repair obligations on the housing, the same cannot be said for those parts of the housing that are the council's responsibility and in need of repair after nearly 30 years of underfunding. Around 25 per cent of the flats have been bought by tenants who have thus become leaseholders, but the value of flats has increased so much that it is most unlikely that this percentage will increase any further. Meanwhile, there are proposals to add another complete floor to the housing and this may help to fund the remaining, long-awaited repairs.

**Top** Aerial view of the refurbished
Brunswick Centre looking north.
**Centre** Views of the main shopping
street.
**Bottom left** Interior of a flat.
**Bottom right** Main circulation area
to the housing.

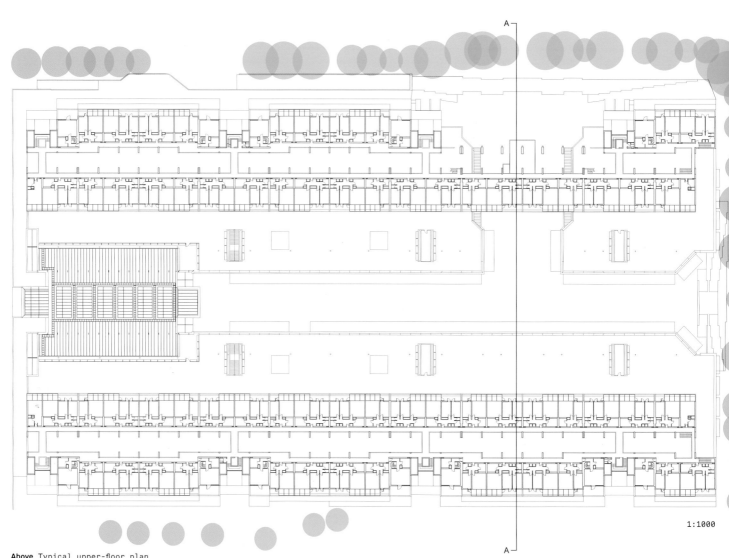

1:1000

**Above** Typical upper-floor plan
showing the circulation cores
to the housing, the residents'
upper-level open space and the
supermarket built across the
northern end of the main street.
**Below** Section A–A through the
cinema also showing both levels of
car parking with service roads for
delivery vehicles on both sides.

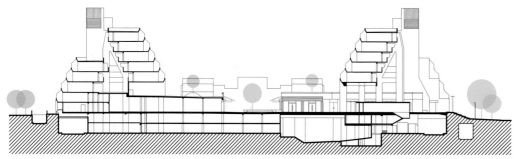

1:1000

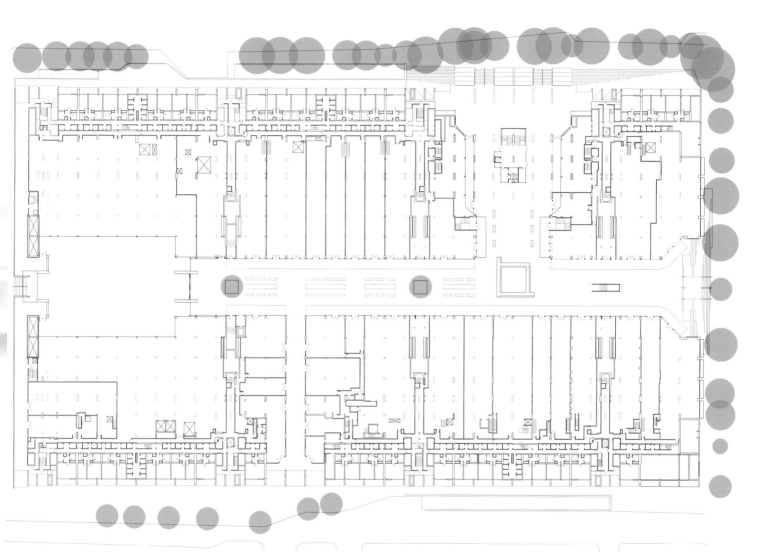

1:1000

**Above** Street-level plan. Flats line the two external street frontages disguising the backs of the shops which face on to the remodelled central street. The supermarket is clearly the anchor for the whole retail centre but its two entrance portals are the only external signs of its presence.
**Below** Plans of typical two-bedroom maisonettes, and one- and two-bedroom flats.

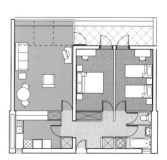

1:250

# Pimlico Village, Victoria, London SW1

With a redundant London Transport bus garage covering the whole site and a very large basement, this was an ideal location for a large new Sainsbury's supermarket. Being just behind Victoria Station, the site was too valuable to be occupied by a single use and Westminster Council, still smarting from bad publicity generated by a gerrymandering scandal of the 1980s, wanted 50 per cent of any housing to be provided as 'affordable'. Eventually a partnership was established between Network Housing Group and Sainsbury's in which high-density flats would be built above a retail floor occupying the whole site at street level.

As costs rose so did the height of the building, especially after it was discovered that two basement levels of parking were unaffordable and the second-floor of parking would have to be sandwiched between the retail floor and the podium from which the housing would rise. Parking requirements were always demanding: a complete floor for the supermarket and a second floor for private residents; the allocation of spaces for the affordable tenancies was much less generous.

Among the design problems were:
• how to integrate in the same building some 180 flats, of which half were to be for affordable rent and the other half large, high-value apartments for private sale;
• how to prevent the street frontage of a large supermarket, essentially an unacceptable blank wall, blighting a residential street of small Victorian terrace houses;
• how to provide access points to the housing at podium level when all supermarket operators want their stores to be clear, uninterrupted spaces with as few columns as possible;
• and finally, how to prevent the building of a solid wall of flats to a height far exceeding any buildings in the surrounding streets. Not surprisingly, the density of the residential parts is high, 267 dwellings or 800 habitable rooms per hectare.

The solution, eventually compromised by several surrounding owners pursuing 'rights to light' claims, was to construct two back-to-back courtyards each served by a

lift and stair core from different streets. This was done in a way that entirely separated the two types of tenure although the external treatment is identical in both cases.

The building spans between two parallel roads, one a shopping street in which the entrances to the new supermarket and a number of smaller retail units were located, and the other residential, which was 'plated' with single-aspect maisonettes with direct access to the street in order to disguise entirely the supermarket behind them.

In an attempt to break up the bulk of such a massive development, much sabotaged by the claims (some spurious) to rights to light, the form was conceived as a series of separate buildings of different heights, rising from a level podium.

After the first five years, it can be seen that the formula is successful for the housing association in management terms. There were initial doubts over whether it would be possible to avoid the security issues that might arise from having a single street entrance serving nearly 90 affordable tenancies. While this approach has failed dismally in the past, the problems seem to have been avoided here by Westminster Council's careful selection of residents.

The scheme does, however, make it possible to see the stark difference between what is achievable in the entrance courtyard and common parts of a high-value block of flats, where the annual service charges are obviously steep, and a similar arrangement for affordable flats, where every effort is made to keep service charges to a minimum.

At street level the private flats have a generous lobby manned by a concierge. This leads to a well-planted and landscaped courtyard, complete with an ambitious water feature, which in turn leads, via various separate lift and stair cores, to the flats themselves; all very welcoming. This contrasts sharply with a modest street-level entrance lobby for the rented flats and a central courtyard in which the landscaped features and much of the planting have been stripped to their bare essentials, so much so

**Architect** Levitt Bernstein Associates
**Developers** Stadium Housing Association (part of the Network Housing Group), Grainger Trust. J Sainsbury plc and Southern Properties
**Site** 0.71 hectares
**Number of dwellings** 160
**Density** 113 dwellings/hectare
**Mix** 57 x 1B + 78 x 2B + 25 x 3B
**Affordable** 50 per cent
**Parking spaces per dwelling** 0.85
**Non-housing uses** retail, 5480 square metres

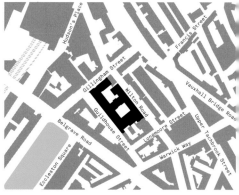

Site plan.

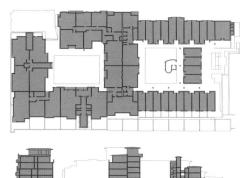

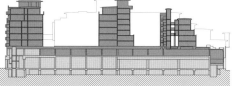

Usage diagrams. ■ Residential □ Commercial

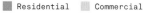

A landscaped courtyard leads to
the private flats.

that there have been residents' complaints
about noise from flats ricocheting round the
walls, passing from one dwelling to another.

Another surprising outcome, given the
location and its excellent access to public
transport, is the number of complaints
from tenants about what they consider to
be a meagre allocation of off-street parking
spaces. It would appear that here, as
elsewhere, many tenants own cars even
if they do not use them every day, while
others – such as nurses on night shifts – need
them when travelling to and from work at
anti-social hours.

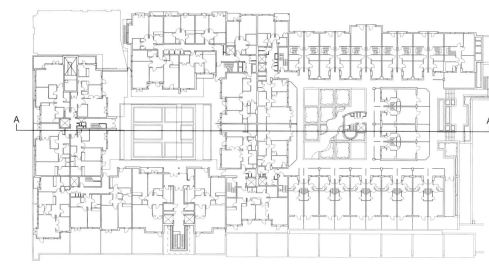

A

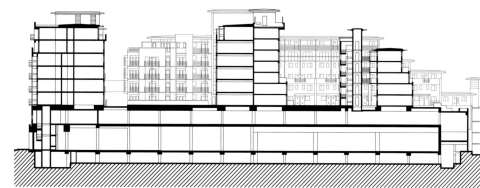

**Above** Plan and section A–A showing the
principal distribution of uses. The whole
street level is dedicated to retail.
The original intention was to have two
levels of basement car parking but costs
determined that the second residents'
parking level was placed above the
supermarket, raising the main podium level
still further above the streets.                    1:1000

**Below** Typical dwelling floor plans.
Note the considerable difference
in size between the high-value,
central-area apartments for sale
and the affordable flats and
maisonettes, designed for the
housing association, separated
by an eight-storey party wall.
Although from outside all tenures
look the same, in fact they never
meet, even having their entrances
in different streets.

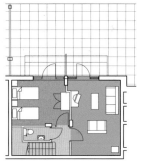

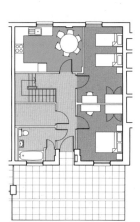
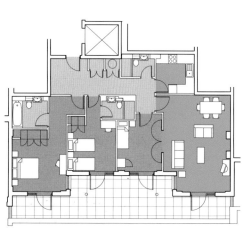

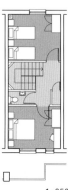

1:250

**Top** Views of the podium-level garden for the affordable flats and maisonettes.

**Above** Affordable single-aspect maisonettes disguising the blank rear wall of the supermarket in an otherwise residential street.

**Above right** Podium-level garden with a large water feature for the private flats.

**Bottom** The supermarket, largely column-free in the sales area, needs a transfer structure at high level to take the loads from the housing above.

# Odhams Walk, Covent Garden, London WC2

After failing to demolish Covent Garden in the early 1970s, the Greater London Council identified just one major site, the redundant headquarters of Odhams Press on the north side of Long Acre, for redevelopment. Fortunately, even at that early stage the potential of Covent Garden for specialist retail had been recognised and in any case the street level was far too lively to be suitable for housing. By the early 1970s high-rise rented housing had already been discredited as a manageable form and the GLC Architects Department set about a layered development of housing above shopping above parking and servicing.

The scheme, completed in 1982, is extremely complex: 150 flats and maisonettes, many of them free-standing structures, rise from a podium level above the shopping. As all roofs are flat, the roof of one dwelling forms a private open space for the one above. Full use is made of sunlight and daylight penetration into all the dwellings, which have their principal windows opening on to private terraces and overlooking a series of internal courtyards at different levels.

By the standards of today the residential density at 154 dwellings per hectare is not high. The maximum building height is only six storeys above street level and as the layout principle resembles a Mediterranean village with four-storey residential structures tightly packed into a small, traffic-free site, it is not a model that could be used to achieve a higher density.

At the time of its completion two completely contrasting critiques appeared in the architectural press (*The Architects' Journal*, 3 February 1982) and the comparison between them is still interesting. One, by Colin Campbell, then chief architect to the GLC, was naturally very supportive of the design and the ideas behind it, only criticising the severity of, particularly, the external elevations. The second piece, by Christopher Woodward, who had been responsible for much of the design of the Smithsons' Robin Hood Gardens in Poplar, pulled no punches. Woodward's view was that by laying out a 'casbah' on top of a podium, little was

achieved that could not have been bettered by repeating the indigenous local forms, dual-aspect terrace housing around the perimeter with a shared upper-level open courtyard in the centre.

In complaining that the housing makes no contribution to the surrounding streets (the phrase 'live frontage' had yet to be invented) he was surely right; the corner treatments are disastrous at street level and not enough is made of potential retail frontages on Shelton Street. But Covent Garden is such a lively place that the absence of a live frontage has hardly been noticed. What he failed to concede, but which is noticeably successful 25 years later, is that by allowing the dwellings to turn their backs to the street, the quality of peaceful and shared enjoyment in the multiplicity of small central spaces, walkways and terraces that are the focus of all dwellings is unusually successful.

Apart from the GLC's use, standard at the time, of a dull dark-brown brick throughout, and the inherent problems of water penetration associated with accommodation ambitiously located directly below trees that have outgrown their large brick planters, Odhams Walk is clearly a great success and is managed by the residents themselves through a tenant management organisation with an on-site manager. Security is achieved with just two gated street entrances leading up to the podium, and these are locked at night, only accessible with fob keys or by remote entryphone.

The layout is probably not a model to be exactly repeated if the aim is to achieve very high city-centre densities but it challenges the more formulaic 'doughnut' alternative, put forward by Woodward, where the courtyards that are so often trapped at the back of continuous terraces make little beneficial contribution to residents' lives. And by arranging the access to all dwellings from the first-floor podium via only two street entrances there is very little interruption to the continuity of the retail frontages.

**Architect** Greater London Council Architects Department
**Developer** Greater London Council
**Site** 0.66 hectares
**Number of dwellings** 102
**Density** 154 dwellings/hectare
**Mix** 61 x 1B + 9 x 2B + 25 x 3B + 7 x 4B
**Affordable** 50 per cent
**Non-housing uses** ground-level retail

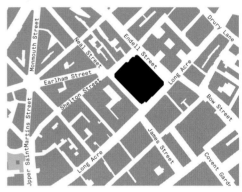

Site plan.

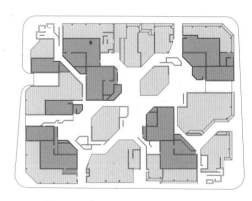

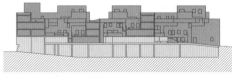

■ Residential  ■ Commercial

**Above** Usage diagrams.
**Right** From almost any view, the housing at Odhams Walk is a riot of planting. Each flat or maisonette has its own terrace and seems remote from the bustle of Covent Garden.

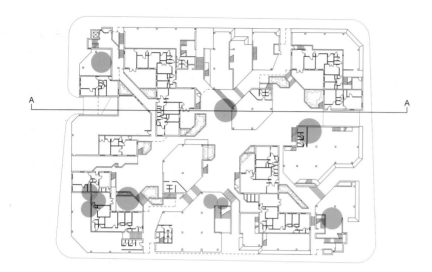

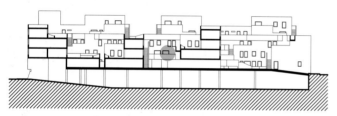

**Above** Key plan at podium level and
section A–A showing the mixture of
flats and small retail units that
line the street frontages. Beneath
the podium is an underground car
park, part of which is rented
commercially.

1:1000

**Below** Examples of flat types.
Mostly single aspect, they are
grouped around private terraces.

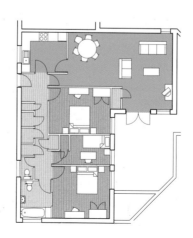

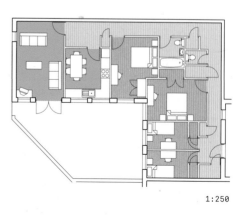

1:250

**Above** View of the exterior looking down the busy Neal Street with shop fronts on to the street itself.
**Right and below left and centre** Views of the podium above the shopping level.
**Below right** One of the private terraces.

The traditional terrace-house plan is as relevant today as it was two centuries ago but the size and shape of the footprint is crucial to its flexibility for future change and to the quality of life of its occupants. It also clearly defines the cut-off between the public and private realms, and it makes good use of land.

Years of experimentation in designing houses on urban sites provide a wealth of different approaches to the width, depth, orientation and appearance of new homes, all of them ultimately related to the questions of density, space standards, the needs of children and the blurring of class distinction. Large estates all of one tenure are now things of the past, prompting the need for a language that is of this century but that also meets the aspirations of both owners and tenants. At the same time, in practical terms the tendency to raise densities has increasingly collided with demands for much greater accessibility. Houses designed 30 years ago with frontages as narrow as 3.6 metres and no provision for wheelchair access would not meet current standards. This section explores the options and the principles behind them to see what

benchmarks emerge and what can be learnt from past examples.

From several points of view – urban design, economy of construction, environmental performance and land use – the terrace house remains the most relevant compromise between the desire of family-size households for space and independence and the unalterable need to regard land as a scarce resource. Among the objectives – subject to frequent change – that affect the way they are designed and laid out are:
• current regulations;
• standards and use of internal and external spaces;
• frontage and achievable densities;
• different kinds of tenure;
• responses to climate change.

## Regulations and their constraints on the terrace house
Today's extensive regulations and guidance have a strong impact on the size and shape of the footprint as well as internal layout. The principal national standards, both regulatory and advisory, that affect the design of terrace homes, are outlined here.

Highworth Cottages, Leighton Buzzard. A recent photograph of terrace housing built in 1954 by Powell & Moya. Note the wide frontage and generous plot size associated with early post-war housing.

# Terrace housing and layout

**Building Regulations** (Department of Communities and Local Government) Part B can be onerous for three-storey houses because a protected staircase route to the main exit must be provided unless there is an approved means of escape from the top floor. This can rule out certain open-plan layouts and make future loft conversions problematic. However, the latest revision to Part B (April 2007) encourages a fire-engineered approach using a combination of fire detection, warning and sprinkler systems, allowing more flexibility in open-plan layouts.

Part E lays down clear requirements for the acoustic performance of the party wall and has an impact on wall construction, which in turn influences street frontages between dwellings. The latest revision to Part E (April 2003) changed the range of frequencies that are tested in an attempt to control bass frequencies from loud music.

Part L limits glazing areas, which can make it difficult to achieve adequate daylighting when deep plans are combined with narrow frontages.

Part M has a major impact on the design of entrances, corridor widths and the location of accessible WCs. Reasonable measures must be taken to enable wheelchair access to the main entrance, and main entrance doors must have a clear width of 775mm, and in all ground-floor corridors and rooms. A wheelchair-accessible WC must be provided at entrance level or on the principal storey of a house that has no habitable rooms at entrance level.

Accessible WCs must be 1 metre wide internally with a clear space 750mm deep outside so that the door can open outwards. This requirement makes it difficult to locate the WC beneath the stairs, which means that it is located either next to the front door, forming a barrier between the two ground-floor rooms, or at the back of the house, blocking a through route to the garden.

**Secured by Design** The rigid recommendations of this non-statutory accreditation scheme for 'designing out crime' in dwellings and housing estates have been the source of considerable disagreement between the police, the DCLG and CABE. One of its key recommendations – street access only to terraced houses and back-to-back gardens —has significant plan implications as access to the garden has to be through the kitchen or, even worse, the living room. These recommendations must be assessed on a case by case basis.

**Design and Quality Standards** (The Housing Corporation, since January 2009 merged with English Partnerships to form the Homes and Communities Agency) These establish requirements and recommendations for all new homes that receive Social Housing Grant. Since April 2007 new schemes have been assessed according to Housing Quality Indicators under three headings: location, site and unit design, and external environment. The requirements for unit size and layout rely on Standards and Quality in Development: A Good Practice Guide from the National Housing Federation, which includes furniture and activity diagrams and implies minimum acceptable dimensions for living rooms, bedrooms and kitchens. While the essential requirements are broadly compatible with Part M and Lifetime Homes (see below), the NHF standards are in some cases stricter, requiring, for instance, that entrance doors be at least 800mm clear and not permitting stair winders.

**Lifetime Homes** (Joseph Rowntree Foundation) Local authorities are increasingly applying Lifetime Homes standards to new homes. For terrace houses, some of the associated recommendations are particularly crucial. By requiring a 300mm-wide space beside the leading edge of doors, the width of the internal entrance area grows to 1.3–1.4 metres. The standards also require provision for a shower to be fitted in the future for the entrance-floor WC: this means that the room needs to be at least 1.4 x 1.8 metres. Additionally, a requirement for stairlifts increases costs and support tracks have longer over-runs.

The main living room has to be at entrance level and while a kitchen/diner is sometimes regarded as acceptable for the 'hospitality'

The terrace-house frontage reinterpreted by Proctor and Matthews at South Chase, Harlow.

aspect of this requirement, it would not satisfy the need for a temporary bed space. The bathroom must be suitable for use by a person in a wheelchair and the need to plan for the provision of a hoist from bedroom to bathroom may mean that the size of ceiling joists or trussed rafters has to be increased.

**Code for Sustainable Homes** (Department of Communities and Local Government) Since April 2007 publicly funded new housing has been required to meet level 3 of the Code for Sustainable Homes, a six-level environmental performance standard for new homes. Solar orientation is a key aspect of the code with impact on terraced housing. The need to optimise passive solar gain is difficult to reconcile with urban-design considerations of streetscape as the optimum orientation from an energy point of view cannot always be achieved. Similarly, as the installation of renewable technologies such as solar panels and photovoltaics becomes common, the built form of terrace houses will need to balance the need for south-facing roof slopes with irregular street patterns. A secondary concern is provision for recycling, cycle stores and individual metering, all of which impact the design of semi-private space on the street side of terraced homes.

**Building for Life** (CABE/Home Builders Federation /Civic Trust) The Building for Life standard is intended to be the national benchmark, encouraging house builders in England to provide new housing projects that demonstrate a commitment to high design standards and good place-making. Most of the 20 criteria in Building for Life apply equally to all types of housing; but question 8 (Is car parking well integrated so it supports the street scene?) and question 15 (Do internal spaces and layout allow for adaptation, conversion or extension?) deserve particular attention in relation to terraced housing.

**Standards and the use of internal and external space: keeping up with lifestyle changes**
Internal space standards continue to be largely unregulated in private housing and there has been no formal attempt at regulating space in social housing since

1979 when council-house building ceased and with it Parker Morris standards. First introduced in 1961, Parker Morris standards have never been a requirement for housing associations, the main providers of social housing in the UK since 1979, although there is much current discussion regarding the imposition of new minimum internal space standards that reflect changes in lifestyle. The initiative for these derives largely, in the UK at least, from ideas put forward by English Partnerships and the GLA.

In the seventeenth and eighteenth centuries the basic terrace house usually had only two rooms on each floor; the nineteenth-century model acquired a third room in a rear extension accessed from the half landing, an efficient plan but one which had a low space-to-external-wall ratio, often resulting in poor daylighting in the narrow slot between two facing extensions.

The terrace house form appeared long before ideas of internal sanitation, and when the bathroom first appeared it was located either at the far end of a ground-floor rear extension or on a first-floor half landing. Both options were a compromise that has still not been satisfactorily resolved in many of the terraced forms in use today.

This section explores how lifestyle opportunities for modern terrace-house dwellers increase with increases in frontage. These might include garden access or naturally lit and ventilated bathrooms, rather than internal artificially ventilated and lit bathrooms, as space becomes available with increases in frontage.

With increases in frontage, however, come reductions in density, and a point is also reached when it is no longer economic to span floors from party wall to party wall without intermediate support and consequent loss of internal flexibility.

**Different kinds of tenure**
Lifestyle and per capita incomes have an enormous effect on the long-term sustainability of terrace houses. The essential and very important design differences responding to the varied lifestyles of different

Reconstructed terrace housing by ShedKM Chimney Pot Park in Salford, Manchester. Parking and shared open space at rear.

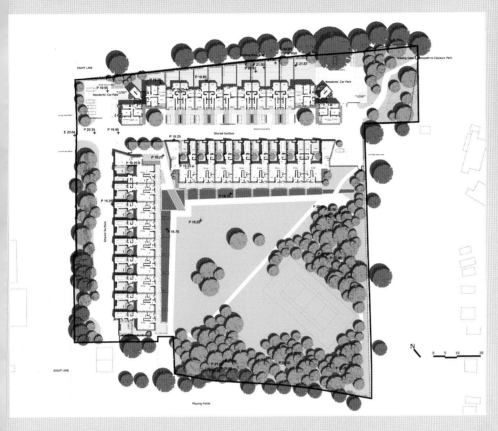

Terrace housing in the Greenbelt.
This 1.6-hectare site at Roding
Lane in the London Borough of
Redbridge was in industrial and
storage use before the original
Greenbelt designation, and the
Borough of Redbridge has been
seeking a solution to this
anomalous situation for years.
In complete contrast to the normal
association of the Greenbelt
and suburban detached houses,
architect Metropolitan Workshop
was commissioned by the landowner
and his agents to transform the
site into an elegant and well-
planned 'hamlet' surrounding a
large 'oasis-like' open space.
The green at its  focus will
be a new managed open space
surrounded on two sides by an
L-shaped development of 26 terrace
houses and 12 flats at an overall
density of 123 HR/hectare. The
terrace houses have their access
from Roding Lane and the newly
created mews, but front on to the
green space from which they are
separated by a swale forming part
of the urban drainage system. The
houses and apartments are tightly
packed on both sides of the mews
but, as the model shows, top-floor
balconies provide private outdoor
space and identify each home in
the terrace. A new route allows
pedestrian and cycle connection
from nearby Repton Park through to
Roding Lane.

tenures are discussed in Chapter 11. They
have a particular impact on the design of
terrace housing.

With the aim of building sustainable terrace
housing designed to have a predicted
lifespan equal to that of any of the historic,
and highly adaptable, traditional terrace-
house forms, certain principles apply not
only to owner-occupation but also to all forms
of tenure if there is a likelihood that houses
built for sale could be rented out at some
stage in their life cycle, or vice versa.

These principles are:
• north-facing single-aspect houses should
be avoided;
• all principal rooms in single-aspect houses
should have natural light and ventilation;
• single-aspect houses should have sufficient
private open space at the front as garden or
patio; parking spaces don't count;
• two-bedroom, four-person houses are
inflexible for households with two children
even if both children are of the same sex;
• suburban terrace houses with gardens

deeper than 10 metres should have an
access route to the garden that is not through
the living room;
• dual-aspect houses with a net frontage of
less than 4 metres should be avoided.

## Frontages and achievable densities

As the summary of regulations implies, the
introduction of Lifetime Homes with the
requirement for a wheelchair-accessible WC
at entrance level has ruled out many of the
experiments in very narrow-frontage houses
beloved by architects in the 1960s, notably
Bill Howell's terrace of private houses in
Hampstead, built around 1960.

Very narrow frontages, such as 3.6 metres,
can only work if there is no separate
circulation, particularly from the front door to
the centre of the house, so the entire width of
the house can represent the width of a living
room or double bedroom, and all ground-
floor rooms are interconnected so that the
stair rises directly from the living space. Such
houses are most unsuitable for affordable
rent or for large families and, in any case, are

limited to two storeys due to the impossibility of meeting Building Regulations without a direct half-hour resisting lobby from the staircase to the street door.

At the opposite extreme, on awkwardly shaped sites where it is the plot depth rather than the frontage that is limited, it is feasible to design wide, double-fronted houses that are only one habitable room deep, with service areas, kitchens and bathrooms at the back. The internal plans work well since circulation is limited to the centre of the house on each floor. The back-to-back distance between houses can be reduced to an absolute minimum of around 10 metres and overlooking can be avoided at first-floor level by having all the bedrooms facing the street, and at ground-floor level by having a 2-metre-high brick wall between back-to-back gardens. In general this arrangement results in uneconomical amounts of roadway and is not a way of increasing densities overall.

Going back to the GLC in the 1970s, various attempts have been made to produce ranges of standard terrace-house types based on different frontages, but none has been widely adopted. Obviously these exercises have concentrated on producing the most economical layouts within given increments of frontage. As the size of terrace houses goes up, the range of potential layouts increases and the imagination of the designer takes over.

The drawings on pages 41–43 show floor plans of narrow-frontage house types starting from an internal frontage of 4.0 metres. These incorporate the current regulations listed above and from them several general principles emerge.

## Responding to climate change

Compared to detached houses, terrace housing is a thermally efficient plan form in terms of the ratio of internal space to external wall. On the other hand, if full advantage is to be taken of measures such as passive thermal gain, solar and PV panels, since by definition terraces follow the line of streets, it is no longer appropriate to use exactly the same house type on either side of a street

running east–west or for those on either side of streets running north–south.

There was a time when architects would simply design one house type and lay them all out with the same orientation, a design solution that might have been sustainable in technical terms but was definitely not sustainable in social or urban-design terms. Taking advantage of passive solar means having relatively large glazed areas to living-room elevations oriented between south-east and south-west. If these elevations face the street there is likely to be a visual privacy problem to be overcome.

These differing sensitivities suggest that, while the bedroom-floor plans in any given scheme of houses can remain pretty standardised, the living-floor layouts need to be capable of a number of different variations.

A similar approach needs to be taken with roof design where simple front-to-back double-pitch roofs will be suitable as platforms for solar panels for water heating and for PVs when either the front or the back of each house faces south. For east–west orientations the same house layout may need double roof pitches with valley gutters running from front to back along the party-wall line.

## Terrace house types and density

A useful range of definitive standard house plans does not exist. Any attempt to introduce one has always proved to be insufficiently flexible to make the most efficient use of a site, except the very largest and most regular in shape.

Different house types can have a significant effect on density. The following diagrams show the footprints and land take (including a nominal parking zone and part of the road) of seven different terrace house plan types. They are ranked in order of relative density, A being the densest. In general, as frontage becomes more generous so do the lifestyle opportunities for the occupants in terms of the sort of issues discussed in the chapter.

In most situations the frontage of each house, measured between the inside faces of party walls, has the most crucial impact on the overall density that is achievable. On sites where frontage is less important than the front-to-back dimension it may be appropriate to place houses back to back but with a much wider frontage in order to make the best use of land.

Almost all of the terrace housing built over the last 50 years has been some variation of types C or D, and for good reason; these are the most practical, simplest layouts and the most likely to suit a wide range of families. Interestingly, they are the most economical in terms of overall floor area, but the least efficient in terms of land use.

With density so high on the agenda but with a recent and vociferous demand for houses rather than flats, the other types – A, B, E, F and G – are examples of the very narrow-frontage, three-storey or single-aspect forms currently being explored in order to push densities above the 50 dwellings per hectare limit achieved by the commonplace C and D types. The effect on density is quite significant (type F occupies a little over two-thirds of the plot area needed for the most greedy, type D). But each of these generic alternatives has significant quirks or limitations rendering them far less suitable as fully accessible, general-needs homes that can be fully occupied and amenable to almost any orientation.

In most situations at initial concept stage, some idea of the relationship between different layouts of terrace house and the densities likely to be achieved on sites that are a regular shape is a useful tool, especially bearing in mind the dimensional constraints imposed by Lifetime Homes, furniture layouts, garden access, whether bathrooms are likely to be internal or not and whether the house is likely to provide 'eyes and ears' on to the street for security purposes.

Facing north, type F would be completely unacceptable but confronted by an east–west site too narrow for a conventional back-to-back garden arrangement, this back-to-back house type has interesting possibilities and considerable commercial advantages.

**Terrace housing and layout**

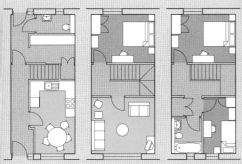

Type A: 4.0 metres internal frontage. 3B5P three-storeys, 103 square metres - not LTH.

1:250

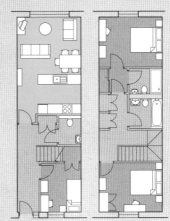

Type B: 4.0 metres internal frontage. 3B5P, two storeys, 95 square metres - not LTH (with en-suite).

Type C: 5.0 metres internal frontage. 3B5P, two storeys, 95 square metres - LTH.

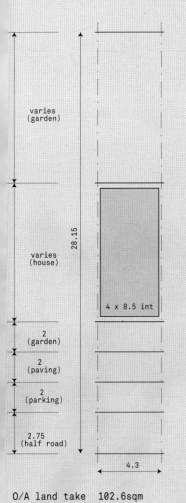

varies (garden)

varies (house)

28.15

4 x 8.5 int

2 (garden)

2 (paving)

2 (parking)

2.75 (half road)

4.3

31.55

4 x 11.9 int

4.3

29.15

5 x 9.5 int

5.3

| | | | |
|---|---|---|---|
| O/A land take | 102.6sqm | 135.7sqm | 154.5sqm |
| density (dw/ha) | 82.9 | 73.7 | 64.7 |
| ranking | 2 | 3 | 6 |

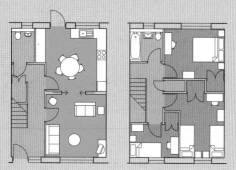

Type D: 6.0 metres internal
frontage. 3B5P, two storeys,
95 square metres – LTH.

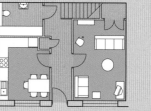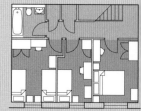

Type E: 8.0 metres internal frontage, single aspect.
3B5P, two storeys, 96 square metres – LTH.

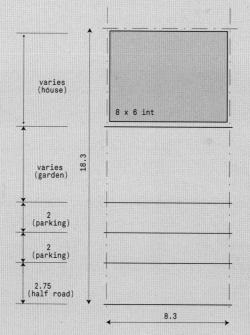

varies
(house)

8 x 6 int

varies
(garden)

18.3

2
(parking)

2
(parking)

2.75
(half road)

8.3

O/A land take   151.89sqm
density (dw/ha) 65.8

ranking          5

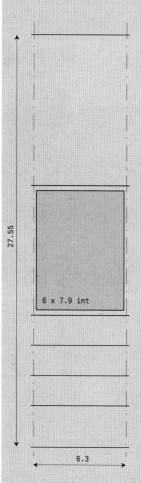

27.55

6 x 7.9 int

6.3

density comparisons
3b5p houses at
4.0, 5.0, 6.0 int front

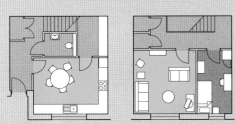
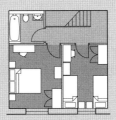

Type F: 6.2 metres internal frontage, single aspect. 3B5P, three storeys 111.6 square metres (LTH?).

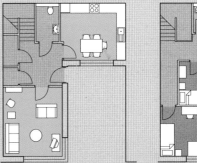

Type G: 7.8 metres internal frontage, single aspect. 3B5P, two-storey courtyard house, 98.7 square metres – LTH.

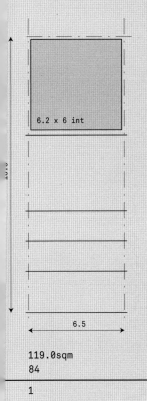

6.2 x 6 int

6.5

119.0sqm
84
―――――――――
1

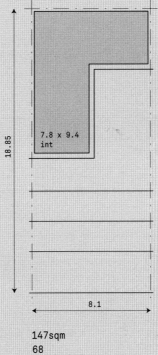

18.85

7.8 x 9.4 int

8.1

147sqm
68
―――――――――
4

density comparisons
3b5p single aspect houses
at 6.5-8.3 int frontage

### Typical 3B5P house for affordable rent

As has been shown, the plans of terrace houses evolve into a wide variety of configurations. Attempts to develop a standard range of house plans for use in different locations usually fail because briefs, sites and design preferences vary so much that it is rarely possible to replicate the same plans on different projects.

But the common denominator for all affordable housing that is in receipt of public subsidy is the need to comply with the requirements of the grant-giving body. In December 2008 this became the Homes and Communities Agency (HCA). Its aim is to ensure that affordable housing is well-designed, sustainable, provides value for money and suits the needs of a wide range of people whose voices cannot be individually heard. In order to measure grant eligibility, design proposals are assessed in relation to a set of standards by converting design and quality performance, into a numerical score.

Standards are continually being revised but, for the time being, the HCA is adopting the Design and Quality Standards published by its predecessor, The Housing Corporation. Essentially, these set minimum standards for the internal environment (under the Housing Quality Indicators) the external environment (under Building for Life) and sustainability (under the Code for Sustainable Homes). Lifetime Homes is also due to become a mandatory standard but probably under the Building Regulations rather than HCA standards as the government intend to apply it to all new housing, not just that for affordable rent.

As a demonstration of the current range of issues and regulations affecting the detailed layout of houses this is a worked example of a typical 'good practice', two-storey, 3B5P house.

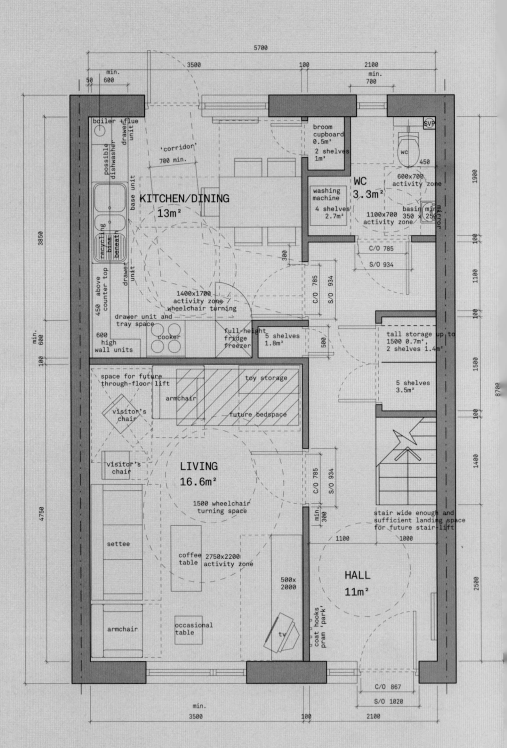

**Good practice 3B5P house**
GLA, 99.2 square metres, 5.7 metres wide, 8.7 metres deep: left, ground floor; right, first floor (dimensions in mm unless otherwise annotated).

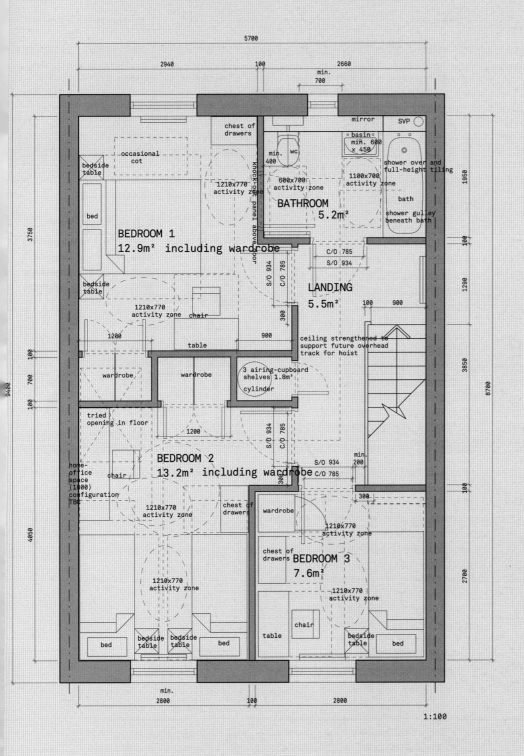

5700

2940     100     2660

min.
700

mirror    SVP

chest of
drawers

basin
min. 600
x 450

occasional
cot

min. wc
400

shower over and
full-height tiling

bedside
table

600x700
activity zone

1100x700
activity zone

1210x770
activity zone

3750

bath

bed

**BATHROOM**
**5.2m²**

shower gulley
beneath bath

100

**BEDROOM 1**
**12.9m² including wardrobe**

knock-out panel above door

C/O 785

S/O 934

1290

bedside
table

S/O 934

C/O 785

**LANDING**

1210x770
activity zone

chair

300

**5.5m²**

100   900

3850

1200

900

table

ceiling strengthened to
support future overhead
track for hoist

100

100

wardrobe

wardrobe

3 airing-cupboard
shelves 1.8m²

700

cylinder

1200

100

tried
opening in floor

S/O 934

C/O 785

home-
office
space
(1800)
configuration
TBC

**BEDROOM 2**
**13.2m² including wardrobe**

300

S/O 934
C/O 785

min.
200

chair

100

4050

1210x770
activity zone

chest of
drawers

wardrobe

300

1210x770
activity zone

chest of
drawers

**BEDROOM 3**
**7.6m²**

2700

1210x770
activity zone

1210x770
activity zone

1210x770
activity zone

table

chair

bed

bedside
table

bedside
table

bed

table

bedside
table

bed

9400

min.
2800     100     2800

8700

1:100

# Holly Street area renewal, London E8

This is the final phase of the renewal of what used to be the Holly Street Estate, now once more merged into the original pattern of streets lying between Dalston and London Fields. A comparison between this development of 151 terrace houses and apartments and the first phase of the original renewal programme dating back to 1992 reveals the sharpest of contrasts – phase 1 compared with phase 6 – and the changes in expectations for the quality of affordable housing that have taken place over the intervening years.

Between 1980 and 1997 there was a huge revolution in the funding of social housing. Gone was the open-ended approach to subsidy that had characterised the preceding three decades, during which many of the most celebrated examples of publicly funded housing were completed only after last-minute injections of additional money. During the years of rule by Margaret Thatcher new housing had to be built under the constraint of subsidy levels that were announced at the beginning of the project and never increased thereafter; additionally, official dogma decreed that 'what was good enough for the private buyer should be quite good enough for a subsidised tenant'.

As a result – and this was the case at the beginning of the Holly Street renewal programme – the successful developer built both houses and flats to the standards then current in the private sector (see Chapter 5). Although the three-bedroom houses were not far short of the Parker Morris standards that had been in use since 1961, the house frontages were narrow, with the result that it was possible to stand in the kitchen, at the front of the house on the ground floor, and reach out to touch both opposing walls at the same time.

As described in Chapter 8, the conservative approach to design of the early 1990s evolved from a period of intense consultation with tenants who wanted nothing resembling modern architecture and who chose what was normally built for private sale at the time. By the end of the competition to select a developer, at a time when the UK was just emerging from recession, there were two

candidates still in the race to redevelop the Holly Street Estate. Although the council's brief stipulated that 20 per cent of new housing should be for private sale, neither of the two shortlisted developers was prepared to entertain the idea of integrating any housing for private sale into the new street pattern. The winning proposal offered to reserve one corner of the 'estate' for private development once everything else had been demolished and rebuilt.

Twelve years on, what was architecturally acceptable to members of the average London neighbourhood had changed radically, greatly assisted by the fact that integrating different tenures in the same street had become the norm, and tenants could appreciate that private buyers were themselves choosing to be more adventurous. But there is another important distinction between phase 6 of Holly Street and the previous five phases, in that the developer of the social-housing component of phase 6 is the local authority rather than one of the housing associations involved in the earlier phases.

From the earliest years of the regeneration project some tenants were resistant to the idea of transferring their tenancy to a housing association, an attitude reinforced to some extent by reservations over some of the standards of the houses and flats built in the early phases. The regeneration programme from the outset up to the completion of phase 5 had been a partnership between Hackney Council, a consortium of housing associations and a developer who withdrew before the final phase began. The council retained all the affordable homes in the final phase, thus fulfilling its obligations to this particular group of tenants.

All apartments have generous balconies. In addition to their rear gardens, the houses have south- or west-facing single-glazed solar sunspaces as a thermal buffer to their living rooms. Other features include:
• U-values down to 0.18 and 0.12 for walls and roofs; these are up to almost 50 per cent better than current Building Regulations;
• airtightness of only 7m³/hm², which is

**Architect** Levitt Bernstein Associates
**Developers** United House Developments Limited with London Borough of Hackney
**Site** 1.2 hectares
**Number of dwellings** 151
**Density** 126 dwellings/hectare
**Mix** 42 x 1B + 59 x 2B + 34 x 3B + 16 x 4B
**Affordable** 26 per cent
**Parking spaces per dwelling** 0.47

Site plan.

**Right** The final phase of the Holly Street regeneration shows a mixture of family houses and non-family flats for both rent and private sale, indiscriminately mixed. Flats line the main road with houses on the side streets. In the distance can be seen earlier phases of the Holly Street development, giving some idea of how residents' tastes have changed over a 12-year time span.

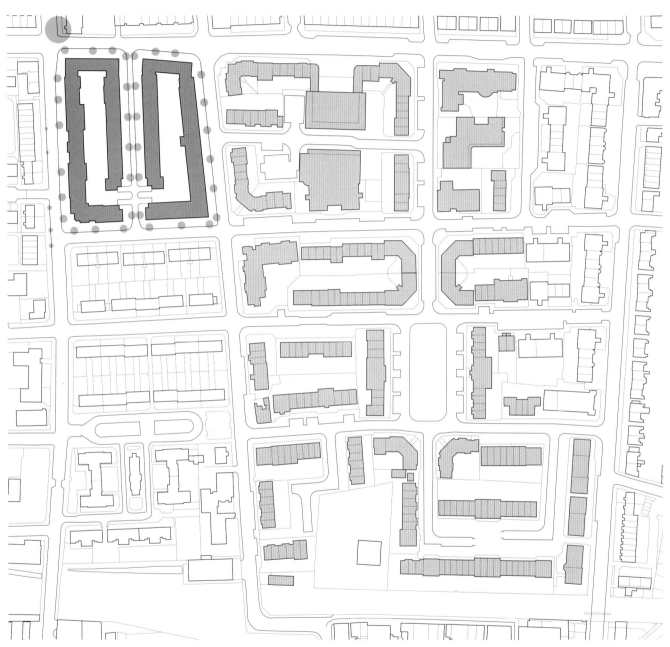

The whole Holly Street
regeneration area masterplan, with
the final phase highlighted.

1:2500

**Above** The layout plan shows a
range of different terrace house
types interspersed with flats on
street corners or along the busy
Queensbridge Road frontage.
**Below** Section A–A.

A ──────────────────────────────────────────────────── A

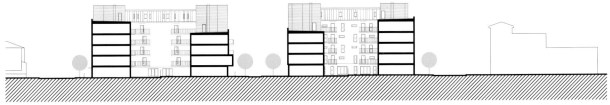

1:1000

30 per cent better than current Building
Regulations;
• entrance/draught lobbies to all houses to
reduce heat loss and to provide useful space
for buggies and boots;
• a utility zone/cupboard separating the
washing machine from the kitchen/dining
room;
• houses for affordable rent were designed
with cut timber roofs rather than trusses, to
allow for storage and/or future conversion to
an extra bedroom/study;
• PV solar panels have been fitted to houses
to meet the requirement for 10 per cent
renewables and the second phase is due to
trial ground-source heat pumps.

Apart from better space standards,
more adventurous architecture and the
indistinguishable integration of tenures, the
other major change over the 12-year period
was an awareness of climate change and
other environmental issues.

 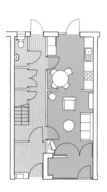 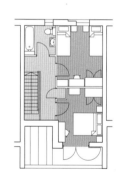

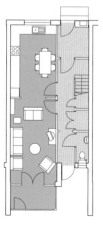 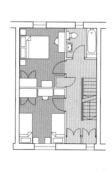 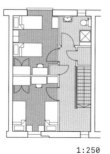

1:250

**Top left** Plan of two-bedroom flat for
sale.
**Top right** Plans of two-bedroom house
for rent.
**Above** Plans of four-bedroom house
with sunspace.

Top View along new Central Street.
Below Kitchen/dining room — house for sale.
Right Massing of houses and flats.
Below right View of rear gardens.

Newhall is a new settlement of approximately 2700 dwellings being created in two phases broken down into approximately ten parcels. The development occupies a greenfield site close to Harlow New Town and the M11 motorway. The proposals developed from the winning submission of a design/developer competition, intended to respond to a masterplan and design code drawn up by Roger Evans Associates.

In the words of the design team, the intention was 'to develop an architectural vocabulary which combines a contemporary aesthetic and response to twenty-first-century living patterns with sensitivity to local materials, colour and texture. The designs also exploit a desire for light and airy modern dwellings and an aspiration to create a sustainable residential community of distinctive character and lasting quality. The architectural language adopted rejects the notion of pastiche in favour of a modern vocabulary which is overlaid into a townscape-driven urban framework to create a vibrant street scene of incident, articulation and variety'.

The houses in this scheme embody many inventive ideas, all based around lightweight steel-framed volumetric construction enclosed in a rendered blockwork outer skin. The basic module is a 4.45-metre-frontage, two-bedroom, two-storey house to which either one or two extra bedrooms can be added. As the plans show, the additional bedrooms are added to the side of each house, forming a courtyard. In the case of the four-bedroom house the extra bedroom is above a carport at the front of the courtyard. All houses have rear gardens and an average of 1.5 parking spaces.

By producing a range of different typologies for the houses – including, in land-use terms, an extremely economical two-bedroom terrace house with a steep and immaculately detailed gabled roof forming a valley gutter along the party-wall line of each house – the architects have been able to develop a plan that has all sorts of variety; some houses are even placed lengthways on to the street with wide frontages and shallow rear gardens. The frequent breaks in the frontage, articulated by the steep white gables, completely remove any of the monotony that is often associated with terrace housing in suburban locations.

The two small blocks of flats are placed on street corners, with the internal corners used as parking courts. This is always an economical use of land, and allows more generous footprints for some of the larger houses.

The public realm promises to be delightful, especially when the tree planting matures. Every street intersection is articulated by a raised platform that adds intimacy and pedestrian priority as well as reducing driving speeds.

Internal planning is equally inventive and is dominated by the open staircase placed down the middle of the house, with circulation down one side. On the other side is the ground-floor kitchen with the bathrooms above it, which makes for an extremely economical service layout. This means that the under-stair area is open and becomes part of the kitchen, while the stairwell is lit from above.

**Architect** Proctor and Matthews Architects
**Developer** South Chase Newhall Limited with Moat Housing Association
**Site** 1.5 hectares
**Number of dwellings** 78
**Density** 52 dwellings/hectare
**Mix** 52 houses, 26 flats
**Affordable** 45 per cent
**Parking spaces per dwelling** 1.5

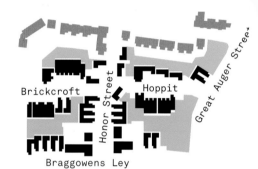

Site plan.

**Right** Modular two-storey terrace houses at South Chase. Houses in this range vary between a two-bedroom version to both three- and four-bedroom houses. Construction is of lightweight steel, externally rendered and with inventive features such as the prefabricated entrance canopy/refuse store/bicycle store.

1:100

**Above** Layout plan showing the variety of
ways in which these modular houses can
be laid out either as narrow-frontage
terraces or sideways on to the street.
**Below** The range of two-, three- and
four-bedroom houses, all based on the
standard two-bedroom module with the
stair located in the centre of the
house.

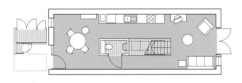

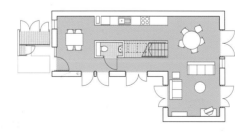

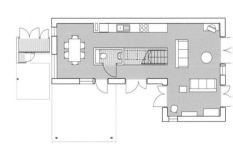

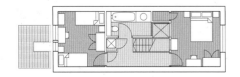

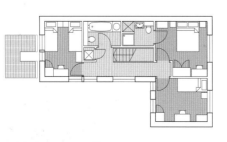

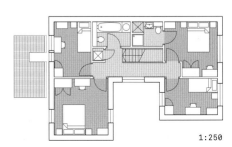

1:250

**Top** Typical street frontage of two-bedroom houses. The steep-pitch gabled roofs are not part of the standard module.
**Above** A standard module placed parallel to the street.
**Right** Views of the unusual interiors created by placing the staircase in the middle of the house rather than along one wall.

# Accordia, Cambridge

This substantial residential quarter is widely regarded as setting a new benchmark for large-scale housing in the UK and was the first housing project to be awarded the RIBA's Stirling Prize, in 2008. It is the result of an unusual collaboration between three of the UK's most highly regarded architects: they and their developer client have taken full advantage of a site that has much to offer. Brooklands Avenue is in a high-value and traditionally secure part of Cambridge and this offered possibilities for the creation of a public realm that can safely break some of the rules about defensible space and Secured by Design that so often stifle innovation in UK housing.

This is a strategically important new residential quarter for Cambridge, sited on the last major undeveloped brownfield site close to the city centre, in a key position between the city and open fields. The site was formerly occupied by low-rise government offices built in the 1940s. The scheme has been masterplanned by Feilden Clegg Bradley Studios with landscape design by Grant Associates. Feilden Clegg Bradley designed 230 of the dwellings, and subcontracted Maccreanor Lavington Architects and Alison Brooks Architects to design 118 and 40 dwellings respectively.

The design includes a variety of innovative house and apartment types in the form of terraces, courtyard houses and set-piece apartment buildings, composed within landscaped public gardens covering approximately 3 hectares – a third of the site.

The buildings are arranged in three dense groups of up to 65 dwellings per hectare, separated by mature landscape, with houses ranging in size from three to five bedrooms (90 to 350 square metres) and apartments of one, two and three bedrooms (45 to 145 square metres). The scheme includes 30 per cent affordable dwellings in mixed tenure, integrated in design and materials with the private housing.

As part of a strong existing landscape framework, including more than 700 mature trees, the principle concept is about 'living in a large garden', informed by contextual references taken from Cambridge college garden courts and the city's public 'greens'. In place of traditional gardens, private open spaces in the form of courtyards, roof terraces and large balconies are designed as an integral part of the architecture. In combination with the generous communal gardens, this aims to reflect the changing aspirations of modern lifestyles and continues a strong tradition of domestic architecture in Cambridge.

The masterplan was designed for pedestrian and cycle demands, with landscaped pedestrian 'streets', mews streets with shared surfaces, discreet car parking and integrated cycle parking for all dwellings. Each dwelling is accessed from an urban shared-surface street side and opens out at the rear on to a communal landscape that includes amenities for passive and active recreation. There is no need for defensible space on the street-entrance side of the terrace and courtyard houses and this gives the streets their mews-like quality, reminiscent of much new urban housing in the Netherlands.

The form of the buildings is not only determined by the relationship and scale of the open space and urban frontages but also by solar orientation. The larger-scale apartment buildings and terraces are associated with the larger-scale open spaces and are typically on an east–west orientation to minimise overshadowing adjacent homes. The lower terraces and courts are arranged around the more intimate landscape spaces with south-facing terraced gardens.

The buildings and landscape have been designed with sustainability in mind, including the environmental performance of each dwelling type, water usage, and the materials and methods used for construction. The external elevations – predominantly an improved imitation of a Cambridge stock brick for the terrace housing – maintain a discipline across the whole site and their success is achieved by the different ways in which openings are treated on the different floor levels. By contrast, the apartments are finished externally with copper and green oak.

**Architects** Feilden Clegg Bradley Studios with Maccreanor Lavington Architects + Alison Brooks Architects
**Landscape architect** Grant Associates
**Developer** Countryside Properties
**Site** 9.5 hectares
**Number of dwellings** 378
**Density** 47 dwellings per hectare, including public open space
**Mix** 212 houses + 166 apartments
**Affordable** 30 per cent
**Parking spaces per dwelling** 1.26

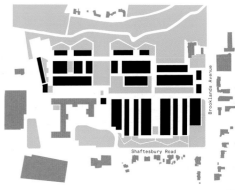

Site plan.

**Right** At Accordia the common areas are characterised by a high standard of planting and landscape.

Overall layout plan. Accordia has
a number of different terrace-
house types and tenures, varying
from high-value semi-detached
houses on the main street
(Brooklands Avenue) to smaller and
more conventional terrace houses
for affordable rent, grouped
together at the rear of the site.
The sale houses are distinctive
for a number of reasons, but
particularly in that their private
patio gardens are contained within
the overall footprint of each
house and most have access from
both front and rear.

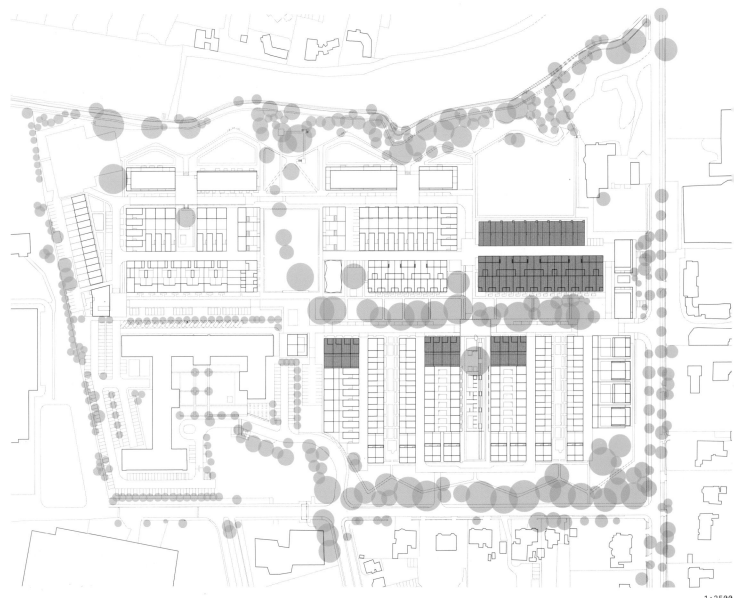

1:2500

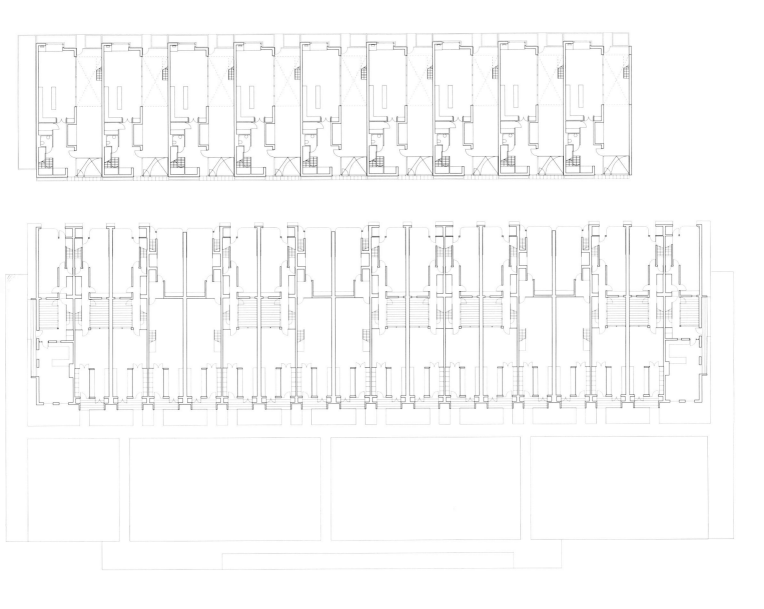

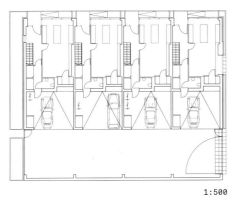

1:500

**Top and bottom** Ground-floor plans of
two house types by Feilden Clegg
Bradley.
**Centre** Ground-floor plans of two
terrace-house types by Maccreanor
Lavington.

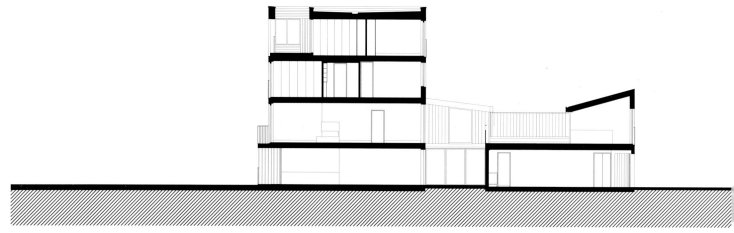

Section A–A of a house type by Maccreanor Lavington
with additional room above the garage and an open
courtyard between the garage and the main house.

1:250

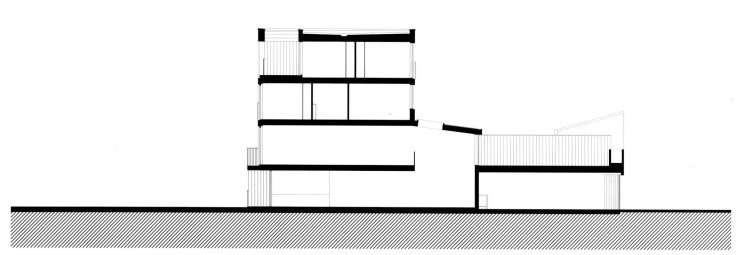

Section B–B of a house type by Maccreanor Lavington
with additional living area at ground-floor level.

1:250

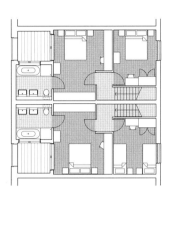

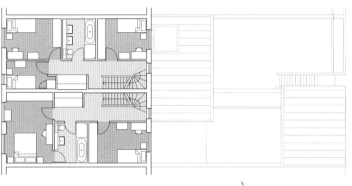

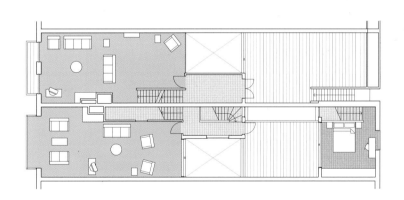

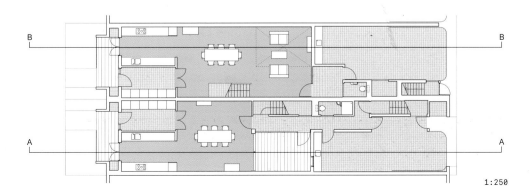

Floor-plan layouts of two
different house types varying
in size between four and five
bedrooms.

1:250

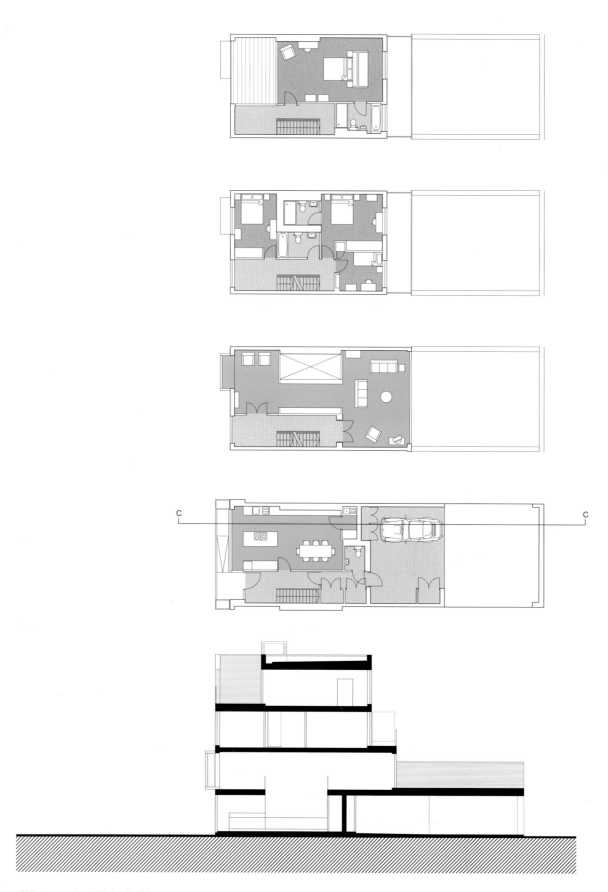

4B7P house, type 08 by Feilden
Clegg Bradley: plans and section
C-C.

1:250

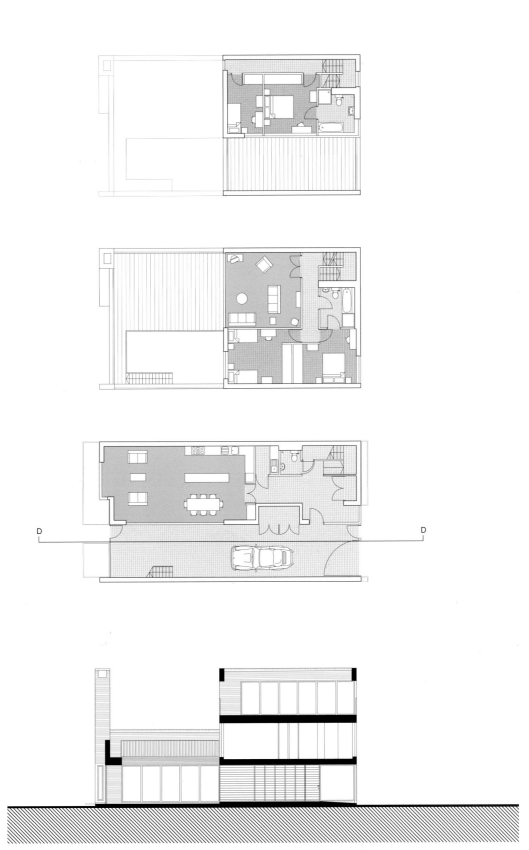

4B7P house, type 12: plans and
section D-D.

1:250

**Top** Rear elevation of Feilden
Clegg Bradley house type 12
opening on to shared green.
**Above** Shared open spaces
throughout.

**Top and centre left** Front and flank elevations of Maccreanor Lavington house types.
**Above** Rear access mews to Maccreanor Lavington house types.
**Left** Terraces to Maccreanor Lavington terrace houses.

This scheme won an open competition between developers in 2005. The design by HTA works within a code established by English Partnerships.

Strictly speaking this is not terrace housing at all but a rare contemporary example of detached and semi-detached houses designed as a group and intended to read together in a formal orthogonal relationship to one another. Although the density is obviously low by comparison with the examples of terrace housing explored elsewhere in this chapter, and the houses are much larger, the layout is economical in terms of making best use of external space.

It is fashionable for the 'style fraternity' of broadsheet readers to decry estates of detached houses placed close to each other with narrow gaps between them. And looking at the average estate of this sort they have good reason, simply because the average housebuilder's product is designed as a stand-alone villa that happens to have landed between two similar villas for no other reason than lack of space.

At Upton, by contrast, everything in the layout is done for a reason, the use of space is economical, the advantage of being able to access your house from front or back is overwhelming, and each house forms part of an ensemble that reads together. Combined with the use of local materials, this should rapidly lead to the development of a collective sense of place. Undoubtedly, the decision to adopt the local configuration of relatively narrow, deep plans provides the perfect form for a street composed of identical steep-pitch gabled roofs, even if the ratio of external wall to internal space is high as a result.

The various different house designs have been unified by the constant gable width and roof pitch. In the same way that additions are added to simple vernacular buildings, simple cubic volumes or smaller gables are added to the one-room-deep house form. This allows the creation of a variety of internal and external living spaces, enables the integration of green roofs, and creates a varied roofline.

The competition for this site was promoted by English Partnerships, the Prince's Trust and Northamptonshire County Council to provide a model for a sustainable urban neighbourhood. So it is perhaps not surprising that the developer has gone to such lengths to incorporate many features for saving both energy and water when most housebuilders still claim that they add nothing to market value.

Although these are either detached or semi-detached houses, the orthogonal layout provides wide south-facing frontages to maximise winter solar gain. Most dwellings front on to streets that are within 15 degrees of east–west and the majority of houses have a sunspace behind the south elevation. Floors and walls are of masonry construction to even out temperature variations.

By combining high-efficency gas condensing boilers delivering locally controlled underfloor heating with solar collectors for hot water, the aim is to reduce $CO_2$ emissions to only 27kg/m$^2$/per year, or less. In addition, six houses are to be fitted with 7.5 square metres of PV panels that are to be grid connected with a total annual output of 115kWh/m$^2$.

With houses of this size, side passages from the rear garden to the street facilitate domestic waste management – including recycling – and there is a purpose-built waste-storage area big enough to allow for more on-site separation in future.

**Architect** HTA
**Developer** David Wilson Homes
**Site** 0.87 hectares
**Number of dwellings** 30
**Density** 34.5 dwellings/hectare
**Affordable** 13 per cent
**Mix** 1 x 6B + 6 x 5B + 13 x 4B + 10 x 3B
**Parking spaces per dwelling** 1.5

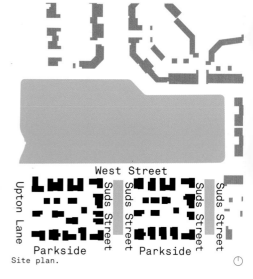

Site plan.

**Right** Houses at Upton have strong unifying features that visually link them. This can be seen in this view of the mews, which is secured from the public but gives rear access to all houses.

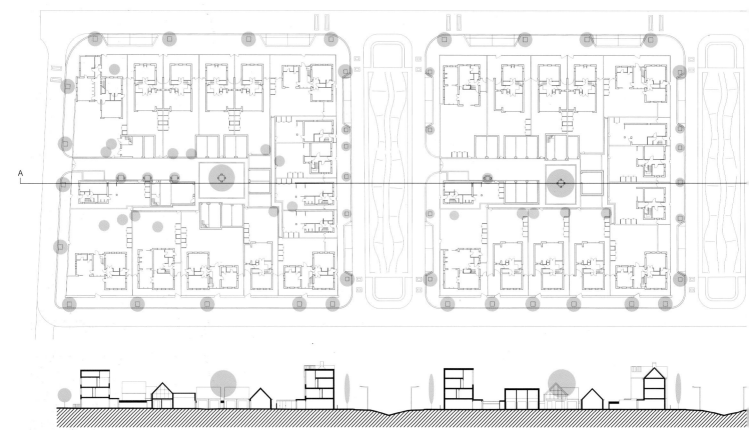

1:100

Above Layout plan and section.
The groups of detached houses
are separated by swales (areas
of low marshy land), part of
the Sustainable Urban Drainage
(SUDS) layout, and are connected
to each other visually by their
repetitive gabled roofs and
physically by their strict
orthogonal layout and garden
walls.
Right Floor plans of a typical
three-bedroom house.

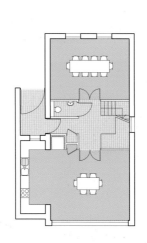
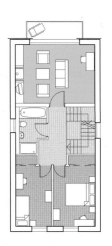
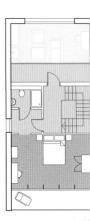

1:25

**Top left** View across the new public open space towards the first completed groups of houses.

**Top right** Although there is more than one external cladding material the palette is small enough to act as a unifying feature and large enough to provide variety.

**Left and above** External views of the street frontages showing the range of different side extensions held together by the strong gabled roof forms.

# Flats: their configuration in blocks, and how to make a flat the home of choice for family living

Roof terrace of private housing
at Freiburg (see Chapter 17).
Note the protection provided by
enclosing the space within the
extended external walls.

Ask a UK city dweller whether he or she would prefer to live in a house or a flat and the response will usually favour the former. But few flats notionally built for families to occupy can compete with the equivalent house: they simply lack the conveniences that houses can offer. This chapter explores those missing facilities and ways through which they can be provided.

In the minds of most people, houses imply, among many other things, direct access to the real ground level and a certain independence of living. Flats, on the other hand, evoke a sense of remoteness from the ground and a definite degree of interdependence. Concerns include density, private open space, access and parking, and there are correspondingly clear implications for security, privacy, waste disposal and the management of shared spaces. More subtle questions arise around the ease with which flat dwellers can make social connections, offer hospitality, develop relationships within the home, enjoy privacy and do practical things like dry clothes, wash the car, store cycles and keep pets.

Closer examination of the issues and implications reveals a confusing mix of benefits and drawbacks. Many could be one or the other depending on how the flats are designed and grouped and who occupies them.

Take security. Many people would feel safer tucked up inside an eighth-floor flat than in a house. Away from the street, with just a few neighbours (all of whom they know) nearby on the landing and at least two locked doors between them and the pavement, it's all quite comforting. But getting to that safe haven has too often involved a convoluted and sometimes threatening journey through the no-man's land of not-quite-defensible shared lobbies and corridors. Of course, good design and layout, high-quality digital entryphones and careful lighting should, and often do, dispel any feelings of insecurity; a concierge, though rarely affordable, provides the ultimate reassurance.

Apart from the question of privacy (see Chapter 9), the critical issues connected with living in flats can be listed under three main headings:

Flats: their configuration in blocks,
and how to make a flat the home of
choice for family living

• quality of internal planning and layout;
• sharing circulation spaces (that is, entrances, lifts, stairs and corridors), common facilities such as refuse disposal and parking, services such as aerial systems and deliveries, and, most importantly, maintenance;
• aspect and orientation.

## Quality of internal planning and layout

As discussed in Chapter 5, designing the layout of flats, like that of terrace houses, involves fewer crucial issues as size increases. As flats get bigger it becomes possible to be less careful in the use of space by providing halls and passages and large rooms whose function, no longer essential, is just to make life more pleasant. Taking the layout of bedrooms as an example, the number of furnishing options in a large room of more than 15 square metres is considerable, whereas in a small room every bit of space counts, while the position of the window and doors and the overall shape are all critical in providing even one satisfactory option.

Commonly, therefore, both developers and users of new flats are engaged in exercising ingenuity, not only in making the most use of the space they can afford to build or buy, but also in organising the planning of flats so that land use is maximised while providing each flat with access to optimum conditions of daylight, sunlight, fresh air and a good view. This is all very well in the design of flats for small households, but when the goal is to squeeze as many people as possible into the smallest possible amount of space it is hardly surprising that families prefer living in houses.

The most radical innovations in the layout of flats for more than half a century have come about when various uses are combined and overlapped through open planning.

There is obviously a distinction between the layout of flats for family (three people and over) and for non-family households (two people and under). There is no such thing as 'one size fits all' in relation to the best place to bring up a family, although most people prefer the idea of a house, with a front door

on to the street and a garden at the back. Examine that preference further and two underlying reasons seem most significant:
• a house is entered directly from the street with no intervening space that has to be shared with anyone else. When children get to an age at which they can be trusted in the street by themselves they are not far from the watchful gaze of a parent. And houses are easier for visitors to find: you don't need to provide a sheaf of special instructions and a map to guide someone to your front door;
• a house invariably has a garden of sorts behind it, conjuring up the possibilities of lazy afternoons surrounded by dogs and happy children playing on sun-filled lawns. However, if you unpack the word 'garden' it can either cover the 30 x 10-metre garden that is found in many traditional suburban streets, or something as small as the 10 x 5-metre patio that comes with a terrace house in a layout of 50 houses per hectare. While either alternative satisfies the aspiration to sit outside and entertain friends while toddlers play and clothes dry, only the larger of the two permits anything like real gardening, a shed for extra storage or space for children's play well into their teenage years.

So there is an argument to be made for bringing up a family in a flat, as opposed to a narrow-frontage terrace house with a 10 x 5-metre patio, if a flat can be equipped with other features that are adequate compensation for not living in a well-designed house. These are:
• a balcony that is large enough for the whole household to use for meals and that gets direct sunlight at some time of the day;
• one extra living space – to make up for the lack of a 'garden', somewhere for teenagers to hang out;
• flexible internal planning so that all children can have a room of their own as they become teenagers;
• a utility room with affordable drying facilities; for example, a tumble dryer with an external vent;
• secure and unthreatening storage at ground level, large enough for buggies and rarely used bulky items;
• secure cycle storage;
• secure facilities for parcel and mail delivery;

Roof-top view of the flats and maisonettes at Odhams Walk in Covent Garden, London. This is urban living that is suitable for families.

Bennet's Yard, Merton Abbey Mills, London SW19, by FCB Studios. Shared circulation in an elegant top-lit atrium.

• good sound insulation to compensate for the lack of two separate floors.

Priorities for non-family flats are different. In addition to cycle storage, a secure place for deliveries and good sound insulation, they usually include:
• making the use of space as economical as possible, concentrating on affordability;
• making the best use of living space through open plans, combining various combinations of living, eating and cooking, either as a single space or two spaces with the dining area as part of the living room or of the kitchen;
• having the bathroom accessible from the bedroom.

## Sharing circulation spaces

Obviously, most flats are in blocks of more than two storeys. Two-storey blocks without lifts used to be quite commonly built for the 'ambulant' elderly, a short-sighted arrangement that inevitably meant a move for older people at the most vulnerable time in their lives, when they could no longer climb stairs. Even for general needs, lift access to every upper-floor dwelling has become essential if the concept of Lifetime Homes (see pages 37–38 and 192–195) is being taken seriously. Where the installation of lifts is not possible because of the economics of a scheme, for instance in a small block with only four or six upper-floor flats, the design should at least incorporate the physical space and the foundations necessary for a lift shaft. Without these simple provisions, retrofitting lifts can be prohibitively expensive.

As buildings with flats rise to seven storeys and above, more than one lift becomes necessary, as six floors are considered to be the most that residents can be expected to climb in the event of lift failure or maintenance.

Assuming that a lift and stair core leads from a single street entrance and lobby, flats can essentially be arranged in one of three different ways. Their front doors can be:
• grouped around the lift and stair core without internal or external corridors;
• accessed from an internal corridor that

leads to the lift and stair core;
• accessed from an external corridor, usually referred to pejoratively as an 'access gallery', which leads to the lift and stair core.

Needless to say, each of these alternatives has both advantages and disadvantages.

**Flats grouped around a core** This can be the ideal arrangement with the shortest distance between lift and stair to the front door; more than five dwellings per floor usually means the lift lobby turns into a corridor. It restricts the number of people sharing circulation space on each floor to a minimum but the total number of households sharing the core depends, of course, on the overall height of the building.

In the case of tall buildings, grouping small numbers of flats around the core may still mean that the lifts, stairs and entrance lobby may be shared by an unacceptably large number of households. In many tall post-war local-authority blocks it was the total number of households sharing a single entrance that became difficult to manage, especially when family-size flats were involved. Where anti-social use of these common areas in new developments is likely to be a problem some form of concierge control has proved to be the only solution, but this has cost implications, especially for residents' service charges. And this is where affordability and security become competing priorities.

The burden of service charges falls much more heavily on shared owners and rent-paying tenants who may be on benefits already and for whom any additional weekly cost should be avoided wherever possible. So at design stage the temptation is to reduce the service-charge element by increasing the number of households sharing each core and, particularly, each lift. As a general principle, however, planning flats for affordable rent so that more than 25 tenancies share a single lift/stair/entrance lobby runs the risk that the scheme may later fail by becoming unmanageable. Even flats built for sale may be risking failure if they have been sold for investment purposes to owners for private renting. Of course there are exceptions and the success of shared

Proposed flat types in small pavilions for Adamstown, Dublin, by Metropolitan Workshop.

entrances and cores can depend on whether incoming residents already know most of their neighbours and on the number of teenagers. Some social-housing developers operate 'local lettings' policies; these assist the formation of strong local communities and are a means of avoiding random letting to homeless households. It may be the difference between success and failure.

A few bold experiments have been attempted that combine tenants and owners sharing the same common access, with very mixed results. In several well-documented cases owner-occupiers, sharing a core with people on affordable tenancies and having their lives disrupted by the activities of neighbours with whom they are of course at very close quarters, have found that they are unable to sell and move away without taking a considerable loss on the resale value of their flat. On the other hand, cores shared between much larger numbers of owner-occupiers and even shared owners, with no affordable tenants, are usually quite sustainable.

**Internal corridors** As the pressures to raise densities and to reduce both construction and service-charge costs increase, an obvious reaction is to reduce the number of lifts and stairs by introducing corridor access. However, this can give rise to an immediate security problem. As the distance between a flat and a sole protected staircase used as the means of escape reaches or exceeds 7.5 metres, unless a fire-engineered solution is achieved it becomes necessary to introduce an alternative means of escape leading directly to the outside. This is covered under part B of the Building Regulations. In affordable housing the presence of a secondary escape route is likely to cause immediate security problems because of unauthorised use by people trying to bypass the controlled-entrance security system.

Although there have been recent examples of private housing successfully planned with generously wide and naturally lit central corridors, it is unlikely the same principle would work as well in schemes containing a high proportion of affordable homes. The dimensions, finishes, lighting and details

of an affordable scheme cannot be as generous as those that can be specified for owner-occupiers. Long, narrow, badly lit and ventilated internal corridors with hard, poor-quality floor finishes can have, and often have had, a most depressing effect on residents whose flats open off them.

But the worst aspect of flats off double-loaded internal corridors is that the flats themselves have a single aspect. This means that for every flat facing south there must be another facing north and therefore deprived of sunlight, while the south-facing flat runs the risk of overheating in summer and has no opportunity for cross-ventilation.

**External access galleries** Most developers of private residential properties maintain that there is a stigma attached to external access galleries and that potential purchasers associate them with often very dreary municipal housing. Their principal advantage, as with central corridors, is to increase the number of flats serviced by a single lift and stair core. They are less efficient than internal double-loaded corridors, although chief among their advantages are the opportunities for natural cross-ventilation that they offer, and, when designed in conjunction with two-storey maisonettes, each alternate floor can have a dual aspect with a consequent reduction in unit frontage.

The justifiable prejudice against narrow access galleries in their normal UK configuration is not shared on the Continent, particularly in the Netherlands. Design subtleties – such as moving the access gallery away from the rear wall of flats or maisonettes with short bridges across to the entrance doors – have enabled Dutch architects to locate the only windows of bedrooms adjacent to the access gallery without an appreciable loss of privacy. Varying the width and providing opportunities for planting and sitting out further humanises such spaces. They have a further advantage as the front entrance door is in the open air.

**Shared circulation at high densities**
As densities increase above 150 dwellings per hectare some of the options already

described become inappropriate or even contradictory. In particular, the principle of limiting the number of affordable rented or private rented dwellings per shared entrance to 20–25 becomes impossible to achieve as the number of storeys increases.

What may then develop is a number of separate, different lift/stair cores, each with its own street entrance, or a single street entrance leading to a number of separate cores, or even a single entrance and multi-lift core leading to a series of corridors or access galleries. From these two last alternatives various types of central atrium have developed that serve several purposes very well. They celebrate the notion of a single controlled entrance for all comings and goings and they also facilitate a much more acceptable version of the access gallery and single-aspect flat. The atrium is usually top-lit and has strategic views out, and it can be either totally enclosed but unheated, or covered but with large enough openings to the outside air to qualify as an externally ventilated space.

Atria perform a useful social and community function as pleasant buffer spaces between the anonymity of the street and privacy behind each individual front door: good places for a chat with neighbours.

In such situations, and where the number of flats exceeds 200, it is possible to consider a manned concierge at the strategic point of entry, rather than simply a secure fob key or similar control on the entry door. Of course concierges can perform other functions such as monitoring underground or covered parking and any other shared facilities, secondary escape routes, cycle stores, etc., but their inclusion largely depends on the level of revenue costs that have to be passed on to residents, particularly to affordable tenants.

## Aspect and orientation

Architects from the 1960s until the start of Postmodernism in the 1980s regarded orientation as a principal determinant in the form and layout of housing, rightly taking the impact of sunlight to be an important factor in people's lives. This was especially true for those who spent most of their time in their homes without any real prospect of holidays in sunny places or of weekending in the country. Making sure that the living rooms of all dwellings would face the sun for a significant part of the day had a higher priority than the formation of real streets lined on both sides with the front doors of houses and flats. In addition, most dwellings had a dual aspect, so flats with east-facing living space almost certainly had west-facing bedrooms that got the afternoon sun and the possibility of cross-ventilation in hot weather.

With the recent emphasis on high urban densities these principles, which had in any case become somewhat discredited as a result of the unsatisfactory priority given to orientation rather than street- and place-making – seem to have been overlooked. Flats in many high-density schemes have not only had their principal living rooms facing east or even north, but by planning them on either side of a central corridor, they only had a single aspect, making those not getting direct sunlight very gloomy and those with a lot of direct sun at serious risk of overheating.

## Guidelines on built form as densities increase

The following eight diagrams describe various low- to medium-rise generic solutions that are typical for the density bands indicated.

To achieve theoretical but comparable densities each is drawn:
• on a 1-hectare plot;
• to include one parking space per dwelling;
• to allow at least 20 metres between principal windows facing each other;
• to include a strip of defensible space between building line and pavement;
• to include private amenity space, balcony, patio or garden for each unit;
• to include shared street-level shared cycle storage, refuse and recycling storage for homes without gardens;
• on the assumption that all dwellings can meet Lifetime Homes standards.

The mix of units shown in each layout varies according to what seems appropriate for the built form. House and maisonette footprints represent three-bedroom, five-person homes and flats are based on either one or two bedrooms. The densities shown would change if the mix were to change.

All layouts set out to test what is possible in relatively low-rise development in order to relate to a hypothetical urban street context.

The diagrams highlight the implications of providing lift access as density rises. The optimum number of units per core in order to make lifts financially viable but keep numbers manageable is between 15 and 25 for affordable rent – and slightly more for market sale. At the lower densities it is difficult to group enough dwellings efficiently around each core to make lift access sensible, but as buildings get taller this becomes easier and, above a certain density, it is desirable to restrict dwelling numbers to just a few units per floor.

In layout 8, which is close to 150 dwellings per hectare, on-street car parking is no longer possible, so a managed solution is necessary.

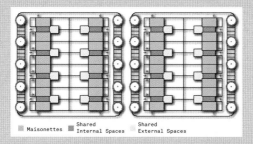

■ Maisonettes ■ Shared Internal Spaces ■ Shared External Spaces

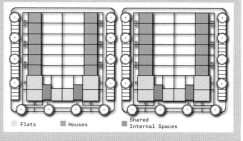

■ Flats ■ Houses ■ Shared Internal Spaces

**Solution 1: 50–75 dwellings per hectare**

Double-stacked family maisonettes with stair cores
64 family maisonettes at four storeys:
• maisonettes double stacked with upper units paired around stairwells;
• no houses or flats;
• lift access not viable;
• two upper-floor units per core;
• shared outdoor space for cycle storage at the rear of stairwells;
• 100 per cent parking on-street and close to homes;
• 50 per cent have own front door to street;
• 50 per cent have private gardens;
• upper dwellings rely on balconies or roof terraces for private amenity.

Management implications very low.

Good solution where predominantly larger family units are needed:
• provide double-stacked maisonettes around stair cores;
• provide balconies or roof terraces to upper-floor homes;
• use ground-floor space for private family gardens rather than for shared gardens;
• consider an alternative arrangement with access galleries where lift access is required.

Additional possibilities: single layer of family maisonettes with small flats over; density, in terms of dwellings per hectare, would remain the same but height would reduce to three storeys.

**Solution 2: 50-75 dwellings per hectare**

Houses and flats with stair cores
24 two-storey family houses + 32 flats at three storeys:
• four shared cores;
• four combined refuse/recycling and cycle stores for flats;
• all parking on street: not well overlooked by flats;
• approximately 50 per cent of dwellings could have own front doors at street level;
• approximately 50 per cent of dwellings have private gardens;
• no shared amenity space for remaining dwellings so these rely on balconies or private roof terraces.

Management implications fairly low.

Good solution where providing some houses is a priority:
• provide terraces of housing with corner flat blocks;
• restrict flat blocks to three or four storeys where lifts are not essential;
• provide stair-only cores serving small numbers of dwellings;
• use ground-floor space for private family gardens.

Additional possibilities: flats could increase to four storeys; density would increase to 68 dwellings per hectare, but lifts not viable at nine units per core. On-street parking would remain possible.

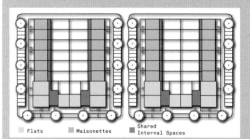

Flats  Maisonettes  Shared Internal Spaces

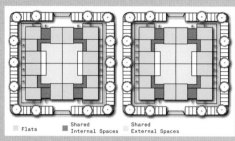

Flats  Shared Internal Spaces  Shared External Spaces

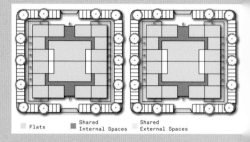

Flats  Shared Internal Spaces  Shared External Spaces

**Solution 3: 75-100 dwellings per hectare**
**Flats and maisonettes with lift access**

48 maisonettes + 32 flats at three storeys:
• four shared cores;
• four combined refuse/recycling and cycle stores for flats;
• all parking on street: not well overlooked by flats;
• approximately 50 per cent of dwellings could have own front doors at street level;
• approximately 50 per cent of dwellings have private gardens;
• no shared amenity space for remaining dwellings so these rely on balconies or private roof terraces.

Management implications fairly high.

Good solution where some larger family units are required, and lift access is needed:
• provide lift cores to groups of flats and extend access galleries to serve upper floor maisonettes;
• restrict each length of gallery to six dwellings or fewer;
• provide secondary security at head of the gallery on each floor;
• achieve at least 10 upper-floor units per core, preferably 15, but not more than 25;
• provide balconies or roof terraces to upper-floor homes;
• use ground-floor space for private family gardens rather than for shared gardens;
• avoid locating habitable rooms on gallery side;
• use sound-resilient flooring to gallery.

Additional possibilities: single layer of family maisonettes with small flats over; density would remain the same but height would reduce to three storeys.

**Solution 4: 75-100 dwellings per hectare**
**Flats with stair cores**

88 flats at three storeys:
• eight shared cores with short internal or external corridors;
• eight combined refuse/recycling and cycle stores – one per core;
• shared outdoor space secured for use only by residents;
• all parking on street well overlooked;
• approximately 25 per cent of dwellings could have own front doors at street level;
• only eight dwellings have private rear patios;
• high-quality shared amenity space to compensate for lack of gardens

Management implications fairly high.

Good solution for lower-rise layouts where lift access is not essential:
• provide stair-only cores each serving small number of flats;
• restrict number of three-bed and larger flats to a minimum;
• retain individual access to street-level/ground-level flats where possible;
• provide balconies or roof terraces to upper-floor homes;
• where more larger family homes are required, make ground-floor units maisonettes or revert to a lower-density solution.

Additional possibilities: could increase to four storeys – see Solution 7; on-street parking would remain possible or some family maisonettes could be introduced at ground level to reduce density, especially as lifts not viable anyway.

**Solution 5: 75-100 dwellings per hectare**
**Flats with lift access**

88 flats at minimum three storeys:
• four shared cores with short internal or external corridors;
• secondary security advisable on landings as eight flats per floor to each core;
• four refuse/recycling stores and four separate cycle stores – one each per core;
• shared outdoor space secured for use only by residents;
• all parking on street, well overlooked;
• approximately 25 per cent of dwellings could have their own front doors at street level;
• only eight dwellings have rear patios;
• high-quality shared amenity space to compensate for lack of gardens – not easy for all ground-floor users to access.

Management implications fairly high.

Good solution for lower-rise layouts where lift access is needed:
• achieve at least ten upper floor units per lift core, preferably 15, but not more than 25;
• keep corridors or access galleries as short as possible by placing cores centrally in a group of flats.

Additional possibilities: floor height could increase, on-street parking would remain possible; introducing family maisonettes to reduce density not advisable as lift viability is marginal already.

# Flats: their configuration in blocks, and how to make a flat the home of choice for family living

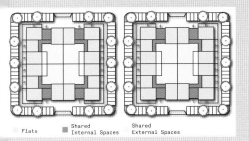

Flats | Shared Internal Spaces | Shared External Spaces

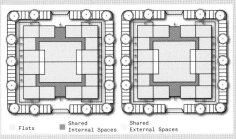

Flats | Shared Internal Spaces | Shared External Spaces

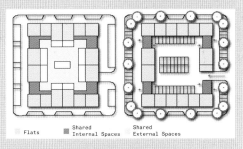

Flats | Shared Internal Spaces | Shared External Spaces

| Solution 6: 100-125 dwellings per hectare | Solution 7: 100-125 dwellings per hectare | Solution 8: 125-150 dwellings per hectare |
|---|---|---|
| **Taller flats with stair cores** | **Taller flats with lift access** | **Flats with raised courtyard over parking** |

**Solution 6: 100-125 dwellings per hectare**
**Taller flats with stair cores**

120 flats at minimum four storeys:
• eight shared cores with short internal or external corridors;
• four combined refuse/recycling and separate cycle stores — one each per core;
• shared outdoor space secured for use only by residents (could be subdivided to provide dedicated space for each core group, but better as a single shared space);
• all parking on street well overlooked;
• approximately 20 per cent of dwellings could have own front doors at street level;
• only eight dwellings have rear patios.

Management implications fairly high.

Good solution for denser layouts where lift access is not essential:
• provide stair-only cores, each serving a small number of flats;
• restrict number of three-bed and larger flats to a minimum;
• retain individual access to street-level/ground-level flats where possible;
• provide balconies or roof terraces to upper-floor homes;
• provide small rear patio gardens to ground-level flats combined with shared outdoor space rather than large private gardens to a few flats;
• restrict height to three storeys where possible, four storeys maximum;
• consider a caretaking service;
• where more larger-family homes are required, make ground-floor units maisonettes, consider top-floor three-bed flats with private roof terraces, or revert to a lower-density solution.

Additional possibilities: could introduce family maisonettes at ground level to reduce density, especially as lifts not viable anyway.

**Solution 7: 100-125 dwellings per hectare**
**Taller flats with lift access**

120 flats at minimum four storeys:
• four shared cores with short internal or external corridors;
• secondary security on landings highly desirable;
• four refuse/recycling stores and four separate cycle stores — one each per core;
• shared outdoor space secured for use by residents (could be subdivided as shown);
• around 20 per cent of dwellings could have their own front doors at street level;
• only eight dwellings have rear patios.

Management implications high.

Good solution for denser layouts where lift access is needed:
• achieve at least ten upper floor units per lift core, preferably 15, but not more than 25;
• keep corridors or access galleries as short as possible by placing cores centrally;
• restrict number of three-bed and larger flats to a minimum;
• retain individual access to street-level/ground-level flats where possible;
• provide balconies or roof terraces to upper-floor homes;
• provide small rear patio gardens to ground-level flats combined with shared outdoor space rather than large private gardens to a few flats;
• balance mix to check that user numbers and child density are within manageable limits;
• consider a caretaking service;
• where more larger-family homes are required, make ground-floor units maisonettes, consider top-floor three-bed flats with private roof terraces, or revert to a lower-density solution.

Additional possibilities: core numbers now at the high end of the optimum range; could introduce some family maisonettes to reduce density and restrict number of users, especially children, per core.

**Solution 8: 125-150 dwellings per hectare**
**Flats with raised courtyard over parking**

145 flats at minimum four storeys:
• eight shared cores with short internal or external corridors;
• four combined refuse/recycling and cycle stores;
• raised, shared outdoor space for use only by residents. Needs ventilation to car park below and may need irrigation to planting;
• on-street parking can no longer provide 100 per cent secure parking; controlled access essential.

Management implications very high but relatively good for this density range.

Good solution where density has increased beyond the point where on-street parking is no longer possible:
• achieve at least ten upper-floor units per lift core, preferably 15, but not more than 25;
• keep corridors or access galleries as short as possible by placing cores centrally in a group of flats;
• restrict number of three-bed and larger flats to a minimum;
• consider maisonettes on lowest two floors with living rooms at first-floor level in order to avoid single-aspect flats here; provide balconies or roof terraces to upper-floor homes;
• balance mix to check that user numbers and child density are within manageable limits;
• provide CCTV and an on-site caretaking service, or consider a concierge;
• where more larger-family homes are required, consider top-floor three-bed flats with private roof terraces or revert to a lower-density solution.

Additional possibilities: could introduce some family maisonettes but now better at first floor as ground-floor units are single aspect without gardens.

**Diagrammatic circulation layouts for flats around lift and stair cores**

This series of diagrams illustrates the relationship between the way that flats are grouped around a core, building height and the affordability of providing lifts.

In order to keep lift-service charges at a reasonable level, it is usually necessary to share the cost between at least ten dwellings, and preferably between 15-20. In lower-density areas, where buildings are three to five storeys high, a reasonably large number of flats must be provided at each floor level, often resulting in extended horizontal circulation.

As density rises and storey heights increase, lifts become viable with far fewer dwellings per floor, allowing circulation to be significantly reduced. But above seven storeys it is considered good practice to provide two lifts - to provide cover in the event of breakdown or repair. That inevitably means that dwelling numbers have to be increased beyond the minimum needed to cover the costs of a single lift, so the optimum grouping patterns change again.

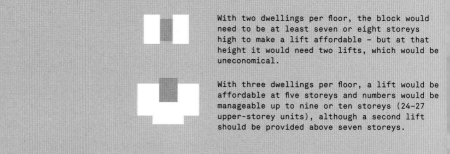

With two dwellings per floor, the block would need to be at least seven or eight storeys high to make a lift affordable - but at that height it would need two lifts, which would be uneconomical.

With three dwellings per floor, a lift would be affordable at five storeys and numbers would be manageable up to nine or ten storeys (24-27 upper-storey units), although a second lift should be provided above seven storeys.

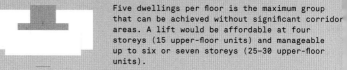

Five dwellings per floor is the maximum group that can be achieved without significant corridor areas. A lift would be affordable at four storeys (15 upper-floor units) and manageable up to six or seven storeys (25-30 upper-floor units).

With eight dwellings per floor, a lift would be affordable at three storeys (16 upper-floor units) but above four storeys (24 upper-floor units) numbers would be difficult to manage.

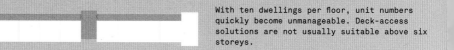

With ten dwellings per floor, unit numbers quickly become unmanageable. Deck-access solutions are not usually suitable above six storeys.

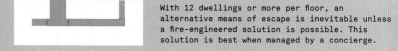

With 12 dwellings or more per floor, an alternative means of escape is inevitable unless a fire-engineered solution is possible. This solution is best when managed by a concierge.

# Flats: their configuration in blocks, and how to make a flat the home of choice for family living

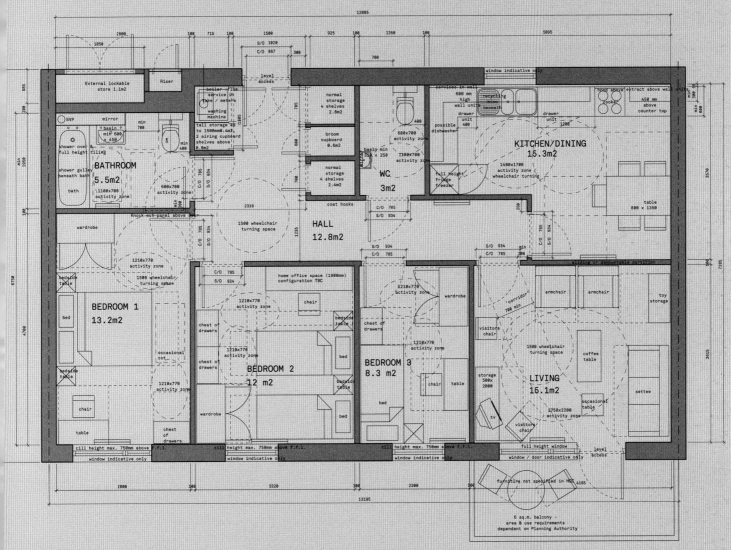

## What needs to go into a typical three-bedroom flat for affordable rent?

This plan shows a typical layout for a straightforward, efficient five-person family flat. Much of what it shows would apply equally well to layouts for flats with more or fewer bedrooms but it serves to illustrate the basic requirements, some of which are easy to forget.

Although designed to have all principle rooms facing in the same direction, it assumes that natural light and ventilation are also possible to the kitchen and bathroom at the rear of the plan, located on an access gallery. A separate kitchen/dining room is therefore possible, giving the family more space to engage simultaneously in different activities.

Internal storage is reasonably generous and easy to access, and there is provision for 'external storage' – space for bulky or dirty items, to be kept close to but outside the home. The Lifetime Homes bathroom and cloakroom each allow for wheelchair access to the WC, and the second or twin bedroom contains a long desk, suitable for homework and large enough to qualify as a 'home office space' under the Code for Sustainable Homes.

The plan is designed for full occupancy: there are no spare rooms and little spare space, but even this unremarkable layout provides some flexibility for the time when children leave home and priorities change. The kitchen/diner could be combined with the living room and the hallway shortened to provide a large open-plan space. Similarly, the single bedroom would work well as a study or dining room or it could be combined with either Bedroom 2 or the living space. As household size reduces, the separate WC may be considered unnecessary and could become a utility space or absorbed into the kitchen and the hallway reduced further.

Structure permitting, the combined effect of these modifications would create quite a different home with two double bedrooms and a very large, almost square living/dining/kitchen space occupying half of the total plan area.

## Good practice 3B5P flat

GIA, 92 square meters,[1] 13.195 metres wide, 7.285 metres deep (dimensions in mm unless otherwise annotated).
[1] area excludes external store and riser

The background to the whole development of what is known as Bermondsey Spa is described in the case study covering the early phases in Chapter 7. This site on the landward side of the railway was acquired from the borough as a result of competitive tender by Hyde Housing Association in 2004. Council policy was aimed at attracting owner-occupiers into the area, as well as increasing the stock of affordable homes.

Southwark was a London inner borough that used to be subject to a 'density ceiling' of 150 dwellings per hectare (500 habitable rooms per hectare). However, the introduction of government guidance encouraging the reuse of brownfield land, coupled with the Mayor of London's lifting of density ceilings after 2000, caused an immediate hike in land values, so that developing housing even to the previous maximum was no longer an option. What would previously have been considered the maximum of about 90 dwellings on this site had to be increased to nearly 140 without, if possible, any reduction in the quality of life of future residents.

The tallest buildings, up to eight storeys, are placed on the eastern edge of the site, mirroring the new buildings of equivalent height on the other side of the railway, and a block of only four storeys is sited along the western boundary. The intention is to temper the abrupt change of scale that would otherwise occur between the traditional estates to the west and the new taller, denser buildings on the other side of the railway. For the flats on the eastern side one distinguishing feature is the circulation system incorporating a covered 'atrium' – a device that has the benefit of reducing the number of separate lift and stair cores without resorting to open-access galleries or, worse still, to long internal double-loaded corridors.

The design incorporates a car park at street level beneath the main amenity space, in the form of a raised courtyard enclosed by housing on all four sides (see Chapter 10). The car park is disguised and the 'live frontage' on to the surrounding streets is preserved by adopting a family maisonette with a single-aspect ground floor, backed against the car park, with a dual-aspect first floor that has a rear patio at the same level as the main first-floor courtyard. This is perforated with openings to accommodate large species trees in the courtyard.

**Architect** Levitt Bernstein Associates
**Developer** Hyde Housing Association
**Site** 0.583 hectares
**Number of dwellings** 138
**Density** 237 dwellings/hectare (682 HR/hectare)
**Mix** 18 x 3B + 69 x 2B + 51 x 1B
**Affordable** 50 per cent
**Parking spaces per dwelling** 0.4

Site plan.

**Right** External detail and general view. The scheme has ground- and first-floor maisonettes. The former are single aspect, backing on to the undercroft car park at the rear but with their own front-door access to the street. On the upper floor they are dual aspect with a rear patio that opens on to the main shared podium above the car park.

1:2500

Tucked into a corner beside the
main railway line from London
Bridge, this is a high-density
mixed-tenure development of flats
and maisonettes. Half of them
enclose a raised podium with car
parking below and the other half
are accessed from a glazed atrium.

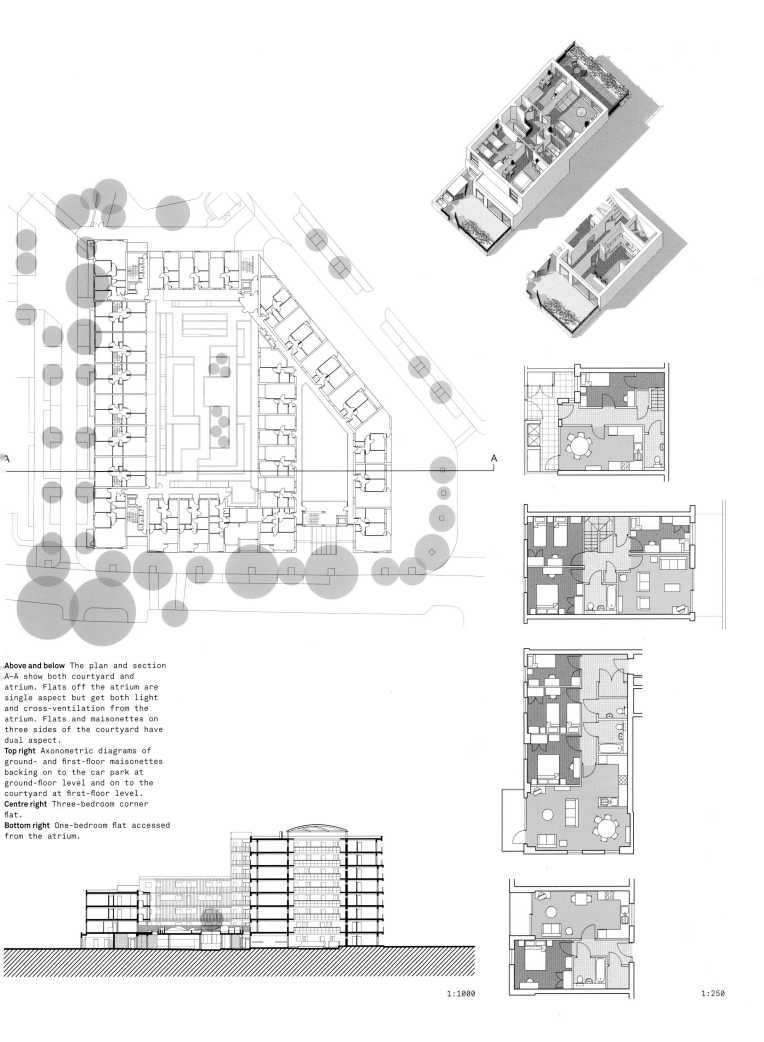

**Above and below** The plan and section A–A show both courtyard and atrium. Flats off the atrium are single aspect but get both light and cross-ventilation from the atrium. Flats and maisonettes on three sides of the courtyard have dual aspect.
**Top right** Axonometric diagrams of ground- and first-floor maisonettes backing on to the car park at ground-floor level and on to the courtyard at first-floor level.
**Centre right** Three-bedroom corner flat.
**Bottom right** One-bedroom flat accessed from the atrium.

1:1000

1:250

# Aylesbury Estate regeneration, Southwark, London SE1

This is the initial phase in the replacement of a very large 2760-dwelling estate bequeathed to the London Borough of Southwark at the dissolution of the Greater London Council in the early 1980s. When completed, this phase will comprise 260 dwellings, a neighbourhood resource centre and some retail. The entire development is being undertaken by a single large housing association.

The estate had defied three previous attempts to rescue it from total demolition but has now finally succumbed and is due to be redeveloped in phases over a period of years to provide 4200 homes, a considerable increase on the original. Several of the earlier proposals failed when the existing residents, mostly affordable tenants, campaigned against what they perceived as the threat to their council homes posed by the involvement of private house-building companies. By the time the third attempt to refurbish the existing flats had failed, due to a combination of cost and the discovery of further structural defects, residents were persuaded that the only possible course of action was to replace the entire estate, much of which is in the form of very large 14-storey system-built slab blocks.

But the council's declared aim of diluting the enormous number of flats occupied by their tenants with a very significant percentage of privately owned homes necessarily meant that overall density had to be increased without resorting to building high. The initial phase averages around six storeys with a taller block of ten storeys overlooking the park on the other side of the road, but the density of around 220 dwellings per hectare, around twice the existing, demanded a built form of urban-scale blocks closely lining both existing and former streets. The latter have been reopened to increase the pedestrian permeability of the estate, as a way of integrating the new buildings into the neighbourhood.

The urban form encloses a series of three open courtyards: one is publicly accessible and uses a converted Victorian school building as an attractive backdrop, while the other two are entirely enclosed shared-amenity spaces.

A 'green route' runs through the site, linking a new urban-scale square at the northern end – which will be the location for the local street market as well as the entrance to the new resource centre – with the open expanses of Burgess Park to the south.

Although each circulation core largely serves a single tenure, in external appearance the three different forms of tenure are indistinguishable from one another (see Chapter 11).

In spite of its high density, the design does not resort to single-aspect flats reached via a central double-loaded corridor. Where the two courtyard blocks converge, an atrium has been formed between them, with dual-aspect flats accessed by a series of bridges and galleries through which light from the roof glazing filters down to the floors below. Elsewhere the flats are served by lift and stair cores but without corridors. Although the design avoids long internal corridors or external access galleries, the number of flats per core is more than the recommended limit of 20–25. The design solution is to introduce a secondary controlled entrance at each floor level as well as keeping the number of affordable rented flats per core to a minimum.

Because of the additional social pressure brought on by high-density living, the affordable flats have been designed to larger than normal space standards (Parker Morris + 10 per cent) and all flats have access either to large private balconies or to terraces of at least 10 square metres.

**Architect** Levitt Bernstein Associates
**Developer** London & Quadrant Housing Trust
**Site** 1.247 hectares
**Number of dwellings** 260
**Density** 209 dwellings/hectare (655 HR/hectare)
**Mix** 26 x 3B + 135 x 2B + 99 x 1B
**Affordable** 35 per cent
**Parking spaces per dwelling** 0.22
**Non-housing uses** Aylesbury Resource Centre, 1500 square metres

Site plan.

**Right** Computer-generated images of the first replacement housing for the Aylesbury Estate Regeneration project, in which tenures are mixed and all flats are accessed from secure individual lift and stair cores. Large areas of common open space are avoided and the entire layout is integrated with existing surrounding streets.
**Far right** Street level on the existing estate is almost entirely dominated by parked cars and lock-up garages. It was designed for all pedestrians to use the upper-level walkway system, which is both inconvenient and insecure. The 14-storey blocks have a single entrance with no access control.

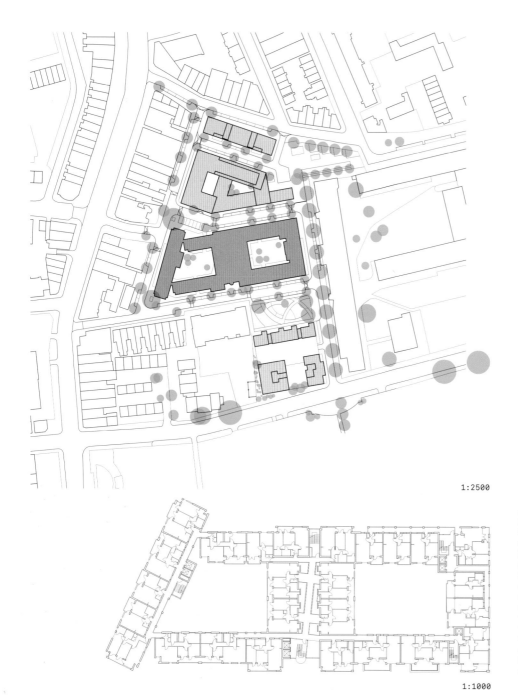

1:2500

1:1000

**Above left** Masterplan.
**Left** Layout of 131 mixed-tenure
flats showing four different
stair and lift cores, the
largest of which incorporates
a covered atrium. Ground-level
flats have their own independent
street access. The four cores
serve 38, 29, 36 and seven flats
respectively. The cores serving
the largest number of flats have
the highest concentration of flats
for private sale. In addition,
each of the three largest groups
have secondary access control at
each landing level.

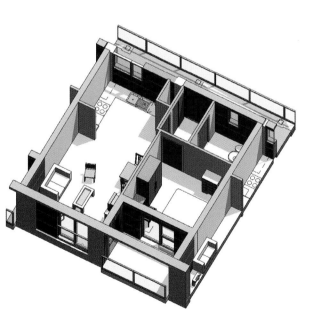

**Top** Section through the same block
showing the two shared internal
courtyards. Entry is restricted to
the flats that surround each one.
**Centre** Typical one-bedroom flat with
inset balcony.
**Right** Perspective of access to flats
from the atrium.

# Internal space: guidance, standards and regulation

Research into the amount of space that households of different sizes need is usually confined to homes at the lower ends of either the private or the affordable market. Given the opportunity, most people rent or buy as large an area as they can afford. At the upper, luxury end of the private market people buy more space so they can have larger living rooms, room for entertaining, separate dining rooms, extra bedrooms, en-suite bathrooms, utility rooms, larger hallways and, of course, more storage capacity. At this end of the market there is no need to codify how much space is needed for any given number of occupants. The situation can be compared with some of the vast nineteenth-century terrace houses with enormous rooms and space for innumerable servants and in which overall occupancy would have been very low. At the same time there would have been every reason to set standards for the minimum nineteenth-century 'two-up, two-downs' that covered vast areas of Victorian cities and in which many people endured miserable, overcrowded lives.

## Merging the standards of different tenures
Where the situation is cost-critical, developers of affordable housing for rent need to be sure they are providing sufficient and well-organised space, while the builders of private homes for sale usually provide just as much space as their first-time, entry-level purchasers can afford to mortgage.

The amount of internal space to be provided in houses and flats in the UK has never been officially controlled as part of Building Regulations. However, standards have been applied as a condition of subsidy in publicly funded rented housing throughout most of the period between the end of World War 1 to the present day. Space standards in private housing, on the other hand, being free of subsidy, have escaped any form of regulation and have consequently been determined by the market.

Recent efforts to blur the social and physical distinctions between private, owner-occupied homes at the lower end of the market and those for affordable rent, in order to create communities that are 'tenure neutral', have been complicated by

the considerable difference in the space standards set for affordable rented housing and what the market usually provides in homes for sale. In both sectors homes have normally been classified by the number of their bedrooms. Whenever there is a straight comparison between the net internal floor areas of affordable homes for rent and private sale, and shared-ownership homes in the first-time-buyers' sector, each with the same number of bedrooms, the affordable rented house or flat is invariably larger than its private-sector equivalent. This causes problems with any attempt to develop a 'one size fits all' approach to building schemes in which tenures are mixed together.

Closer examination of the way households in the two sectors actually use their homes reveals an entirely different method of comparing them and also reveals why they tend to have different sizes for the same number of bedrooms. Affordable tenancies are usually occupied up to the maximum number of bed spaces provided and there is little chance of moving as children grow older and need more space. In contrast, the private sector can very often afford to under-occupy by using at least one bedroom either for guests or for storage or as an office/workroom. And when the owner-occupier grows out of one home he or she has the option of trading up to something bigger. Once comparisons are based on the amount of space each member of either type of household actually needs for everyday living or to sleep comfortably, there should be no difference between the two types of tenure.

## Standards of social (affordable) housing regulated through subsidy
Internal space standards for rented social housing have, until recently, only been expressed in the relatively crude terms of overall net internal floor area per dwelling, and there has been a long history of tying them tightly to the amount of subsidy receivable per house or flat. Parker Morris standards applied to the development of social housing by local authorities were regulated in this way until the Thatcher government abandoned both the standards and the housing they were designed for in

Designers need to be acutely aware that furniture for bedrooms and living rooms comes in a surprising variety of shapes and sizes! The shape of rooms and the positions of openings in them are therefore crucial, as well as their overall size.

the early 1980s. After that, responsibility for
providing social (now known as 'affordable')
housing passed to the housing associations,
regulated by The Housing Corporation.
This effectively dodged the issue of space
standards, introducing instead a space
banding system, known as Total Cost
Indicators, tied to the subsidies that were
made available.

Affordable space standards now form part of
a complex briefing document called *Housing
Quality Indicators*. Though the relationship
between unit size and subsidy is not a direct
one, designers need to understand it in
order to ensure that dwellings comply with
the minimum standard required for grant
eligibility, and that where they exceed the
minimum they optimise their 'point scoring'
position in the higher bands defined by
percentage increase. Realising that there
has to be some flexibility, The Housing
Corporation (since January 2009 replaced
by the Homes and Comunities Agency)
publishes bands of normal range areas for a
variety of dwelling types. These are based on
the number of bed spaces and the number
of storeys for each type with a subsidy figure
based on accumulating points, as long as
plans fit somewhere above the minimum and
below the maximum. Of course, this leads
clients and designers to fix their dwelling
layouts fractionally above the minimum in
each band in order to attract the maximum
subsidy with the minimum buildable area
and, therefore, cost of construction.

## Guidance on dwelling layout

The imposition of minimum overall space
standards per dwelling on their own is no
guarantee of good internal layouts and
permits designs that feature awkwardly
shaped rooms and space wasted through
inefficient circulation. The standards
introduced in 1961 as *Homes for Today
and Tomorrow* (better known as the Parker
Morris report) were based on allowances
for net internal floor areas for different
sizes and types of dwelling. Intentionally,
it contained no guidance on the sizes of
individual rooms, as the idea was to leave
all such decisions to designers. Either early
results were considered quite unsatisfactory
or designers themselves wanted guidance on

how much space should ideally be allocated
for various functions: whatever the reason,
*Homes for Today and Tomorrow* was rapidly
followed by further government clarification
in various Design Bulletins. In particular,
these covered the layout of kitchens and
bathrooms and generally gave optimum sizes
and arrangements for internal layouts. Parts
of these were published in an expanded form
in *The Architects' Journal Metric Handbook*.

These were, and still are, usable tools.
However, throughout the 1980s and the
first half of the 1990s the Conservative
government had been philosophically
opposed to the idea of reviving any notion
of space standards in social housing and
it formally ceased to refer to Parker Morris
standards, on the principle that whatever 'the
market' produced for sale was good enough
for social housing.

It was not until 1998 that the Joseph Rowntree
Foundation prompted the National Housing
Federation to get round this embargo by
looking at the activities that new homes
needed to accommodate, rather than
reviving minimum space standards.
The National Housing Federation duly
published *Standards and Quality in Housing
Association Development*, now in its second
edition. Although this document is only for
guidance, and avoids any reference to actual
space standards, it does for the first time
set out guidance on how to accommodate
essential activities in all the principal rooms
of a house or flat, expressing minimum
space requirements for those activities and
the furniture needed in each room. These
standards are now incorporated into Housing
Quality Indicators and are the basis for
scoring points under 'unit layout', another
criterion for which a minimum score is
essential for grant consideration.

## Space standards applied to both private
## and affordable housing

Useful as the first edition of *Standards and
Quality* was, it was not convenient as a
design tool in the early stages of new housing
design. It was only the second edition,
published in 2008, that provided something
more up to date for this purpose than the
1961 Parker Morris standards.

As recently as 2006 the Greater London Authority became increasingly alarmed by the large number of very small dwellings – particularly one- and two-bedroom flats in the private sector – that had been appearing in the planning applications it reviewed. Consequently the GLA commissioned an entirely new report on space standards that set out to resolve the apparently conflicting approaches of the private- and affordable-housing sectors by proposing that internal space allowances should be related not to the number of bedrooms a dwelling contains – the traditional measure – but to the expected occupancy of each dwelling, applied across both social and private sectors. It went further and suggested allowing more design flexibility by not attempting to set space standards for individual rooms but to break down the internal floor area of dwellings into just three 'zones'. It concluded that as long as circulation and bathrooms are adequate, what really matters to occupants is the amount of usable space in the main functional areas, and that this is a more reliable means of achieving reasonably spacious dwellings than simply dictating overall floor area.

At the same time, it set out to allow more flexibility in design by defining two main 'zones' within the dwelling rather than by setting fixed standards for individual rooms. This encouraged different types of living space and combinations of bedrooms:
• 'cooking/eating/living space'; that is, kitchens, dining rooms and living rooms;
• sleeping space; that is, bedrooms.

Internal storage requirements were also defined as, unlike bathrooms, it was felt that they must necessarily increase for each additional person.

For guidance purposes, a percentage add-on was applied to the sum total of the zone areas in order to achieve a set of minimum internal dwelling areas, known as IMDAs. The report makes clear that this is to be a secondary standard and one which is conditional on demonstrating that the minimum area had been achieved for the two main functional zones and for 'internal storage' for each dwelling.

Originally it was intended that these proposals for the GLA should be bound into the latest version of the London Plan for application in both housing sectors, but strong representations from the house-building industry succeeded in limiting the publication merely to an advisory document. However, at the time of going to press it seems likely that the GLA will adopt a set of mandatory space standards for all tenures across the board – it is not yet clear what these standards will be.

In November 2007 English Partnerships, a body set up by government, now also part of the Homes and Communities Agency (and with its influence growing through the merger with The Housing Corporation to form the HCA), published its own standards: *Spaces Homes, People, English Partnerships' Quality Standards*. These are intended to apply to all housing schemes, regardless of tenure, over which the organisation has any control, usually through ownership of the land. In terms of internal space the English Partnerships' document sets out higher standards than anything previously available including all but one of the 'normal range' standards of the Housing Corporation's HQIs; however, it is clearly a work in progress. For instance, generous as they appear, these standards cover only a small range of dwelling types, with fixed couplings of occupancy and numbers of bedrooms. They make no distinction between the space allowance for houses as opposed to flats and generally ignore any provision for external storage, although this was a Housing Corporation requirement.

The impact of the introduction of Lifetime Homes on housing for sale and for rent generally is complicated. Since their introduction, the measures advocated in Lifetime Homes have generally been welcomed, from government downwards, as expressing a thoroughly sensible social objective, that of making it possible for any member of a household to continue living an independent life in their own home for as long as possible through old age or infirmity. But moving from intent through interpretation to implementation is less straightforward. Although originally conceived for

## Comparison of space standards

| Dwelling type | | HQI 2003 | EP 2007 | NHF 2008 | PM 1961 | GLA 2006 | LHDG 2010 |
|---|---|---|---|---|---|---|---|
| | | Housing Corporation (legacy) standard: Housing Quality Indicators normal range | English Partnerships (legacy) standard | National Housing Federation: indicative minimum dwelling area | Parker Morris standard | Greater London Authority: Draft standards issued as guidance only | London Housing Design Guide: Interim Edition |
| 1B2P | 1-storey | 45–50 | 51 | 50 | 45.5 | 44 | 50 |
| 2B3P | 1-storey | 57–67 | 66 | 61 | 57.8 | 57 | 61 |
| 2B4P | 1-storey | 67–75 | 77 | 70 | 71.1 | 67 | 70 |
| | 2-storey | – | – | 82 | 73.8 | – | 83 |
| 3B5P | 1-storey | 75–85 | 93 | 86 | 80.7 | 81 | 86 |
| | 2-storey | 82–85 | – | 96 | 84.1 | – | 96 |
| | 3-storey | – | – | 102 | 96.1 | – | 102 |
| 3B6P | 1-storey | 85–95 | – | – | 87.8 | – | 95 |
| | 2-storey | 95–100 | – | – | 94.2 | – | – |
| | 3-storey | 100–105 | – | – | 99.8 | – | – |
| 4B6P | 1-storey | 85–95 | 106 | – | 87.8 | 92 | 99 |
| | 2-storey | 95–100 | – | 108 | 94.2 | – | 107 |
| | 3-storey | 100–105 | – | 114 | 99.8 | – | 113 |
| 4B7P | 2-storey | 108–115 | – | 117 | – | 105 | – |
| | 3-storey | – | – | 123 | – | – | – |
| 5B7P | 2-storey | 108–115 | – | 120 | – | – | – |
| | 3-storey | – | – | 126 | – | – | – |

Notes

1 All figures are internal floor area in square metres.

2 HQI and PM only give areas per person; for example, a 3B6P unit has the same area range as a 4B6P unit.

3 PM and EP do not go above six people.

4 HQI areas here exclude external storage.

5 PM figures here include an allowance for internal storage; additional external storage not shown.

6 In 2006 the GLA commissioned independent research into minimum space standards. This concluded that minimum standards should be applied uniformly across all tenures, and that in determining dwelling mix for planning purposes, flats or houses should be categorised not by the number of bedrooms but by the number of people to be housed. This was in order to prevent, for instance , construction of large numbers of small two-bedroom flats for sale that were never intended to house more than two people, when the planning intention was to create two-bedroom family homes for up to four people. These proposals, in spite of the very modest areas proposed, were considered too radical to impose on all sectors of housing at the time. They were not incorporated as mandatory into the London Plan, but the report was later attached as an advisory document only.

incorporation into the design of two-storey, wide-frontage suburban houses, most of the requirements fit relatively easily into flats. But they are much more difficult to fit into narrow-frontage, two-storey terrace houses, and it can be argued that they are unsuitable in principle for three-storey houses, as domestic stairlifts are only designed to rise through two floors.

Lifetime Homes measures are normally accepted by housing associations for affordable housing for rent. On the other hand, developers resist the idea in housing built for sale as the provisions tend to increase space for circulation and bathrooms at the expense of living and sleeping areas, and they don't want to make flats bigger overall. In flats, the connection for a future shower is also very difficult to achieve within the depth of the floor finish (without encroaching on party-floor construction) while prefabricated bathroom pods often do not achieve level access into showers.

En-suite bathrooms are often required in houses for sale, and this, coupled with the upstairs family bathroom and the Lifetime Homes downstairs WC plus future shower, results in three bathrooms. Applying Lifetime Homes criteria in homes for private sale usually results in bigger houses than the market optimum; sometimes even bigger than their affordable equivalent. It is possible that Lifetimes Homes will be adopted across the board by including its provisions as part of Building Regulations.

## Summary

Whether for regulation and enforcement of minimum dwelling sizes, or for guidance to prevent designers having to reinvent the wheel each time they embark on a new project, both space standards and guidance documents are invaluable design tools and are a way of passing on accumulated experience. That is not to say that rules and standards are not made to be improved upon or that tried and tested ideas can not be bettered, but progressive innovations need to be founded on a thorough knowledge of the current benchmarks.

**How much space do two people need to live in?**

This series of three unremarkable one-bed flat plans show why it remains difficult to produce a single set of space standards. Setting any kind of standard inevitably focuses on defining minima but, just as inevitably, minimum standards too often become the norm.

The first plan shows a basic one-bedroom flat designed to meet Lifetime Homes standards and the minimum requirements of the Housing Quality Indicators for affordable housing. It provides an acceptable solution and might well be appropriate for areas where land values are high, density is a priority and the neighbourhood offers a good range of amenities. It would work for any tenure and would be a good low-cost starter home. But as a generic model for good housing, it feels inadequate.

The second plan provides two social spaces as the kitchen is large enough to eat in. It could, of course, be combined with the living room if the occupiers prefer, but the provision of separate spaces provides more flexibility.

The third plan is simply a larger version of the second though it is still not luxurious. There is space for two chests of drawers and two medium-sized wardrobes in the bedroom, considerably more space in the living room and modest gains elsewhere.

With an overall range of .10 square metres, this group of plans demonstrates that there isn't a simple answer to the amount of space needed to house two people.

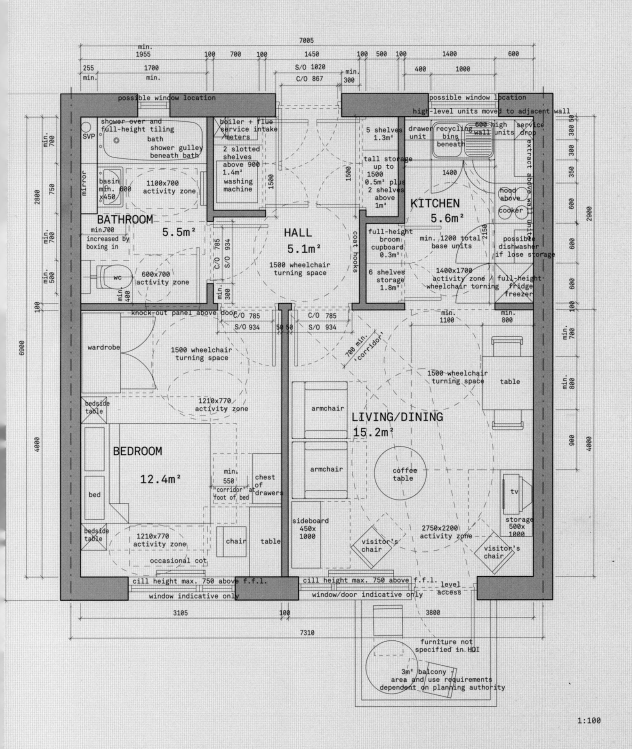

7005

min.
1955
100  700  100       1450       100  500  100      1400         600
255      1700              S/O 1020      min.       400    1000
min.      min.            C/O 867       300

possible window location                    possible window location
high-level units moved to adjacent wall

shower over and              boiler + flue      5 shelves    drawer recycling 600 high service
full-height tiling          service intake     1.3m²         unit   bins  wall units  drop
SVP        bath            meters                            beneath
          shower gulley    2 slotted          tall storage                    hood
          beneath bath     shelves            up to                           above
                           above 900          1500                            cooker
mirror   basin             1.4m²              0.5m² plus                  1400
         min. 600   1100x700                  2 shelves
         x450      activity zone  washing     above
                              machine         1m²
BATHROOM                                                                    possible
                                          full-height          min. 1200 total  dishwasher
          5.5m²             HALL          broom               base units    if lose storage
min.700                     5.1m²         cupboard
increased by                              0.3m²                            full-height
boxing in                  1500 wheelchair                    1400x1700    fridge
          600x700          turning space    6 shelves         activity zone  freezer
wc        activity zone                     storage           wheelchair turning
                                            1.8m²

KITCHEN
5.6m²

knock-out panel above door C/O 785    C/O 785             min.        min.
                           S/O 934  50 50  S/O 934        1100        800

wardrobe                                                                      table

          1500 wheelchair
          turning space                        700 min.
                                               'corridor'      1500 wheelchair
bedside                                                        turning space
table     1210x770
          activity zone                    armchair    LIVING/DINING
                                                        15.2m²
BEDROOM
                          min.     chest              coffee
12.4m²                    550      of                 table                  tv
bed                       'corridor' at  drawers                             storage
                          foot of bed                                        500x
bedside                            sideboard  2750x2200                      1000
table     1210x770        chair  table  450x  activity zone
          activity zone          1000         visitor's           visitor's
          occasional cot                      chair               chair

cill height max. 750 above f.f.l.    cill height max. 750 above f.f.l.    level
                                                                          access
window indicative only          window/door indicative only

3105              100              3800

7310

furniture not
specified in HQI

3m² balcony
area and use requirements
dependent on planning authority

1:100

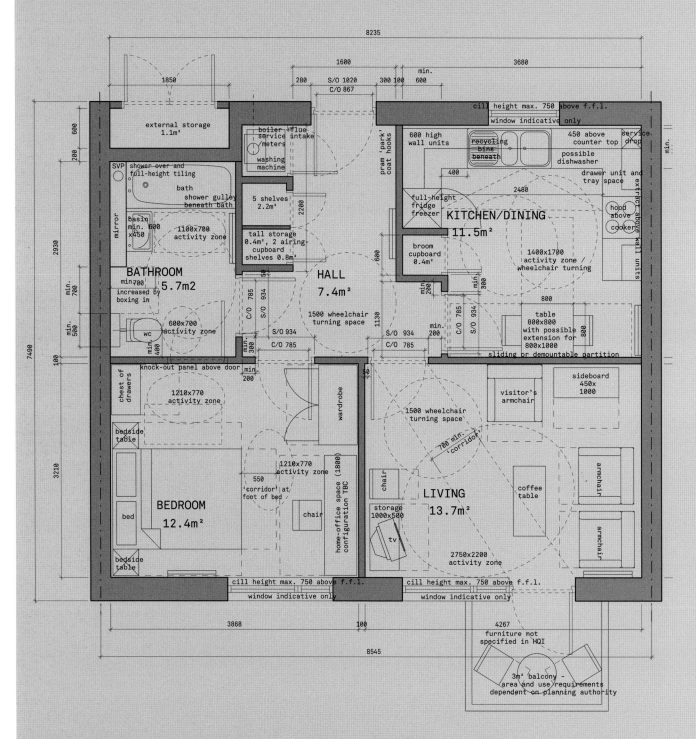

8235

1850                    1600          min.                3680
                   280   S/O 1020   300 100   600
                        C/O 867

600                                          cill height max. 750 above f.f.l.
200                                          window indicative only

                                  600 high        recycling      450 above      service
external storage      boiler+flue  wall units     bins           counter top    drop
1.1m²                 service intake                beneath                      min.
                      meters                                     possible
SVP  shower over and  washing                                   dishwasher
     full-height tiling  machine                                              drawer unit and
              bath                                                            tray space
              shower gulley                    full-height                    hood
              beneath bath    5 shelves        fridge      KITCHEN/DINING     above
     basin    1100x700        2.2m²            freezer     11.5m²             cooker
     min. 600 activity zone
2930 x450                     tall storage
mirror                        0.4m², 2 airing-            1400x1700
              BATHROOM        cupboard                    activity zone /
              5.7m2           shelves 0.8m²   broom        wheelchair turning
     min.700                                 cupboard
     increased by              HALL          0.4m²
     boxing in                 7.4m²                                           800
min.                                                           table
min. 600x700                   1500 wheelchair               800x800
700  activity zone             turning space                 with possible
min.          C/O 785                                        extension for
500  wc 400   S/O 934                                        800x1000
                              S/O 934                S/O 934  sliding or demountable partition
100           C/O 785         C/O 785               C/O 785
                                    knock-out panel above door  min.200
     chest of                                                  sideboard
     drawers   1210x770                            visitor's   450x
               activity zone                       armchair    1000
     bedside
     table                    wardrobe    1500 wheelchair
3210                                      turning space
                                                   700 min. corridor              armchair
               1210x770
               activity zone  home-office space    coffee
     bed       550            configuration TBC    table
     BEDROOM   corridor at              chair                                     armchair
     12.4m²    foot of bed            storage    LIVING
                              chair   1000x500   13.7m²
     bedside                          tv
     table
                                               2750x2200
                                               activity zone
     cill height max. 750 above f.f.l.      cill height max. 750 above f.f.l.
     window indicative only                 window indicative only

3868                    100                4267
                                           furniture not
7490                                       specified in HQI
8545

                                           3m² balcony -
                                           area and use requirements
                                           dependent on planning authority

                                           1:100

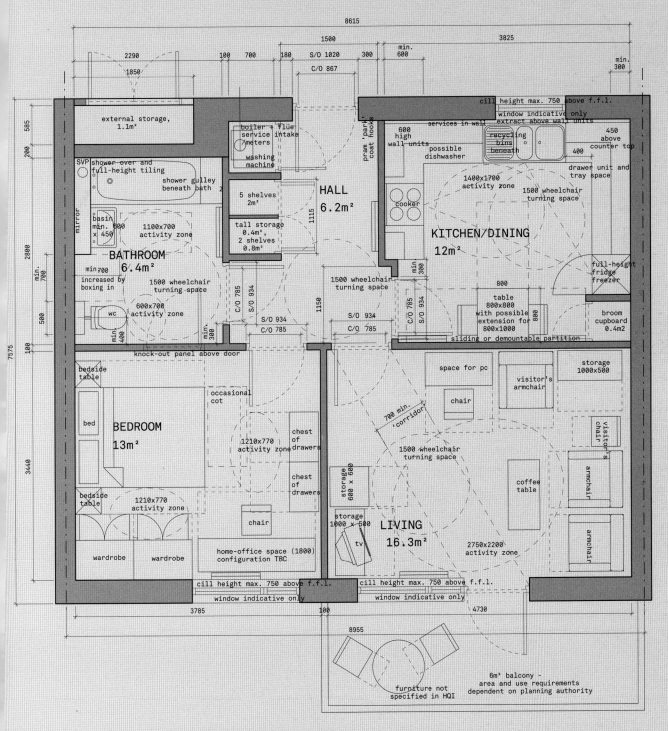

8615

1500 · 3825

2290 · 100 · 700 · 180 · S/O 1020 · 300 · min. 600 · min. 300

1850

C/O 867

585

200

external storage,
1.1m²

boiler + flue
service intake
meters

cill height max. 750 above f.f.l.
window indicative only
extract above wall units

600
high
wall units

450
above
counter top

SVP shower over and
full-height tiling

washing
machine

services in wall

recycling
bins
beneath

400

possible
dishwasher

shower gulley
beneath bath

5 shelves
2m²

HALL
6.2m²

drawer unit and
tray space

basin
min. 600
x 450

1100x700
activity zone

tall storage
0.4m²,
2 shelves
0.8m²

1400x1700
activity zone

1500 wheelchair
turning space

cooker

2800

BATHROOM
6.4m²

min 700

KITCHEN/DINING
12m²

full-height
fridge
freezer

mirror

min. 700

increased by
boxing in

1115

1500 wheelchair
turning space

min. 300

min. 300

800

table
800x800
with possible
extension for
800x1000

800

500

600x700
activity zone

1150

800

broom
cupboard
0.4m2

wc

1500 wheelchair
turning space

min. 400

C/O 785
S/O 934

S/O 934
C/O 785

S/O 934
C/O 785

C/O 785
S/O 934

sliding or demountable partition

100

7575

knock-out panel above door

space for pc

storage
1000x500

bedside
table

occasional
cot

visitor's
armchair

chair

chest
of
drawers

visitor's
chair

bed

BEDROOM
13m²

1210x770
activity zone

700 min.
'corridor'

bedside
table

1210x770
activity zone

chest
of
drawers

1500 wheelchair
turning space

coffee
table

armchair

chair

storage
600 x 600

LIVING
16.3m²

3440

wardrobe

wardrobe

home-office space (1800)
configuration TBC

storage
1000 x 500

tv

2750x2200
activity zone

armchair

cill height max. 750 above f.f.l.

cill height max. 750 above f.f.l.

window indicative only

window indicative only

3785 · 100 · 4730

8955

furniture not
specified in HQI

6m² balcony -
area and use requirements
dependent on planning authority

1:100

One of many conundrums about gardens and balconies is the contrasting preferences of different households when they try to assess their need for private open space. Clearly many people make private open space an important factor in their choice of house or flat; some want more outside space and others less, while some don't want any at all. Some have an acute need for privacy while for others getting as much sunlight as possible is the over-riding factor. Some, especially those with children between the ages of, say, three to eleven years, enjoy having access to a large shared garden while others consider that this type of increasingly prevalent 'semi-private' space is no compensation for not having a proper outdoor space of their own.

Designing a bespoke house gives an architect the opportunity to establish a precise relationship between outside and inside, interpreting as closely as possible the wishes of the client. But when the architect is designing speculatively (for persons unknown) it is only possible to generalise and to make assumptions about what an average resident will want, trying to anticipate as many eventualities as possible. All too often people long for somewhere outside in which to sit and to grow plants but live in flats where neither is possible, while other people have generous balconies that have either been barricaded off or are used only to store unsightly objects such as cycles and defunct household objects.

However, there are several relatively safe bets. One is that nearly everyone who aspires to live in a house also aspires to a garden of sorts, even if it is small; another is that whereas flats used to be turned out without any private outside space, lifestyles and expectations have changed and balconies or roof terraces have become the norm rather than the exception. Although it has implications for service charges, flat dwellers now also tend to be provided with shared or semi-private outside space.

From the eighteenth century the average private house sat with its own land on all four sides and was linked to its grounds on at least one elevation by double doors and usually a flight of shallow steps or, in the case of a grand house, a terrace. This implied little relationship between inside and outside except for recognition that inside was warm, protected and clean. The transition between inside and the landscape outside was

This terrace of listed eighteenth-century houses in Bloomsbury was converted into flats – some of which were for families – in 1979. As there was no possibility of providing any private open space beyond the smallest possible balconies on the rear elevation, it was decided to create maisonettes at the top of each house and to disguise these highly prized roof terraces between the original central valley roofs.

simply a door or pair of doors with the steps or terrace doing little to soften the abrupt contrast between the two.

As the relationship between inside and outside developed through the nineteenth and twentieth centuries the gradation became more subtle, often with a conservatory acting as a buffer between house and garden. Then, as terrace housing became the urban norm, there was an additional problem in supplying and maintaining a garden without having to use the main reception rooms of the house as the service route. Except in poor-quality workers' housing, the gardens of nineteenth-century terrace houses were often as much as 15 or 20 metres long, large enough for serious gardening, and they were sometimes designed with a shared rear alleyway for access. Even where this method of access to gardens was not provided, house frontages were wide enough to allow a passage as a direct link from the front entrance to the garden, leaving the formal rather than the functional relationship between a living room and garden, inside to outside, via a pair of semi-glazed french doors.

Not until the Modern Movement arrived in England in the 1930s (early examples include works by Connell Ward and Lucas, and Berthold Lubetkin) was there any further celebration of the relationship between house and garden or flat and balcony, a relationship cemented after World War 2 in America through the work of architects like Richard Neutra in California: a benign climate and wall-to-wall glazing defied easy identification of what was house and what was garden in his designs.

Given the densities to which even houses now need to be built and given also that every square metre of space inside and out is an important commodity, designers of gardens and balconies are faced with several challenges:
• to design gardens and balconies as usable extensions of the main living space, addressing both privacy and sunlight;
• to try to make sure that the only route to the garden with a large bag of compost is not over the sitting-room carpet;

• to design for wildly differing levels of commitment in terms of how each household wants to use their space without annoying their neighbours. Five uses come to mind: small-children's play, drying laundry, sitting out, growing things, and keeping cats, dogs and other pets;
• to design gardens, particularly front gardens, and balconies so that one occupant's lack of interest in their space does not become a neighbour's eyesore;
• to deal with the issue of 'defensible space';
• to top up the limited amenity provided by small gardens, patios or balconies by providing secure shared semi-private space for groups of residents (see Chapter 7).

**Front gardens**
To describe the strip of space in front of most houses and flats as a garden is to employ something of a euphemism. In most cases, although not private in themselves, these spaces between the street and the building line provide a useful privacy buffer to the home itself. Much has been written about its role in defining 'defensible space' and it can be handled in a number of ways, depending on tenure, neighbourhood and the approach to maintenance.

Where a developer chooses not to define the separating boundaries but to leave a continuous strip of grass or planting, punctuated only by pathways – and sometimes parking spaces – leading to each front door, the capital cost is clearly relatively low but the long-term service-charge obligation on owners and tenants is relatively high. For this approach to be successful the developer needs to be confident that future residents and those in the wider neighbourhood will observe all the basic rules, parking only in dedicated spaces and not littering or destroying the soft landscape. Even so, in terms of 'defensible space' this approach is of little value in areas of social stress: if the management structure needed to provide day-to-day maintenance is missing, the long-term prognosis is invariably disastrous.

The alternative approach by developers of terrace housing, irrespective of tenure, is to provide a physical barrier that assigns and defines the area in front of each house so that responsibility for maintenance clearly lies with individual owners or tenants. Although the cost of good boundary treatment is high, the landlord's ongoing responsibility is much reduced.

Front gardens clearly defined by a robust combination of walls, railings and limited amounts of timber have a number of other advantages, affording privacy, improving security and disguising instances where residents have failed to look after their patch, which would otherwise become an eyesore.

Boundary treatments also have a function in incorporating stores for refuse and recycling as well as gas and electricity meters without necessarily obstructing views out to the street from ground-floor windows. There is a fine balance to be struck between adhering to the principle of 'live frontages' by keeping views out as open as possible while screening untidy front gardens from the public gaze.

### Rear gardens

As has been noted, the term 'rear garden' can designate anything from a small 25-square-metre patio to something ten times the size, large enough to accommodate a vegetable patch.

Like all small spaces that one wishes were bigger, patios need to be designed so that every bit of space counts. Choices of paving and drainage are crucial. Patios need to receive direct sunlight, with adequate privacy and security and a positive link to the main living space via a well-designed glazed screen and not obstructed by doors when they are open. It then becomes almost an extra room with all sorts of uses for adults and very small children.

Servicing a patio is not as challenging as getting a wheelbarrow into a proper garden and access from one of the principal living rooms is an acceptable solution, although access from the kitchen with a hard, washable floor is to be preferred. But the combination of narrow-frontage houses, in which there is no possibility of reaching the garden except through the living room or kitchen, with a garden that is at least

12 metres deep is unsatisfactory. The current approach of police liaison officers, supported by housing managers, usually results in a veto over any idea of a rear alleyway on security grounds. However, it seems ludicrous to condemn future generations of occupants to such an unsatisfactory arrangement without considering how rear access via an alleyway could be made secure using locked gates protected by fob keys.

### Balconies and roof terraces

Flats are still being built without any sort of outside space. However, pressure has been increasing, especially in affordable housing, for all of them to have some kind of private open space that is accessed directly from the flat, space that receives sunlight for some part of the day and is large enough for all members of the household to sit out and take a meal together. Roughly, this means at least 4 square metres for a couple and an extra 1 square metre for each additional person. The so-called 'Juliet balcony' – full-height windows with a balcony rail on the outside allowing them to open to the floor – does not qualify; its only possible merit is to improve the quality of light and sunlight entering a room.

Apart from the size, orientation and relationship with the internal living spaces, the effectiveness of balconies and roof terraces is affected by issues of privacy, wind protection, level thresholds, safety, and also waterproofing in the case of roof terraces above other accommodation.

Terraces and projecting balconies facing south or west with no overhead shading can suffer from excessive sunlight, but the alternative of recessing them adds to cost, especially in meeting thermal-performance requirements.

Roof terraces differ from balconies in that they have living accommodation immediately below them. Special care needs to be taken in their design to ensure that whatever waterproofing method is chosen is totally protected from the uses to which roof terraces are normally put. Historically, roof terraces have been problematic because

Old Royal Free Square, Islington. With rented housing it is hard to predict whether a garden, once provided, will be valued or not. And if this garden is in a conspicuous place and neglected it can blight a whole street. Happily, in this instance the garden has clearly been a great joy to the tenant concerned for more than 12 years, both to her benefit and to the benefit of everyone else.

One of the great dilemmas about providing private gardens is that for every one resident like this there are at least five others who do not share his enthusiasm. The process of allocating tenancies has to share some of the responsibility for this.

of water penetration through the flat-roof membrane or round the rainwater outlet, made worse as they have to be able to bear traffic as well. Difficulties have been compounded by the tendency of designers to conceal rainwater downpipes. The crisis of confidence in construction methods that accompanied the flight from Modernism in the mid-1970s included an aversion to flat roofs in any form. Horror stories accumulated over the cost of tracing and remedying leaks, many of them avoidable had the original designers used more forethought.

The history of failures of flat roofs and roof terraces from the 1960s resulted in a reaction against any type of flat roof that has lasted for a whole generation. In the rush for growth from 2000 onwards, marked by increases in density and a return to building flats, many of the lessons of that period have been forgotten, although the materials now in use are far superior and the likelihood of failure has been reduced. Development of the 'upside down' method of building flat roofs – where the waterproof membrane is located below the wearing service and the insulation – has improved their working life. The membranes themselves have become increasingly flexible and effective, compared with traditional asphalt, but are still vulnerable around their edges and rainwater outlets.

Most designers prefer to cantilever balconies, stacked one above the other, and to avoid visible rainwater downpipes. Both these features, compounded by the need to eliminate cold bridges, are relatively expensive as a proportion of overall construction costs. Steel or timber decking without any form of piped drainage is the most economical method of construction but means that balconies stacked one above the other can't be used when it rains, and furniture has to be stored inside – a big disadvantage. And downpipes somehow need to be incorporated into the design without being built into walls, as the number of 30-year-old buildings that have had to have them added later testifies.

The safety of balustrading is covered by Building Regulations and is an issue of vital concern to households with small children. But clumsy detailing that ends up looking and feeling like a cage is to be avoided and there are subtle alternative solutions for the crucial top 150–200mm.

The insulation needed to avoid a cold bridge makes achieving level thresholds from balconies (a requirement of Lifetime Homes) difficult, whether they are inset or cantilevered.

The need for privacy and wind protection usually go together. Adjoining balconies should always be screened from each other where they abut and the subtle use of timber or perforated-metal screening to part of the fronts of balconies can enhance privacy and cut down exposure to strong winds, especially in tall buildings, without reducing sunlight penetration. It also provides somewhere for the storage of balcony furniture. A useful variant of the inset balcony, much used in the Netherlands, is the creation of a virtual sunspace by the addition of an extra line of glazing on the outside face of the building so that it combines the utility of a balcony in summer and an enclosed sunspace in winter.

The era of shared laundry facilities seems to have entered the annals of welfare provision, gone the way of communal bath houses for the poor, except for some categories of housing for single, mobile people for whom ownership of washing and drying facilities is unrealistic. Drying clothes is an affordability issue for many households in flats and, unless some provision – such as the partial timber screening of balconies – is made for them, breaking the rules with clandestine washing lines on balconies in full view will always be infinitely preferable to watching the electricity prepayment meter rushing round to keep pace with a tumble dryer.

Balconies to housing-association flats in Bermondsey. All the flats in this building have generous balconies, large enough to take meals on.

Balcony at the Brunswick Centre.

# Naish Court regeneration,
# Islington, London N1

Naish Court, an estate of 200 flats, was built for the London Borough of Islington in the late-1940s. This area, between the Caledonian Road and the new development on the King's Cross Railway Lands, consists of a monolithic series of post-war council estates, in contrast to the area to the east of Caledonian Road, which has some of the best and highest-value streets and squares in North London. Locating so much council housing in one place, in stark contrast to the prosperous 'gentrified' streets on the other side of what is affectionately known to locals as 'the Cally' has created a pocket of deprivation, with all that implies, particularly in terms of low-grade youth crime and mindless vandalism.

In 1999 the residents of Naish Court felt persecuted and embattled by young vandals. Nothing was private except their flats once they were safely inside them, but getting there meant crossing tarmac courtyards full of abandoned cars to reach squalid and graffitied entrance lobbies, then using vandalised lifts, or more often than not walking up six flights of stairs because the lifts were broken. Long dingy corridors then led to front doors that looked like they had been built to withstand a siege.

Naish Court residents, knowing that the council could not afford a radical solution to this impossible situation, voted for the estate to be transferred to a large and well-regarded housing association. This was on the understanding that the whole estate would be knocked down and rebuilt, that residents would have a say in the design of their new homes, and that no-one would have to move more than once.

The original estate consisted entirely of flats and maisonettes roughly arranged around the perimeter of a rectangular 2.2-hectare site, distributed in blocks varying from four to eight storeys, with the largest families being housed in two eight-storey blocks of maisonettes sitting in the middle of the development. The architects of public housing in the 1950s were obsessed with the notion that healthy communities should live in blocks of flats; however, so little thought went into the design of the public realm that each block sat like an island surrounded by open areas designated for no useful purpose whatsoever. Given the relatively large areas of unusable open space, both in the central courtyards and in a 5-metre-wide strip of grass running round the whole perimeter of the site between the pavement and the flats themselves, it was not difficult to design a new development that increased the number of dwellings overall but also included terrace houses with private gardens for the largest families and flats for smaller households in blocks of not more than 13 flats off a single core, each with its own lift. This has resulted in 88 per cent of all dwellings achieving Lifetime Homes standards and 5 per cent being fully adaptable for wheelchairs.

The original developers of Naish Court, feeding their obsession with isolated blocks each surrounded by a *cordon sanitaire* of space of indeterminate use, were not alone in creating a community that was completely cut off from the surrounding neighbourhood of streets and squares. This reinforced the stigma associated with 'public housing'. An immediate requirement for the new plan was to make new streets and squares that join up with those that already existed and to make sure that good use was made of every scrap of outdoor space. What is therefore not usable shared space has been given over to private gardens: these now represent 33 per cent of the whole site area.

The original residents, many of whom were already well into middle age, insisted on the need to have lifts to every flat and a private balcony large enough for them to sit outside at a table for meals in warm weather. These two demands created a funding problem that was only solved by a masterplan that reprovided the same number of homes on only 85 per cent of the site followed by the residents' agreement to sell the southern portion to a developer to meet the then insatiable demand for small private flats.

**Architects** Levitt Bernstein Associates and Pollard Thomas Edwards architects
**Developer** The Guinness Partnership
**Site** 1.9 hectares
**Number of dwellings** 232
**Density** 122 dwellings/hectare
**Mix** 55 x 1B + 100 x 2B + 54 x 3B + 20 x 4B + 3 x 5B
**Affordable** 88 per cent
**Parking spaces per dwelling** 0.3

**Right** Before regeneration, which involved demolishing 200 flats entirely, there was no private open space anywhere. On the same overall footprint and at an even higher density, it was possible to provide three- and four-bedroom family houses with their own rear gardens.

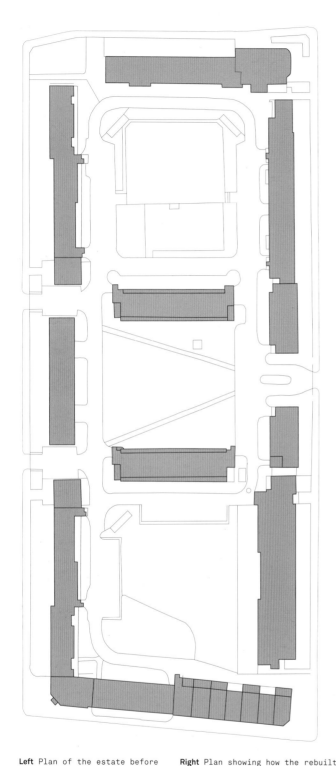

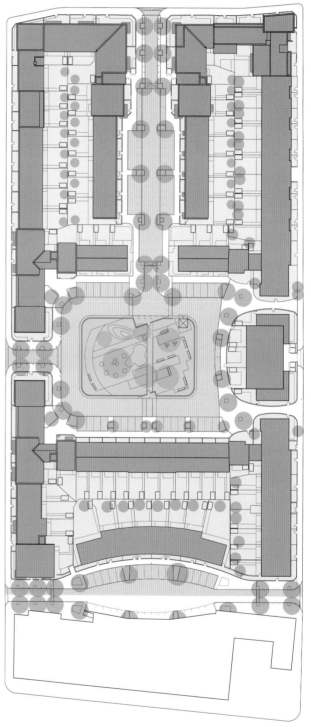

1:1250

**Left** Plan of the estate before demolition. There was no private open space at all, either at ground level or in the form of balconies. Instead there were three areas of communal tarmac open space in the centre mainly used for parking, and an unusable strip of communally owned grass between the back of pavement and the blocks themselves.

**Right** Plan showing how the rebuilt estate introduces conventional roadways into the scheme (pale grey), which together with 30% on street parking, accounts for 14% of a total site area, itself reduced by 10% (white area at the bottom of the plan, released to a private developer) while still providing the same number of units as the original. 33% of the site area is now private gardens (pale green) and a further 8% (dark green) as a landscaped square and childrens' play area.

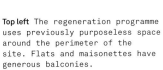

**Top left** The regeneration programme uses previously purposeless space around the perimeter of the site. Flats and maisonettes have generous balconies.

**Top right** Conventional streets and squares have been extended into the new development.

**Bottom right** The estate as it was before demolition. The left-hand image shows a new terrace of houses being built in the spaces between the existing blocks. This enabled the entire estate population to move just once, in phases, from their old flats into a new home.

# Granville New Homes, Kilburn, London NW6

This initial phase of the rebuilding of the South Kilburn Estate is the result of a design competition, held in 2004, promoted by the local authority and supported by residents of the estate, some of whom will be its first occupants. Like most schemes that win design competitions, Granville New Homes is bristling with innovations but in this case the innovations are sanctioned by future residents and there is every chance that they are fully committed to making them work effectively.

The design deliberately avoids any version of the vernacular; instead it seems, refreshingly, to take its point of departure from examples in the Netherlands, Denmark or Sweden, which is perhaps appropriate following a residents' visit to Rotterdam at the briefing stage. It certainly represents a sea change in residents' ideas of how they see the future, compared with the lifestyle they might have chosen ten years earlier.

However, first impressions can be deceptive. The generous openings at upper levels were indeed borrowed from similar (but much tighter) air and sunlight gaps in between the Victorian terraces and semi-detached houses in the area. This historic reference is translated into a modern 'vernacular' and exploits the generous gaps to maximise light in the back gardens and reflect day- and sunlight into the living spaces facing the generous 'breaks', while simultaneously breaking up street and façade repetition.

As the first phase of a regeneration programme for the replacement of the grim adjoining South Kilburn Estate, put up in the 1970s, the new buildings are situated on long, narrow and rather awkwardly shaped slivers of road frontage that were previously a park, and mostly back on to the gardens of a terrace of fine nineteenth-century semi-detached villas. This is an urban-design exercise in 'town mending' since the old street pattern had been fractured by the building of the South Kilburn Estate, leaving the backs of Victorian terraces exposed to an untidy area of public open space – literally 'space left over after planning' (SLOAP). Seizing the opportunity offered by an irregular site plan, a delightful irregularity

runs right through the design, using every piece of available land, including awkward corners. By avoiding any idea of symmetry the design fits neatly on its irregular infill site.

The massing changes as the buildings rise up to their highest point at seven storeys. There are three separate mixed-tenure buildings in an L-shaped plan, which incorporates a community building on the corner site, rising from five storeys at one end to seven storeys at the other. The massing and roofline are complex so that, unlike most housing rising to this height, the number of storeys at the highest point is relatively unobtrusive and this is helped by an abrupt change of external wall treatment, from brick tiles to self-finished white cladding to the two upper storeys.

Generous balconies project from the external skin at apparently random points and these are balanced by equally generous openings that seem to be punched through the external skin. These allow daylight and fresh air into the common circulation at upper levels.

Most of the ground and first floors are taken up with maisonettes. These have their own front doors leading directly on to the street and small private patios at the rear so that, solely in terms of their accommodation, they are identical to terrace houses. Interspersed at intervals between the maisonettes at street level are shared entrances leading to lifts and stairs serving small groups of dual-aspect upper-floor flats varying in size from one to three bedrooms. Unusually, the upper-floor landings to flats are external spaces with openings in the frontage to admit light and air, a device that makes the front door to each flat feel like a true front door and not simply a door off an internal corridor, as in a hotel.

Every flat has its own balcony, which is large enough to eat meals on; internal space standards are generous, with well-shaped rooms and circulation areas.

But the innovations are not limited to planning and physical form; they boldly address the challenge of climate change in a variety of ways over and above (15 per cent) Building Regulation requirements, achieving

**Architect** Levitt Bernstein Associates
**Developer** London Borough of Brent
**Site** 1.215 hectares
**Dwellings** 130
**Density** 107 dwellings/hectare
**Mix** 13 x 4B maisonettes + 14 x 3B maisonettes + 8 x 2B maisonettes + 12 x 3B flats + 44 x 2B flats + 39 x 1B flats
**Affordable** 100 per cent
**Parking spaces per dwelling** 0.4
**Non-housing use** children's centre

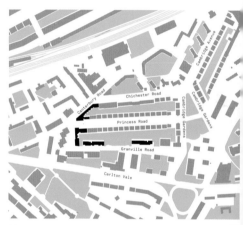

Site plan.

**Right** One of the principles enshrined in the competition-winning design of this replacement housing for the South Kilburn Estate was that all upper-floor flats should have generous balconies and, where necessary, projecting canopies to minimise summer solar gain.

approximately Code for Sustainable Homes level 3, of which the principal features are:
• a high-performance external envelope designed to reduce residents' running costs as well as the carbon footprint (SAP rating 120, U-values of external walls 0.19–0.23, roofs 0.15, ground floor 0.25);
• central, block by block, gas-fired condensing boilers, supplying low-temperature, individually metered underfloor heating to all flats, a system designed for conversion to CHP as the primary heat source in future;
• solar collectors mounted on the flat roofs able to offset 30 per cent of hot water needs and a total of 15 per cent of the development's estimated heating energy needs. These solar collectors are linked both to small individual thermal stores in each dwelling and to large communal water-storage tanks, which can be topped up by the communal block boilers if necessary;
• underground rainwater collection for use in irrigating landscape and gardens;
• mechanical heat recovery from kitchens and bathrooms, mainly to heat dwelling corridors;
• external lighting using energy-efficient compact fluorescent fittings controlled by central timers and photocells;
• building materials selected from renewable sources and with minimum environmental impact;
• all flat roofs planted with sedum except those used for mounting solar collectors or roof terraces;
• generous dedicated areas in all blocks for waste recycling and cycle storage;
• reduced off-street parking.

Managing and servicing features that are in any way innovative is much easier in large commercial or private housing installations where the budgets for day-to-day maintenance are higher than those for affordable-housing schemes, particularly those that are mainly for rent. Housing associations and local authorities have to tread the narrow path between, on one hand, keeping tenants' service charges as low as possible and, on the other, providing the necessary levels of specialist skill required to maintain new and unfamiliar equipment. A high priority is the need for good access

to all mechanical services, particularly common services accessible from the shared circulation, as well as accurate 'as-built' information assembled on completion.

Given that the performance (and complexity) of Granville New Homes is expected to be far higher than that of the average new affordable housing, it will be important to monitor all aspects of this in order to gain experience for future projects. Inevitably, it will take some time for all the new systems to bed down and there will be much more need to familiarise residents with the ways to get the best out of the systems in their new homes.

Ground-floor layout plan. New houses built on a narrow strip of unused former open space leaving an area in the centre of the terrace as a landscaped pocket park.

1:1250

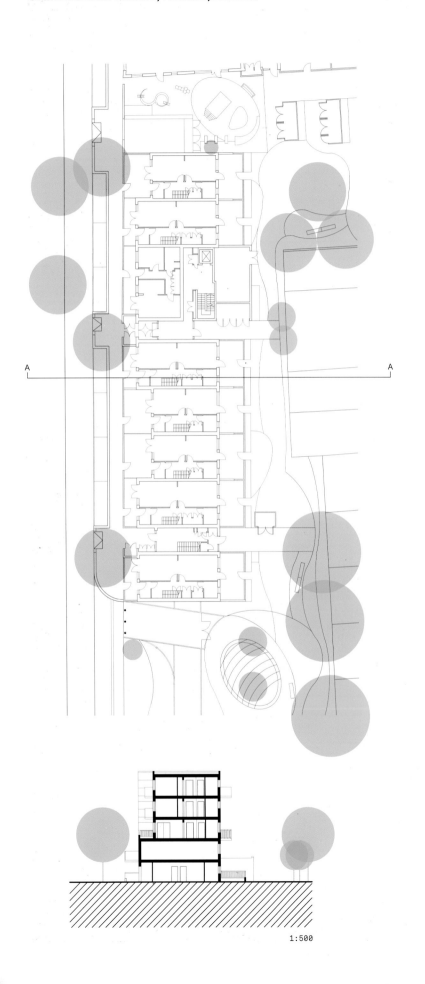

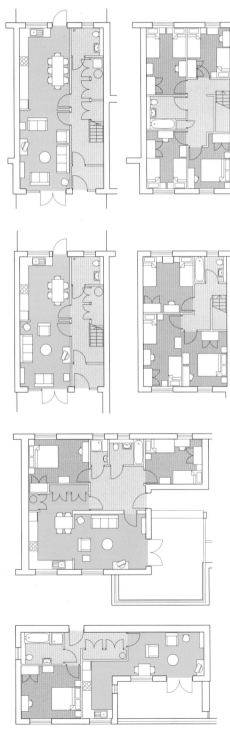

**Left** Typical plan and section A–A of new terrace housing showing the ground- and first-floor maisonettes – each having a small rear patio opening on to a shared open space. Between these maisonettes are the entrance cores to flats on the upper floors.
**Below** Three- and four-bedroom maisonettes.
**Bottom** Typical upper-floor flats with generous private balconies.

1:500

1:250

Street elevation and details
showing the massing broken up
to provide well-lit balconies
and roof terraces to upper-floor
dwellings.

# Shared amenities, indoor facilities and outdoor spaces

The shared roof terrace to the
high-density key-worker housing
at Nile Street in Hackney, by
Munkenbeck + Marshall Architects.

The need for specific amenities for residents as built-in components of successful and sustainable housing is now as widely recognised as it was previously ignored. From the end of World War 2 onwards in public, that is social, housing, as part of a drive to improve public health, large shared open spaces were provided on housing estates, which now had much larger numbers of families housed in flats. This policy became a byword for all that subsequently proved to be misconceived – large areas of unused, unkempt asphalt or grass became breeding grounds for all kinds of anti-social activity. To address this failure the principle of 'defensible space', first propounded by Oscar Newman, was enthusiastically embraced, not only as a way of creating secure environments but also because it conveniently reduced the landlord's obligations in terms of management and maintenance.

There is a difference between true public open space, to which anyone and everyone has access, and shared communal space – such as a central courtyard, garden or pocket park enclosed by terraces of houses or flats – access to which is restricted to certain groups of residents.

If the pendulum swung away from large amounts of shared space and facilities after 1979, pendulums can swing too far: a whole generation of schemes built in the 1980s and 1990s with almost no common facilities has proved to be almost as problematic as the earlier generation, when an attempt had been made to provide facilities but without any idea of how to manage them. What is now emerging is a more sophisticated policy under which spaces are more thoughtfully designed and equipped, and the means of securing them and running them properly are also provided. This means not only finding the capital to build them into the physical framework, but also the revenue necessary to run them without adding an intolerable burden to the residents' service charges. Current examples can demonstrate the value of providing areas of shared open space for specific uses and activities, designed with their future management and upkeep in mind. The emphasis should be on access and the quality of provision, not just fulfilling notional obligations of 'enough space'.

Many local authorities have started to define an amount of shared or private amenity space as a planning requirement. In theory this is a good thing but standards can be very onerous. Bigger is not necessarily better, and this planning approach can also lead to 'box-ticking' and increasing reliance on shared roof terraces with little evidence that they will be either useful or manageable.

As schemes increase in size and reduce in density the design of outside spaces becomes more indeterminate; external spaces are looked at not so much as 'outdoor rooms' but as simply the space between buildings, landscaped with grass, trees and the ubiquitous bushes, which tend to be planted where no better idea has occurred. By contrast, higher-density schemes can benefit from shared external spaces that are often more purposeful, more valued and more secure.

The idea that external areas should be laid out as communal gardens with benches and rose beds has been around since the earliest days of housing on estates, whether private or subsidised. However, they usually matured into unkempt and sad places, partly because there was insufficient money to look after them properly, but also because the spaces themselves were not identified as belonging to any small, particular group of residents and were thus popularly supposed to harbour all kinds of unpleasant detritus, from dog waste to used hypodermic needles.

This naive approach, which saw soft landscape simply as scaled-up private gardens but with municipal-type planting, was largely discontinued from the 1960s onwards without necessarily being replaced by anything more positive. People, especially those living in flats or with small children, do appreciate having somewhere convivial to meet up with neighbours, but planning anything resembling a shared garden needs careful forethought about how it is to be maintained. Forming community development trusts as mechanisms for tapping the voluntary efforts of residents is an attractive idea, but hugely difficult to realise and sustain.

There are relatively few successful examples to use as models for this approach to semi-private/semi-public shared space. As has already been shown, the small entirely

private garden/patio has its uses but also its obvious limitations, one of which is the impossibility of forming any kind of social connection, particularly for children, with neighbours except via the street. The model established by Victorian developers in the West London suburb of Maida Vale was to provide each terrace house with its own garden but to link, via a gate in the back fence, the rear of each garden to a landscaped shared open space that was thus landlocked behind a group of houses and inaccessible to non-residents.

Although the scale of this could hardly be repeated at today's densities, smaller versions have been tried recently in a mixed-tenure scheme at Chapel in Southampton and at Greenwich Millennium Village in London. There is an equivalent version for high-density flats surrounding an internal courtyard, often raised one floor above street level to accommodate parking underneath, which is accessed from the common stair and lift cores. The second phase of Coin Street on the South Bank in London and the schemes at Bermondsey and Pimlico are examples.

All flats in blocks need some shared space but for a typical scheme of more than, say, 100 new homes the shared external facilities should include:
• play areas, including space for informal football games, for children of all ages;
• peaceful places in which older people can congregate outside;
• dedicated areas for dogs.

Indoor facilities should include:
• storage for bulky items, such as flat-dwellers' cycles;
• provision for a crèche;
• youth clubs;
• meeting rooms;
• a multi-purpose hall.

### External facilities

Family households need places for small children to play together and, if the scheme is large enough, play areas or adventure-playground facilities for older children as well. Satisfying the needs of teenagers is the most elusive of tasks: their iconoclastic

Broadclose in Bude, Cornwall by Trewin Design Partnership. High-quality shared space in a rural setting.

Residents in Granville New Homes chose to have a large shared garden rather than long private gardens exclusively for the lower units. Each ground-floor unit has its own patio with a gate giving access to the shared space.

instincts propel them away from things organised for them in favour of more clandestine activities.

The needs of children and young people tend immediately to bring the interests of families into conflict with childless households, especially older residents. The concept of NIMBYism might have been invented for this situation. No-one seems to want a small-children's playground on their doorstep except during the few years when they happen to have children of the right age, still less an enclosed ball-game area or adventure playground. Where possible, consultation with residents usually produces a 'least-worst' compromise and avoids complaints from people who feel that they have had a playground plonked on their doorstep without being able to protest. To some extent, as children get older their activities can (and arguably, as part of growing up, should) take place further and further from their own front doors but play spaces still need to be safe and overlooked. Crossing streets is usually the first major hazard, which is one reason for laying out streets as child-friendly 'home zones'.

Experience of providing small-children's play areas, even when large sums have been spent equipping them, shows that their shelf

life can be quite short as the children for whom they were designed outgrow them. Often, especially in neighbourhoods with lots of new affordable family tenancies, there are age bulges with many children of nursery age growing out of facilities provided for them at the same time. This suggests that the design of play facilities needs to include some flexibility, with an eye towards adapting spaces for different future uses as the community goes through its lifecycle.

Informal football is an even more contentious activity than small-children's playgrounds but another one that won't go away. Children like playing football in the street, close to home and to other people. They seem to be basically gregarious and noisy when playing ball games and half the expensively laid out ball-game courts on large estates are unused once their novelty has worn off, often because they are tucked away out of sight. So the best compromise seems to be small enclosed courts planned into the overall layout of the neighbourhood, close to family houses and remote from non-family flats, ideally in such a way that they neither completely dominate nor are completely hidden.

The design of adventure playgrounds is outside the scope of this book, but where space allows their value is beyond question.

They need to be large and are often unsightly. Unlike play areas for smaller children, they are usually staffed when they are open, so it is reasonable for them to be tucked away.

And last but not least, dogs and their owners can generate much bad feeling. The determination of some to keep dogs is outweighed by a majority who are even more determined to make sure those dogs are controlled on grassed areas, especially where their waste is concerned. Dedicated dog-exercise areas have been tried but they offer no benefit to those without dogs, so general spaces in which owners are required to pick up waste seem to offer a more pragmatic solution.

## Internal/indoor facilities

As part of a general approach to making living in flats more attractive as well as encouraging cycling as opposed to driving, new efforts are being made to build stores that won't get vandalised, both for cycles and for other bulky household possessions that don't fit easily into flats. Past attempts were usually dismal failures for reasons that invariably involved a combination of vandalism, rough sleeping and drug taking, unwittingly facilitated by poor management and security. Shared stores will always be problematic so planning individual stores within the secure envelope of a scheme, accessed either from within each lift and stair core or from an external courtyard, works best. In very large schemes where each stair core gives access to more than 25 flats, storage needs to be covered by CCTV as well, ideally linked to a concierge who will probably also be monitoring the car parking and other common areas.

Funding from independent sources for a crèche in schemes of several hundred dwellings is now more frequently available. A crèche needs self-contained ground-floor space and a secure external play area, probably located along with meeting rooms, a management office and a large multi-purpose hall; this needs to be designed to serve social functions as well as large gatherings involving the whole community. Traditionally, this complex of uses was combined into a standalone building but, since most of the functions needed to be at ground level, the result was a single-storey structure, unoccupied at night, prey to window smashing and graffiti, and very expensive in terms of land take. One solution is to combine the whole complex into a building with flats above. This can deal with the vandalism problem but letting out a hall used for social functions underneath flats can produce complications of noise nuisance that severely limit its use in the evenings.

Making space available for youth activities can be all-important, although what constitutes the right kind of facilities in one instance can be completely inappropriate in another. A brief to cover the various alternatives is beyond the scope of this book, but the provision of suitably soundproofed and flexible space, with generous ceiling heights, in the location least likely to annoy the neighbours is a good way to start. Genuine engagement during the design stage with the young people most likely to use the facility is almost essential to its ultimate success.

Adelaide Wharf: central courtyard equipped for play in a mixed-tenure development. Architect AHHM.

Designs from the 1950s and 1960s, where successful, have all-enduring popularity, as at Golden Lane in the City of London. Architect Chamberlin Powell & Bon.

# Chapel, St Mary's, Southampton

St Mary's was a challenging area in terms of security and car crime, as well as being in the floodplain of the River Itchen. Chetwoods' competition-winning scheme addressed those issues and several others at the same time.

Consultation with the local community has resulted in a genuinely mixed-tenure development in which all of the houses and flats are built to the same space standards and specification: the different tenures are indistinguishable. The design is refreshingly contemporary with a genuine appeal to both owners and tenants. The days when tenants felt they were being stigmatised by living alongside modern architecture while those who could afford to buy chose traditional homes are long gone.

The long thin site has been divided into three sections by two new streets, and the three resulting blocks have been developed around their perimeter to leave a courtyard at the centre of each, beneath which is semi-underground parking. This has the benefit of raising all the housing above the flood-risk level. Ramps lead up to the fronts of houses, which therefore enjoy the additional advantage of having their ground floors raised above the surrounding streets.

As the scheme is a mixture of houses and flats, Chapel has a relatively large population of children. All flats have balconies while the houses have both front doors on to the street and rear patios that include their own individual storage sheds. But what makes the layout exceptional from the amenity point of view is the treatment of the rear courtyards above the parking areas.

The gaps at the corner of each courtyard are secured by railings and gates. These allow householders to access the rear of their houses and their stores without having to take everything through the house. This has been a cause of controversy with crime-prevention officers since Secured by Design – the police much prefer gardens to be placed back to back as this is one of the fundamental planks of defensible-space strategy. At Chapel the design goes even further by providing a shared/communal space in the centre of

each courtyard to which all the surrounding houses have access through their rear. This could be a source of disputes between residents over responsibility for the upkeep of shared space and the cost of doing so when it becomes a service-charge issue. But when it works, the hierarchy for children's play is almost perfect. Very small children can play in their own private rear patio before graduating around the age of four to being able to play with children of the same age in the shared courtyard/garden, which should still be secure from outsiders provided the right controls are in place on the gates. As children grow older at Chapel there is a linear public park nearby, but beyond the protected shared courtyards.

Invariably there are teething problems with any progressive idea of this kind, but the long-term quality-of-life advantages must outweigh any disadvantages.

**Architect** Chetwoods
**Developers** Persimmon Homes with Swaythling Housing Association
**Site** 1.694 hectares
**Dwellings** 174
**Density** 100 dwellings/hectare
**Mix** 23 x 3B + 111 x 2B + 40 x 1B
**Affordable** 37 per cent
**Parking spaces per dwelling** 1 private; 0.7 affordable

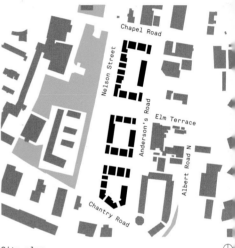

Site plan.

The scheme was designed around these communal courtyards: each is accessible only to the residents who live surrounding each courtyard. The ground-floor dwellings also have their own private patios.

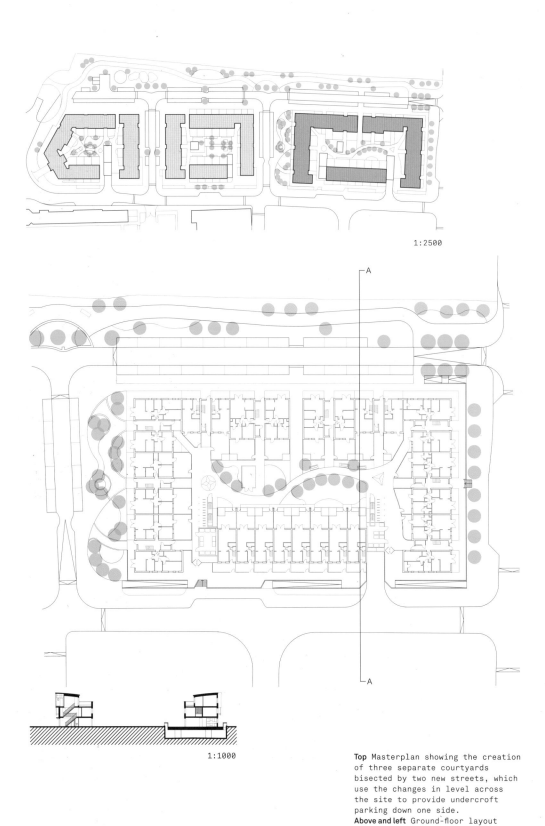

1:2500

1:1000

**Top** Masterplan showing the creation of three separate courtyards bisected by two new streets, which use the changes in level across the site to provide undercroft parking down one side.
**Above and left** Ground-floor layout plan and section A–A.
**Right** Typical plans of three-storey three-bedroom houses and one-bedroom flats.

1:250

RESIDENTS
PLEASE PARK
IN ALLOCATED
PARKING SPACES

External views to surrounding
streets. In each courtyard the
ground-floor units have their own
patios opening on to a shared
courtyard that is protected from
outsiders by lockable gates (as can
be seen in the top photograph).
Also visible are the two cycle
stores for each courtyard.

# St James Square, Bermondsey Spa, London SE16

For many years the old borough of Bermondsey, associated with London's docks but now absorbed into the London Borough of Southwark, had become a quiet sort of backwater. Given that it is only a 10-minute walk from the now expensive residential area of Butler's Wharf and the south end of Tower Bridge, its nature was bound to change, especially after it gained a station on the Jubilee Line extension in 1999. Most housing in the area around the church of St James, one of the famous 'Waterloo churches' built as a job-creation project for returning soldiers at the end of the Napoleonic Wars, is still owned by Southwark Council. Mostly pre- and post-war low-rise flats, they are punctuated here and there by 20-storey towers from the 1970s. But the borough also owned land that it had acquired when in low-grade industrial use, in and around the railway arches of the massive viaduct bisecting the area that carries all the rail traffic for London Bridge station.

In 2001 Southwark Council received a successful tender for a large area (1.95 hectares) of derelict industrial land to be developed for a mixture of private and affordable housing. The winning team consisted of Hyde Housing Association in a partnership led by Kennedy Hayward, a private developer which then had to withdraw. This posed a dilemma for those who wished to remain involved, and the borough agreed that Hyde Housing Association could take over the whole scheme, which now consisted of 627 dwellings, as developer of housing for sale as well as for rent. A third of all dwellings are affordable and the rest are to be disposed of in the private market.

Southwark was one of those inner boroughs of London that used to be subject to a 'density ceiling' of 150 dwellings per hectare (500 habitable rooms per hectare). But the introduction of government guidance encouraging the reuse of brownfield land, coupled with the Mayor of London's lifting of density ceilings after 2000, caused an immediate hike in land values, so that developing housing even to the previous maximum was no longer an option. What would have previously been considered the maximum of about 300 dwellings on this site had to be increased to nearly 630, plus a local supermarket and a large primary healthcare centre without, if possible, any reduction in future residents' quality of life.

When seeking precedents for housing at this sort of density in London you don't have to look very far, in fact just across the road to Shad Thames, the majority of which consists of converted nineteenth-century warehouses separated by narrow cavernous streets. And the principle of this form of housing was continued in The Circle, a scheme just behind Shad Thames designed by Piers Gough of CZWG in the 1980s. Of course the large, well-appointed private apartments behind these façades, many of which hardly ever receive direct sunlight, are occupied by privileged people who can afford to spend their holidays and weekends elsewhere, and are attracted to this area because of its convenient location, its history and the chic combination of uses. Nevertheless, the atmosphere in the streets around Shad Thames provided the idea behind the new masterplan for the Bermondsey Spa sites, several of which are only 12 metres wide from building face to building face.

The two blocks known as St James Square have large private balconies to provide open space. In addition each is built around a central landscaped courtyard at first-floor level with parking below, and these spaces are shared by residents. The lower-floor family units have small private patios that partly surround and overlook the courtyards, but Hyde Housing Association is committed to managing and maintaining these small but important shared spaces in a scheme where the density is very high.

**Architect** Levitt Bernstein, Associates
**Developer** Hyde Housing Association
**Site** 0.71 hectares
**Dwellings** 207
**Density** 291 dwellings/hectare (877 HR/hectare)
**Mix** 49 x 3B + 76 x 2B + 82 x 1B
**Affordable** 33 per cent
**Parking spaces per dwelling** 0.3

Site plan.

**Right** As at Chapel in Southampton, St James Square is based around two shared courtyards with a central street between them on the axis of the church built as an employment project after the Napoleonic Wars.

Masterplan of new development
between Spa Road and Jamaica
Road, Bermondsey, London. The
new buildings are deliberately
set to enclose narrow streets in
the manner of the nearby historic
streets of the Shad Thames area
near Tower Bridge. All flats have
generous private balconies while
those at the lowest levels have
private patios opening on to a
shared central courtyard raised
above the parking undercroft.

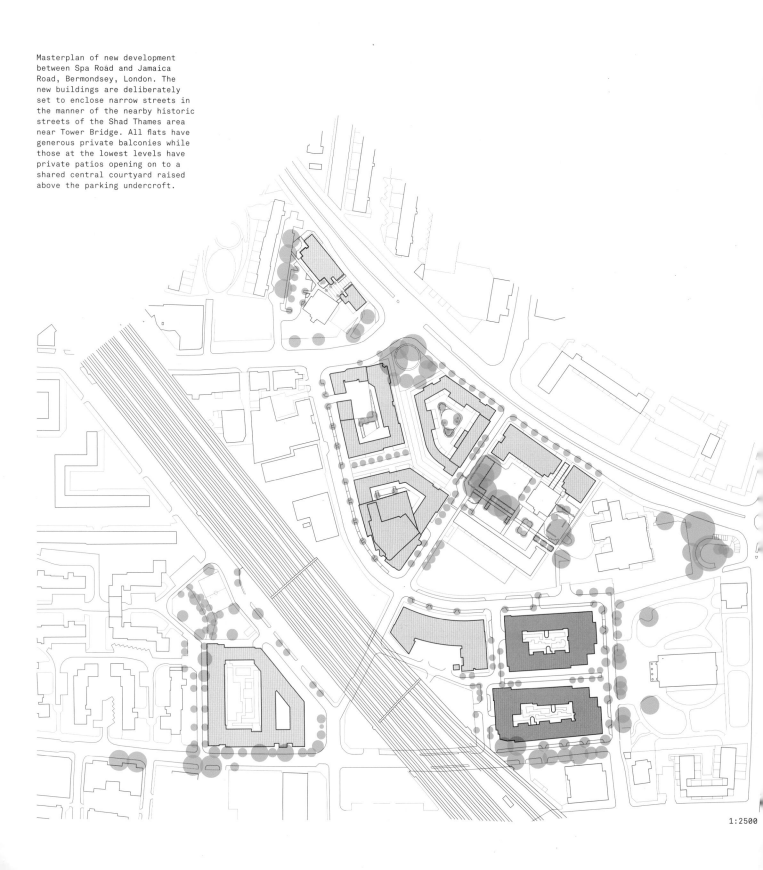

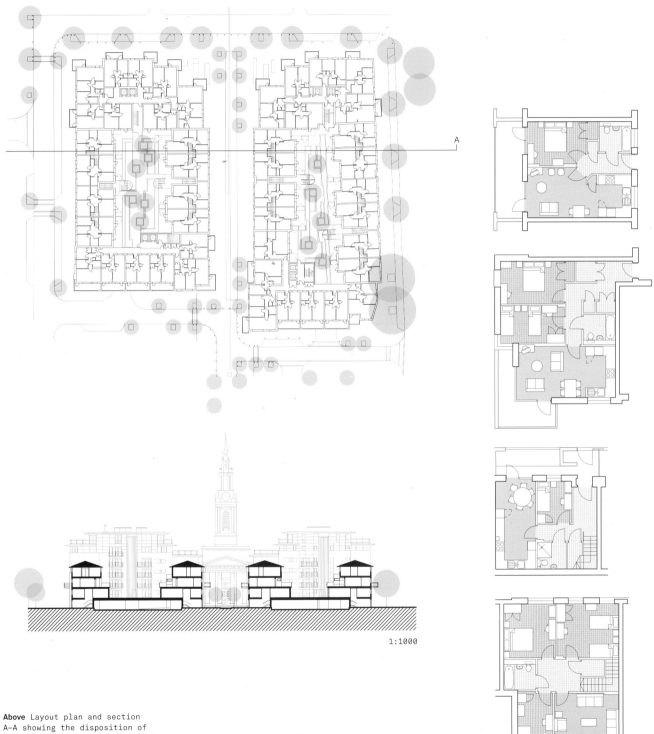

1:1000

**Above** Layout plan and section A–A showing the disposition of flats and maisonettes around their internal courtyards with St James Church on the main axis.
**Top right** Typical one- and two-bedroom flat plans.
**Bottom right** Plans of four-bedroom maisonette.

1:250

**Above** View from the churchyard of St James.
**Left** General massing as seen from the top of a tower block in Jamaica Road.
**Above right** The new square formed in front of the church.
**Below right** View of the internal courtyard, accessible to all residents.

A block of 46 apartments developed by a housing association on a busy main road heading west out of London might seem a recipe for something quite conventional. However, the design of Oaklands Court is anything but that. The end of a block formed between the intersection of two side roads, the site has three road frontages: the basic configuration is a mixture of rented and shared-ownership houses, maisonettes and flats developed around the three-sided perimeter.

Enormous care has been devoted to both the concept and detail design for a previously undeveloped site that had been valued highly by the local authority for its environmental contribution to an area with very little open space. Mindful of this, the design uses as much of the site area as possible (67 per cent) as open space. At ground level a secure area, enclosed at the rear on three sides by the U-shaped building, is devoted to parking space and a playground equipped for small children. At the very top of the building, shared amenity space is provided in the form of a communal roof garden running parallel to Uxbridge Road.

The family houses and maisonettes have their own door access to the street, while a single entrance on the main Uxbridge Road serves all the shared-ownership flats. The remaining flats for affordable rent are split between two entrances: this reduces the number sharing each entrance and keeps communal circulation to a minimum. One lift serves the general-needs accommodation while the shared-ownership flats have been provided with a shaft to allow the installation of a lift if it is considered necessary in future. The design provides every dwelling with private open space, either in the form of a patio for family units or generous balconies for flats.

As described so far, the provision of accommodation is both generous and thoughtful, but what makes this high-density urban development so particularly unusual is the treatment of the main roof, which has been laid out in the form of a large landscaped roof garden and is directly accessible to all the dwellings except

the ground-floor family maisonettes and houses.

As an example of shared amenity space the roof garden at Oaklands Court is unusually ambitious, for this is no windy terrace but a landscaped garden in every sense, complete with grass, generous planting and a shelter equipped with benches. It is clearly not intended for teenage football but as a refuge where adults and those with very small children can escape the impact of the traffic-dominated street. At a time when housing associations as landlords are so concerned to balance the need to reduce the service charges they have to levy on their tenants against the very real need for better amenities, this facility is a bold experiment.

**Architect** Monahan Blythen Hopkins
**Developer** Catalyst Housing Group
**Site** 0.08 hectares
**Dwellings** 46
**Density** 656 HR/hectare
**Mix** 7 x 3B + 39 x 1 and 2B including four wheelchair
**Affordable** 100 per cent
**Parking spaces per dwelling** 0.25

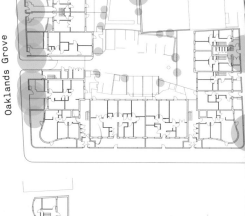

Oaklands Grove

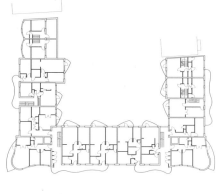

**Top right** Street-level plan. Flats and family maisonettes packed around three street frontages with a small central courtyard and children's play space. Every centimetre of open space used to its maximum with nothing left over for quiet relaxation.
**Centre right** Typical intermediate floor with four stair cores and short access galleries to reach each flat.
**Bottom right** Top-floor plan. Two staircases reach the roof level, one from the general needs and the other from shared-ownership flats. Between them is a garden complete with mown grass, trees and a shelter.

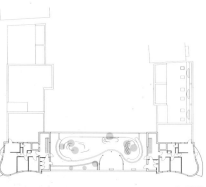

1:1000

The roof-garden design follows the
geometry of the building itself.

Private houses in the prosperous
Los Angeles suburb of Eagle Rock
have no need for front boundaries
and their owners have incomes
large enough to pay for someone to
cut the grass.

This chapter deals with what has become the biggest growth area in the syntax of UK housing since the late 1960s, a time when designers still assumed that everything that was not completely private could be shared equally by everyone else. The chaos that followed, exacerbated as densities increased and echoed in many post-industrial North American cities, was first captured in the public imagination early in the 1960s by Jane Jacobs in *The Death and Life of Great American Cities*. Not even the vast growth in CCTV and other electronic security systems has prevented shared facilities, from car parks to useful things like laundries, storage and roof gardens, from being comprehensively vandalised or closed down because their security was too expensive to manage.

Of course it was the growth of large publicly funded post-war social-housing schemes on both sides of the Atlantic that first brought the phenomenal amount of anti-social behaviour they engendered to general attention. The greatest sufferers were not the occupants of wealthier areas surrounding these estates but the relatively poor occupants of the estates themselves. This is not to say that petty crime was not exported – it was, and the presence of a disreputable council estate in an otherwise peaceable neighbourhood would reduce the value of privately owned property to well below average market prices in the wider area. Conversely, after the once infamous Holly Street Estate in the London Borough of Hackney had been entirely dismantled and rebuilt in the 1990s, the value of surrounding property shot up disproportionately as car crime, street robberies and burglary decreased.

To suggest that the climate of fear and anti-social behaviour was caused entirely by poor design decisions would be a huge over-simplification. The best, and in some cases the most celebrated, designers and their publicly funded clients in the period following the end of World War 2 were more excited by the ideals and ideas for high densities first promoted by architects like Le Corbusier in the 1930s than by home-grown planners like Barry Parker and Raymond Unwin, who pioneered the ideas behind many of the first-generation post-war New Towns. Bold idealism about 'machines for ving in' was matched by assumptions about the social make-up of the inhabitants of brand-new estates, assumptions about full employment and the conforming behaviour of young people, all of which proved to be over-optimistic. At the same time, central government fuelled the expansion of new estates with high levels of subsidy, leading to large numbers of schemes that were naive in their approach to security and adopted a second-rate style of often brutal, municipal architecture that hastened their slide to the condition of 'sink estates'.

By the end of the 1970s the era of maintaining full employment at all costs, which had persisted since the end of World War 2, had come to an end. So did subsidised construction of new housing by local authorities, while public ownership was eroded under the government's 'right to buy' programme. And as unemployment rose so did the demand for social housing. The inevitable result was a concentration of the poorest benefit-dependent households in the remaining stock – a situation that still obtains. While all this activity in the social sector was going on, enormous post-war demand meant that tenures had never been more obviously polarised or more problematic, and the private market was almost exclusively being supplied by an uninspiring expansion of cosy low-density suburbs in 'safe' neighbourhoods.

The clearest indication of failure in housing of any tenure is that residents who are able to make the decision to sell up and move away do so; if they are tenants, they do their utmost to be transferred elsewhere. At the end of the 1970s and during the early 1980s, as now, the most common reasons for wanting to move were fear of physical assault or fear of burglary and damage to property. Three factors contributed to this situation. The first was a culture of crime fostered by a concentration of poverty, inadequate education, unemployment and, in the case of young people, poor role models and inadequate parenting. The second was a shortage of the revenue funding needed to provide services to deal with these issues. The third was a physical environment that, at best, had been designed for an entirely

different clientele, and at worst had slavishly followed some outmoded planning dogma, and which in any case fostered crime and feelings of insecurity.

By the time council building stopped at the end of the 1970s and before the shortage of rented housing, combined with rising unemployment, had begun to bite, housing experts had recognised the symptoms and had begun to come up with some solutions, based on sound urban-design principles such as:
• no more high-rise housing;
• a return to building houses rather than flats, arranged with their gardens back to back, rather than the obsession with south-facing orientation for all dwellings that prevented a logical return to street-based layouts;
• fewer flats in smaller blocks not exceeding 20–25 flats per core, used to articulate and enliven corners;
• recreating a traditional street pattern, with roads bounded (preferably on both sides) with the 'live frontages' of houses and flats, with eyes and ears on to the street;
• no more underground garages, or long stretches of street-level undercroft parking;
• no larger families above the second-floor;
• a clear delineation between the public realm, shared/communal space and private 'defensible space';
• as little communal circulation as possible;
• effective door-entry/security systems to flats;
• more intensive management;
• higher levels of investment in the public realm; safer, well-used routes, better street lighting, more imaginative and useful public spaces;
• a greater attempt to consult tenants and involve the wider community at the design stage.

While a very few wealthy local authorities managed to sustain their ambitious 1960s and 1970s estates through good and well-resourced management and maintenance – the Barbican in the City of London and Lillington Street in Westminster are good examples – the new developers of affordable rented housing were housing associations. In the period between 1980 and 2000 housing associations were encouraged to follow these new guidelines and to copy the efforts of volume housebuilders in a simplistic attempt to avoid the stigma that had become associated with concrete and high rise, and what was popularly regarded as 'flat-roofed Modernist architecture'. By reducing densities back down to an average of around 30–50 dwellings per hectare with parking ratios approaching 1:1, most of the measures listed above could be achieved in developments consisting mainly of houses with small blocks of three-storey, non-family walk-up flats and with cars parked within sight of their owners' homes. By adhering to the principles of defensible private open space and the approach to car parking described in Chapter 10, as well as such things as avoiding flank walls of houses being exposed directly to the temptation of potential footballers, many security issues were avoided. Many formerly unmanageable estates have been redeveloped in this way and the principles listed above have been employed to great effect. But returning to street-based layouts of predominantly family houses limits achievable densities.

In order to meet the enormous demand, particularly in south-east England, without spreading beyond the boundaries of existing settlements, government policy has been to concentrate new housing on brownfield land wherever possible. The effect of this, and the consequent rise in the value of land, has been to encourage, once again, considerable increases in density and the abandonment of many of the principles that had been introduced largely to address the issue of security. With higher-density schemes once again firmly on the agenda, designers need to ensure that shared circulation, the external environment and essential shared facilities never again become no-go areas like their predecessors, whose densities they already exceed. Where building affordable flats in taller schemes becomes unavoidable, the number of flats sharing a core may need to exceed 25, coupled with providing secondary controlled entry at each landing.

Success also largely depends on not concentrating large numbers of affordable rented homes together. Keeping affordable housing distinctly separate from any private housing still risks the creation of social ghettoes. So from around 2000 on, increasing efforts have been made to mix tenures together and to make them indistinguishable from each other (see Chapter 11).

Other chapters deal with the security of, and shared facilities inside, blocks of flats (Chapter 7), the hazards associated with car parking (Chapter 10), and the front curtilage of houses and ground-floor flats (Chapters 3 and 6), some of which is covered in the police resources of Secured by Design.

Right at the start of any neighbourhood-planning process it is very important to assess the approach that needs to be taken to make it 'safe'. In existing neighbourhoods that have had a problematic history, or in new neighbourhoods on brownfield land where location means there could be a problem, it is essential to make a clear-cut distinction between the 'public' and the 'private' realms. This is usually done by inserting physical features such as walls, fences and gates along the dividing line, something it would be almost impossible to add as an afterthought, due to the cut off of capital funds once a project has been completed and occupied.

In making the distinction between public and private it is important to distinguish further between security on the one hand and privacy on the other. To preserve someone's privacy, simply making the boundary clear with a low wall or railing is usually sufficient; anything more would be over-fortification. If an anti-social person is really determined to invade someone's privacy by opening the front gate and walking up the path to their front door very little can be done to stop them. On the other hand, allowing the design to blur the dividing line to allow that same anti-social person easy access to the back of a house or flat is likely to create an untenable situation – the separation needs to be marked by a substantial barrier, 2 metres high.

Having successfully corralled people into a defined public realm, much is made of the self-policing effect of so-called 'live frontages' where a street is faced on both sides by the windows and front doors of homes, in the belief that, particularly at night,

This has a deterrent effect on street crime and burglary. Compared with streets defined only by the blank end walls of apartment blocks, car parks or commercial buildings, this type of 'live frontage' is clearly credible, except that many examples don't stand up to much scrutiny. Simply positioning living-room or kitchen windows parallel to the street is unlikely to act as much of a deterrent to a criminal, especially if the view up and down the street is partially obscured by cars parked 'in curtilage' or by bits of the building such as porches projecting outwards. It is rendered even more futile by the British obsession with net curtains.

Taking the opportunity seriously in design terms offers opportunities for first-floor living rooms with bay windows as one possible solution. Or various tenures, dwelling and room types can be mixed along each street frontage, coupled with different window types, including bays, to diversify the pattern of occupation and observation.

# Holly Street, Hackney, London E8: the early years, phases 1–5

Nineteenth-century Ordnance Survey maps of this part of London show a dense network of streets with small, closely packed, narrow-fronted houses. Cleared in the late 1960s, the area was later redeveloped, becoming the infamous Holly Street Estate. Looking at the old maps, very little imagination is needed to see why Holly Street was targeted for redevelopment. Some houses were grouped around small backyards, one even operating as a knacker's yard. Others backed closely on to one of the main commuter rail lines into the City of London – the smoke, grime and filthy conditions are easy to imagine.

Around 1970 the London Borough of Hackney's Architects' Department, with central-government encouragement, came up with a scheme to clear the existing housing and to replace it with four 22-storey system-built towers and a vast five-storey interconnected block of system-built maisonettes. At the time this would have been hailed as progress towards a physically healthier community. But the damp, poverty and squalor that existed in the 100-year-old terrace houses were nothing compared with conditions in the unmanageable concrete-clad monsters that replaced them. After only 25 years the Conservative government of the day decided that money set aside for improvement under an 'Estate Action' initiative would not solve the deep-seated problems, which were largely determined by a totally flawed design. Instead, it was decided to consult residents on the possibility of a second, complete redevelopment.

Out of a thousand flats, all but a handful belonged to Hackney Council. Unemployment, crime and fear of crime were high on the list of deprivation suffered by an understandably depressed and suspicious community. The government decided that redevelopment should be led by a private housebuilder and Laing Homes was selected as the result of a competition, with a brief to maintain the existing density and to transfer ownership of the majority of rented homes to housing associations. And although the government was encouraging the idea of home ownership as an alternative to monolithic social renting, the winning scheme offered little in the way of a genuine social mix, apart from a small percentage of shared ownership and a contractual undertaking to develop 20 per cent of the area as an all-private enclave at the end of the process, once the stigma of the old Holly Street Estate had gone for good.

The underlying principle of the masterplan was to reintroduce as much of the original street grid as possible. The goal was to obliterate the notion of an 'estate' by normalising the public realm into a series of streets and squares linked to the surrounding streets. The residents wanted homes that represented as far as possible the private homes they would own had they been in a position to do so, and the architecture is intentionally conservative. This is understandable given residents' hostility to the kind of Modernism represented by Holly Street, constructions that could hardly have been described as architecture at all.

The main issue was personal security. Car crime and the fear of car crime had been big issues for residents, who parked their vehicles whenever there was space in one of the streets surrounding the estate. Even after rebuilding the same total number of dwellings and with a ratio of one parking space for every two dwellings, all parking is now provided in the street within sight of residents' windows. A new problem is posed by non-residents now choosing Holly Street as a safe place to park.

At another level the early phases of the new Holly Street, now almost 15 years old, make an interesting comparison with the changes in policy that have become enshrined in current housing-association practice. Admittedly the first phases were planned to fit into the redundant green spaces between and around the infamous 'snake blocks', and this imposed its own constraints. Some of the first council tenants to move from their existing flats into new houses complained that their kitchens were so narrow they could touch opposite walls at the same time. As well as adopting a modified version of the national housebuilder's standard house or flat, of brick and block construction, with gable walls and shallow pitched roofs, government policy on space standards

**Architects** Levitt Bernstein Associates
**Developers** Laing Homes, London Borough of Hackney + a consortium of housing associations led by Circle 33 Housing Trust
**Site** 11.18 hectares
**Number of dwellings** 833
**Density** 92 dwellings/hectare
**Mix** 27 per cent x 1B + 38 per cent x 2B + 23 per cent x 3B + 12 per cent x 4B
**Affordable** 70 per cent
**Parking spaces per dwelling** 0.5
**Non-housing uses** sports centre + general practice + Sure Start/Early Years centre

Site plan.

Learning from its grisly
predecessor, in 1991 the new
Holly Street had, above all, to
feel secure. The chosen remedy
was to discover as many of its
lost streets as possible and to
link them together. Each terrace
house had its own clearly marked
boundary fence and gate and each
flat shared its front door and
common hall with no more than
seven others, while cars had to be
parked in the street where they
could be watched over by their
owners. This photograph, taken in
2008, some 15 years after this
first phase was built, shows that
the solution chosen is working.

was governed by the notion that whatever
was adequate for private purchasers must
be suitable for tenants as well. Of course
this ignored the fact that when owners'
houses became too small for their needs
they could swap them for something larger,
an option totally unavailable to the average
tenant. Comparison between three-bedroom
houses in phase 1 and the latest equivalent
house types in phase 6 reflects the official
recognition of the need for better space
standards for affordable housing over the
intervening 15 years.

But the success of the new Holly Street is
overwhelmingly due to the design of a public
realm in which every open space, shared
or private, is defined and enclosed by the
building frontages that surround it. The layout
is legible for visitors since every home now
has a number in a street that is on the A–Z.
By creating a distinction between the public
and private realms and clearly articulating
the 'defensible spaces', the streets are no
longer the threatening places they once
were, where even the police were only
prepared to patrol in force and most of Holly
Street was a blank white space on the map.
Parts of Hackney may still be threatening but
Holly Street is not one of them.

**Above** Masterplan with special-need
housing for the elderly shown in pale
blue and community buildings in dark
blue. This is the area covered by the
1970s Holly Street Estate (photographs
opposite). The new plan is based on
extending and joining up the original
surrounding street pattern as far as
possible. Each phase contained a mix of
terrace houses and flats with gardens
placed back to back, and with particular
emphasis on overlooking on street
corners.

**Right** Phase 1 three-bedroom terrace
houses. Simple plans very much influenced
by the builder/developer's experience
of value engineering simple two-storey
houses for sale. Although the overall
floor areas approximate to those of Parker
Morris standards, these houses predated
Lifetime Homes. They also suffer from the
lack of built-in storage space but still
retain their popularity with families.

1:2500

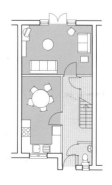 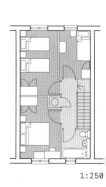

1:250

**Top** The central square serves both as
a children's play space and a garden.
Enclosing it with railings makes it possible
to lock the square at night if there is
anti-social behaviour or vandalism.
**Above left** Street corners are dominated by
flats designed to overlook street activity.
**Above right** Conventional three-bedroom terrace
houses are protected by robust brick walls
and bin stores that provide a degree
of defensible space between house and
pavements.
**Bottom right** Unkempt and vandal-prone space,
and view from one of the four tower blocks,
three of which have been demolished, showing
the infamous 'snake blocks' that covered
the whole estate in one long inter-connected
access-corridor system.
**Bottom left** The whole street level was
dominated by parked cars and lock-up garages
– a breeding ground for crime.

# Abbotts Wharf, Tower Hamlets, London E14

Here primarily as an illustration of good practice in secure parking and the security of shared circulation, the development at Abbotts Wharf – winner of a Housing Design Award – was a first for many of the parties involved. A joint-venture partnering contract between an experienced East London housing association and a developer/builder, it was also the architect's first commission for this client.

Although their markets are obviously different, East Thames Housing Group and Telford Homes shared a vision for the site: the resulting development consists of four separate buildings placed at right angles to the canal and arranged around a new mooring basin on the Limehouse Cut as it nears its junction with the Thames. This arrangement optimises east–west orientation and gives all residents views of the park on the other side of the canal.

There is a total of 201 dwellings in a mix of affordable rent, shared ownership and private sale. Externally, in terms of design quality and materials nothing distinguishes one tenure from another, and it was the deliberate intention of both clients that all residents should benefit from a uniformly high-standard urban development.

The initial brief was for 140 dwellings but it was possible to increase this by varying the height of each of the four blocks, from four storeys to match existing neighbours at one end, to eight storeys on either side of the mooring basin and a 13-storey tower for private sale at the other end.

All buildings are constructed with in-situ concrete frames and floor slabs. External walls comprise lightweight steel-framed and highly insulated panels finished externally with self-coloured render. Mastclimbers were used instead of conventional scaffolding. Bathrooms – lightweight steel-framed 'pods' – were prefabricated off site.

The steel-framed balconies to each flat were hoisted into position complete with their frameless glass upstands and handrails. They were then bolted to prefabricated 'jigs' cast integrally into the floor slabs.

The topography of the site meant that there was a difference of a whole floor level between the access road and the canal towpath. This allowed the construction of almost invisible 'podiums' beneath the two central eight-storey blocks to house 95 cars. The often-prohibitive expense of creating a full basement has been avoided and all flat entrances can be at street level – an enormous advantage. It also means that all parked cars can be concealed from the street and that there is a single secure entrance and exit to each block, which is closely monitored by a full-time concierge.

The security system built into the design from the outset is one of the most distinctive features of the scheme. Had Abbotts Wharf consisted entirely of housing for private sale, like, for example, many developments by Urban Splash in Manchester and Liverpool, it could probably have been successfully managed without 24-hour on-site security. As a mixed-tenure development in an area of social deprivation, in spite of the very high design quality, it could have failed in the same way as the resounding failures of so many similarly configured social-housing schemes of the 1960s and 1970s.

Opinions vary about the number of homes needed to make a 24-hour on-site concierge affordable from service-charge contributions, but the development partnership at Abbotts Wharf built their whole brief around this principle. The continuous technical advances in effective remote door-entry systems and CCTV coverage do make it possible, as in this case, for a single member of a security team on duty to monitor the comings and goings from more than one entrance and exit as well as all the shared amenity spaces. At Abbotts Wharf this presence has proved to be a sufficient deterrent to would-be intruders bent on stealing or vandalising cars or illegally entering the entrance lobbies and common circulation areas in the blocks of flats themselves.

**Architect** Jestico and Whiles
**Developers** Telford Homes with East Thames Housing Group
**Site** 0.62 hectares
**Number of dwellings** 201
**Density** 330 dwellings/hectare
**Affordable** 50 per cent
**Mix** 77 x 1B flats + 110 x 2B flats + 8 x 3B flats + 6 x 3B maisonettes
**Parking spaces per dwelling** 0.43

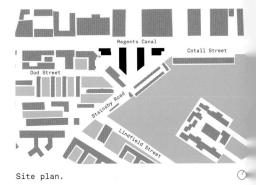

Site plan.

**Right** Successful collaboration between a housing association and a developer/builder to meet the security challenges of a high-density development of flats in an area where crime rates have traditionally been high.

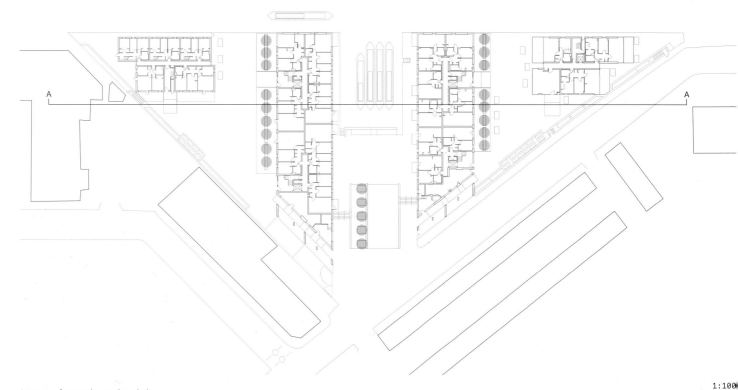

1:100

Layout plan and section A–A
showing all four blocks. The
tallest is privately owned and
the four-storey block is for
affordable rent; the two central
blocks have a mixture of shared
ownership and affordable rent.
There are two points of entry for
pedestrians and two for cars, all
four being controlled by the 24-
hour concierge system.

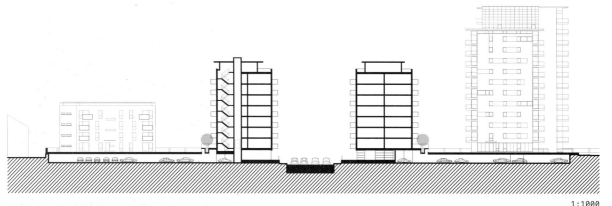

1:1000

**above** Looking from one side of the newly formed canal basin to the other showing ground-floor openings to the parking undercroft.

**top right** A concierge monitors all comings and goings on a 24-hour, seven-days-a-week basis.

**right** Secure vehicular entrance to podium, secure pedestrian entrance and concierge observation window.

St James Square, Bermondsey.
Conventional ideas of visual
privacy are challenged in this new
pedestrian-only street, which can
be as little as 12 metres wide
between opposite building faces.

This chapter deals with the issues of visual and acoustic privacy between adjacent dwellings. Other issues affecting privacy such as personal security and privacy within the home are dealt with in Chapters 6 and 8.

Within the home and garden, privacy is largely a matter of personal expectation and the relationships between neighbours or household members. Adherence to an absolute condition of being unable either to hear or to see neighbours may represent complete perfection to one person but isolation and loneliness to another. Anecdotal evidence of disputes arising from noise leaking through poorly insulated party walls is matched by anecdotes from close communities that value some connection, for instance a mother's scream alerting a neighbour after she has fallen downstairs with her new baby.

In visual terms there is clear evidence from dense urban areas that, while some people want to prevent others looking into their windows from the street or access gallery or shared courtyard, other single flat dwellers feel less isolated if their kitchen windows overlook other kitchen windows where from time to time there may be some kind of human contact. The ideal therefore seems to be a situation in which privacy can be controlled – you can have it when you want it.

**Visual privacy in the home**
Few subjects have been treated with less sensible attention than visual privacy. The out-dated and arcane regulations imposed by many planning authorities have meant that visual privacy has conventionally been addressed by imposing minimum distances between the principal windows of dwellings, regardless of whether the windows are those of bedrooms, living rooms or kitchens. However, other design solutions can be more effective while also making better use of outside space. Without this more imaginative approach to the issue, we cannot achieve higher densities or intimacy in place-making.

At their most conventional, planning authorities stipulate that the distance between principal windows should not be less than 21–22 metres, which suggests streets of uniform width, and back-to-back rear gardens of around 11 metres in depth. This approach, imposing privacy by regulation, entirely misses the subjective aspects of visual privacy and has led to many very dreary housing solutions.

The subject is complicated and closely related to the expectations of neighbours, depending on whether they live in a dense urban or a leafy suburban neighbourhood. Contrary to expectations, people living cheek by jowl with their neighbours seem less concerned about overlooking than their suburban counterparts. They don't expect what they are doing in their kitchens, living rooms or bedrooms to go unnoticed by their neighbours, and if they prefer to remain private they take steps to use blinds of various kinds to control how much they can be seen from outside.

Experiments in urban housing built more than 20 years ago show that kitchen and even bedroom windows facing each other only 7 metres apart can function perfectly satisfactorily, with the aid of suitably adjustable blinds. However, such an arrangement in a suburban context would be considered quite unacceptable. Privacy must therefore be thought of as relative, not absolute. One satisfactory solution when the overlooking distance is extremely limited is to form a projecting bay with windows on either side at right angles to the outside wall and only clerestory windows, or none at all, on the central section.

There are significant differences in the approaches to privacy taken in the UK and some other European countries. For example, in the Netherlands – which in many other respects has design policies parallel to those of the UK, although Dutch residents are less inherently conservative – the treatment of privacy in balcony-access flats is more imaginative. In the UK balcony access is associated with municipal housing and is considered a narrow and unattractive method of getting from lift to front door in as little time as possible. In the Netherlands it carries no such stigma. The received view of balcony access in the UK stipulates that designs should not require the occupants of one flat to have to pass a bedroom or living-room window of another flat in order to reach their front door. In the Netherlands the access balcony is rightly compared to a normal footpath, generously wide and provided with planting. Where privacy for bedroom windows is necessary the balcony

walkway is pulled away from the façade, and thus away from any windows, by an amount sufficient to provide privacy from strangers or neighbours. This allows night-time ventilation without compromising security. Short bridges then connect the walkway to individual front doors.

Part of the reason that overlooking has been receiving so much recent attention can be understood by looking at changes to the size of windows: despite thermal regulations driving window areas down, they are still much larger than they were 50 years ago. Floor-to-ceiling windows in living rooms and bedrooms are now common and, although a system of integrated venetian blinds can control both glare and privacy, many new homes both for rent and sale are handed over to their first occupants without blinds or the financial means to install them. Different kinds of blinds are now available. It is possible to control banks of louvres independently and roller blinds can pull up from the bottom so occupants don't need to lose all the light and view.

No description of methods for gaining privacy can avoid mentioning the net curtains so beloved by UK householders and to many a cultural necessity. As well as being part of a deeply entrenched tradition, they are obviously a much cheaper alternative to any system of blinds, and much easier to install and maintain. From a functional point of view their use is strictly limited for although net curtains stop people looking in – except at night when they don't work – they effectively prevent anyone inside from looking out, or carrying out 'passive surveillance' of the street, which is the main objective of so-called 'live frontages'.

## Visual privacy and private open space
If there is a variety of approaches to the question of visual privacy between one house or flat and another, the way to treat balconies and back gardens is equally uncertain. On gardens, opinion seems equally divided between those who want complete privacy from their neighbours with 2-metre-high walls or fences all the way round, and those who look forward to a congenial chat with neighbours 'over the garden wall'.

In sought-after urban locations ingenious solutions to issues of privacy are to be found through careful detailing. Newbury Mews, Kentish Town, London, by Brooks Murray.

In the case of ground-floor flats or maisonettes with several floors of flats above, the height of fences is relatively academic, as the whole garden or patio can be seen from above. But in general terms 2 metres of solid 2-metre-high fencing projecting on both sides from the rear wall of a house or ground-floor flat is enough to stop next-door neighbours having a direct view into the ground-floor rear room, or a view of any terrace immediately outside the house. If the remaining sides and the rear boundary are built up as solid fencing to 1 metre, with an additional metre of trellis above that, there is a degree of privacy from all but the most intrusive neighbour. Trellis is either transparent enough for contact with someone next door or a good framework for climbing plants to form a completely private enclosure.

In some situations, such as shallow sites around 20 metres deep and sandwiched between two roughly parallel streets, it is possible to line both streets with wide, double-fronted houses that are only one room deep and have a 'back to back' distance of as little as 10 metres. The first-floor bedroom windows would all face outwards and overlook the street, while the ground-floor rooms would open out on to a 5-metre-deep patio at the back as well as the street. In such a situation, where privacy at the back of each house would only be as good as the permanent boundary between them, a brick dividing wall is a sensible alternative to the relative impermanence of timber.

The issue of visual privacy in relation to balconies is discussed in Chapter 6.

**The transfer of sound**
Recent research shows that for most people acoustic privacy is an even higher priority than visual privacy. Protection against structure-borne sound transmitted from one dwelling to another through party walls and party floors is now largely a matter of technical specification dealt with under Building Regulations, Part E. The 2003 revision of Part E changed the spectrum of sound measurement for determining the required insulation of party walls, in order to take account of the annoyance caused by the bass frequencies of loud music.

While the issue of what is acceptable is highly subjective, noise nuisance is almost certainly the greatest cause of disputes between adjoining owners and between landlord and tenant. Therefore standards of soundproofing can never be treated lightly and risks should never be taken.

Apart from standards dealt with under Building Regulations, the principal issues are:
• stacking and handling of plans;
• choice of structures;
• impact sound transmission and reverberation from common circulation;
• airborne sound leakage from one dwelling to another;
• conflicting sound levels within dwellings.

**Stacking** There are common-sense steps that can be taken in terms of stacking rooms of similar function in flats one above the other, as well as handling plans so that a party or tenancy-separating wall does not have to come between the bedrooms of one dwelling and the living room of another.

**Structure-borne sound** Acoustic separation is achieved by using mass to absorb sound or by isolation/separation. Heavyweight construction is the most effective means, but only if backed by sound workmanship; for instance, a brick party wall built with mortar omitted from the perpendicular joints provides a sound path through the joints.

A requirement for pre-completion testing has been introduced into the Building Regulations to ensure that the designed performance is achieved in practice. However, the house-building industry's response to the burden of pre-completion testing has been the introduction of a scheme in which developers and manufacturers propose standard forms of construction and pay for them to be tested, after which they are adopted as 'Robust Details' and avoid the need for pre-completion testing. This process has enabled developers to demonstrate innovative forms of construction, such as timber-frame party walls that are capable of achieving the necessary levels of acoustic performance if built correctly. If the construction adopted fails to perform after completion the adoption of 'Robust Details' is no defence when a dispute arises.

Certain types of framed structures perform differently in terms of structure-borne sound transmission. Overcoming sound transmission through different types of frame has cost implications.

**Impact sound transmission** Most noticeable in the evening and at night, this is usually caused by hard-soled or high-heeled shoes on hard external surfaces and can easily be transmitted via the structure directly into bedrooms on the floors below. By far the most cost-effective remedy is to avoid hard – concrete or ceramic-tiled – surfaces, simply stopping creation of the noise. If hard surfaces are unavoidable both they and the screed to which they are fixed need to be isolated by cushioning from the supporting floor structure. The 2003 revision of Part E of the Building Regulations introduced a statutory requirement to control the level of reverberated sound in the common parts of residential buildings.

**Airborne sound transmission** As densities are inevitably on the increase in schemes where flats predominate, the chance of airborne sound transmission through open windows reaching nuisance proportions also increases. Nuisance from airborne sound caused by noise passing from one dwelling to another through open windows is a particular problem in summer. Obviously, rooms that overheat in summer temperatures are only rendered tolerable if it is possible to open windows. Every possible step to avoid overheating needs to be taken, using external shading and passive ventilation where practicable. Schemes built around courtyards are particularly vulnerable to sounds reverberating between hard reflective surfaces via open windows. Intensive planting, particularly of trees, and absorbent external wall surfaces need to be integrated into the design from the outset.

**Internal sound transmission** Noise nuisance is often generated inside dwellings themselves and passes from one room to another. It can be particularly acute in flats or houses with open-plan living spaces.

An obvious step to avoid in triple-function cooking/dining/living rooms is the sound from washing machines, tumble dryers and boilers that need to be located elsewhere than in the kitchen. In addition, the need for older children to be able to create noise independently of their parent(s) is now partially taken care of within the Building Regulations specification for insulation in partitions and intermediate floor voids in houses.

# Old Royal Free Square, Islington, London N1

**Background + sense of place, Chapter 1**

From the outset it was important to combine the provision of family houses with a density that was as high as possible within the still sacrosanct density ceiling of 250 habitable rooms per hectare for new buildings. The cost of purchasing such a strategic site in a high-value area needed to be spread over as many dwellings as possible and there was therefore pressure to increase the numbers. This was achieved by excluding the dwellings fitted into the retained hospital buildings from the density calculation because, curiously, density ceilings do not apply to refurbished buildings, even when they involve a change of use to housing.

Not only was this is an area of very high property values, the brief demanded a high proportion of family dwellings with their own street entrances and private rear open spaces. It was not designing out of character with the area when, to achieve the target density, with 70 per cent on-street car parking, involved reducing the scale of the spaces between buildings and adopting the scale of buildings most commonly found in mews housing. The result was a street with houses on both sides just 7 metres across, one third of the normally accepted minimum, which requires around 21 metres between 'principal windows facing each other' for the purpose of achieving an acceptable level of privacy.

Although this street forms part of a public pedestrian route through the development, linking a considerable area of nineteenth-century housing with Islington's main shopping street, there has been no hint of complaint about lack of privacy. On the contrary, since occupants of these houses have their ground-floor kitchen windows overlooking the street it is arguable that the intimacy reduces the sense of isolation experienced by members of households who spend much of their time alone at home.

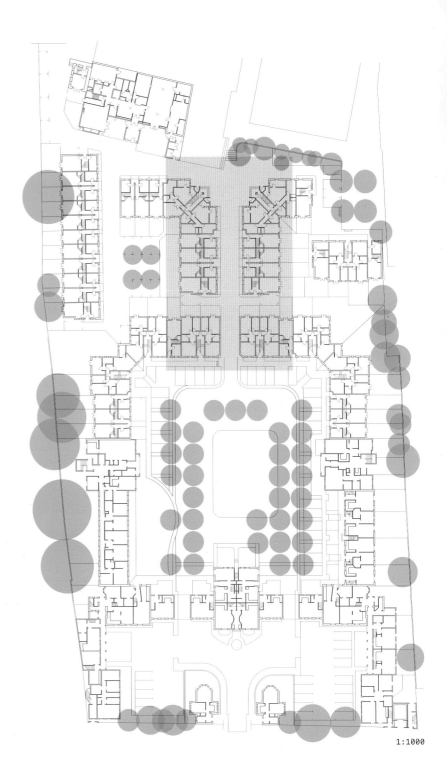

1:1000

**Above** Ground-floor plan. The pedestrian street, shared with service and emergency vehicles only (shaded), is only 7 metres wide but each terrace house has its own private patio garden at its rear. Kitchen windows at the front overlook the street so a close eye can be kept on activity in the street itself.

**Right** Although the street is deliberately narrow and is a shared surface with no pavements, it has some of the qualities of a mews. Regular public foot traffic through the site adds to the feeling of security, rather than reducing it.

**Background + shared amenity space, Chapter 7**

The background to this development is described in Chapter 7, which explains why such a high density has resulted from a competitive-tender process based on the maximum capital receipt to Southwark Council, which owned the land, combined with a density ceiling way above the previous maximum of around 160 dwellings per hectare (494 habitable rooms per hectare).

For affordable flats the aim is to reduce the number of tenancies entered from a single core to not more than 20–25. This avoids over-dependence on electronic systems as the only means of providing security and preventing vandalism in common areas. Except where it is possible to avoid lift access to flats altogether, a measure now almost impossible if designing to Lifetime Homes' standards, every entrance and circulation core requires at least one lift. A general guiding principle for manageable mixed-tenure housing, as distinct from developments of all-private housing, suggests that the optimum height should not be more than seven storeys. Above this, access to two lifts instead of one is required, in case of breakdown and to allow for maintenance.

The St James Square scheme combines these storey-height principles with a very high density, and this inevitably puts pressure on the width of streets and the spaces between the buildings themselves. A precedent for housing at this sort of height and density was available just across the road: most of Shad Thames consists of converted nineteenth-century warehouses separated by narrow, cavernous streets. The principle was continued in the 1980s by Piers Gough in CWGZ's Circle scheme just behind Shad Thames. The new masterplan for the Bermondsey Spa sites includes several streets that are just 12 metres wide from building face to building face.

The resulting scheme aims to combine a high standard of amenity for individual flats with an approach to visual privacy – principal windows facing principal windows – that challenges the normal requirement for 22 metres between them. Each flat has a generous balcony and the larger family dwellings on the ground and first floors have rear patios each with direct access to a shared courtyard (see page 123). Inevitably, the orientation of some flats provides for better access to sunlight than others but the plan arrangement of multiple cores allows all units to have a dual aspect and this means that each receives sunlight for part of the day.

If this approach to privacy proves to be successful, and numerous examples (including Shad Thames and Old Royal Free Square) suggest there is no reason why it should not, the logical conclusion must be that people living in high-density urban situations do not expect to enjoy the same degree of visual privacy they would want in the suburbs. At the same time, in narrow streets where daylighting is an issue, the trend is towards larger windows combined with various types of venetian blinds. Blinds, although beyond the means of many tenants in affordable homes, provide excellent privacy without cutting out too much light or entirely blocking the view.

**Right** Although these balconies overlook each other, and it is possible to see into adjoining living rooms from the balcony of a neighbouring flat, the balconies are clearly well-populated and privacy is protected by either roller or venetian blinds.

The Peabody Trust acquired the Nile Street site at full market value from the London Borough of Hackney in March 2003. It had been the site of a car park and a derelict community centre known as the Blue Hut. From the outset the development was conceived as a high-density mixed-use scheme that was intended to meet the needs of both the council and community. Although Peabody's offer for the land was not the highest in value, the quality of the scheme and the high level of affordable housing proposed made it the most attractive.

The council's aim was to generate small flats as part of an initiative to deal with unmet demand for affordable keyworker and shared-ownership accommodation in central areas of London. The Peabody Trust undertook to develop the Nile Street site for a mixture of tenures – affordable for rent was the smallest proportion.

The Blue Hut site had, for a number of years, been contentious as local residents were disappointed with the dilapidation and eventual loss of a valuable community facility. For more than five years a well-organised group of residents had been lobbying the council to provide the community facility again, rather than simply disposing of the site and losing the resource for ever. The council required Peabody to provide the facility as a condition of sale; the trust worked with council officers, councillors and, importantly, local residents to guide its exact nature.

At 790 habitable rooms and 438 dwellings per hectare, and an average of six storeys, the accommodation is highly concentrated. The astonishingly high density in terms of dwellings per hectare is a product of the considerable number of studio flats for keyworkers. Of the 174 dwellings, 137 are either studios – single-room flats – or one-bedroom flats.

To the south of the site is a standalone block of flats for owner occupation, half of which face out, and half face in to the internal courtyard. The studio and shared-ownership flats occupy an L-shaped block, double banked with a central corridor, half of which again face out and half towards the

central courtyard. This internal courtyard is not accessible to residents but is a visual amenity based on a water feature by artist Antony Donaldson. All residents do, however, have private balconies and access to a shared roof terrace.

At this density on the fringe of the City of London, this is sophisticated urban living with flats for owner occupation, shared ownership and keyworkers, predominantly small households, and larger family flats for affordable rent by tenants of the Peabody Trust. And although the shared entrance to the flats for affordable rent is in a different street from the entrance to the majority of the flats, the sheer proximity of all the households creates an awareness of different lifestyles without creating the kind of flashpoint that could so easily occur between larger households with children and those without.

Apart from the density and the boldness of the architecture, one of the most astonishing features of this development is the calm assumption about privacy, clearly endorsed by the Peabody Trust's great experience. In several instances the principal windows of flats face each other across the courtyard with a distance of only 9.5 metres between them. This is urban housing at the upper end of the density scale. Its occupants clearly have to abide by the rules about sound transfer through open windows. If they are sensitive about being overlooked, they deal with the problem by installing blinds.

**Architect** Munkenbeck + Marshall Architects
**Developer** Peabody Trust
**Site** 0.4 hectares
**Number of dwellings** 174
**Density** 438 dwellings/hectare (790HR/hectare)
**Affordable** 11 per cent affordable rent + 62 per cent shared ownership and keyworker
**Mix** 10 x 3B + 27 x 2B + 59 x 1B + 78 studios
**Parking spaces per dwelling** none
**Non-housing uses** youth club, 250 square metres

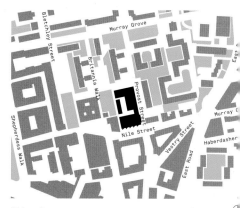

Site plan.

**Right** This view from the balcony of one flat across the narrow courtyard towards the living area of another on the opposite side, shows how some occupants choose to have blinds while others do not. It can also be argued that single people – and this is predominantly a development for key workers, many of whom are single – prefer to be able to have some kind of visual contact with their neighbours.

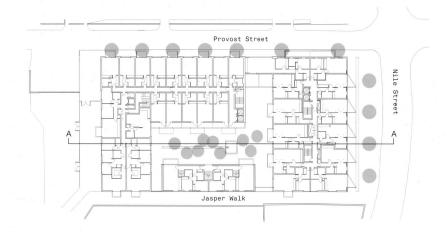

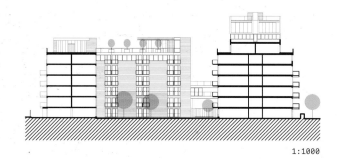

1:1000

**Above and left** Layout plan and section A–A of the Peabody Trust's high-density scheme at Nile Street, showing the narrow internal courtyard. This is inaccessible even to residents, and is only 9.5 metres wide. Reflecting the extremely high density, many non-family flats are single aspect, looking only into the central courtyard.
**Below left** Plans of one-bedroom and single-person studio flats.
**Below right** Plans of three-bedroom and two-bedroom flats.

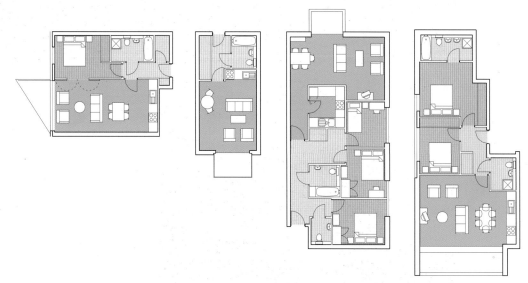

1:250

ove External elevations.
ove right The internal courtyard.
t Entrance to private flats.

### Wanting to own a car/needing to own a car

Car ownership and housing is a subject that has endless ramifications: developers and authorities have to make judgements over the difference between new residents wanting to own a car and needing to own one.

Dealing first with the issue of those who want to own cars regardless of their necessity, some authorities have been veering away from over-generous parking provision to the opposite extreme of car-free developments, in an effort to discourage car ownership and therefore unnecessary car use. However, a significant number of households, regardless of their economic circumstances, want to own a car even if they don't want to use it every day. Making the right decisions about parking provision therefore becomes a critical design problem that cannot realistically be solved by imposed planning decisions restricting parking spaces.

Buying a car is no longer an issue of affordability: virtually any household can aspire to own one, the cost of a cheap second-hand car as a proportion of household income having steadily reduced over the past 50 years. But as average densities increase car ownership is bound to decrease. The availability of parking and the high cost of underground or undercroft parking, insurance, congestion charges, metered parking and fuel make the cost of owning any car, however cheap to buy, much more significant.

As average densities increase the aim to 'provide a space in the street where residents could park one car per dwelling within sight of their homes' is no longer remotely practicable except in schemes of up to 50 dwellings per hectare if 100 per cent houses, or up to 125 dwellings per hectare if a mixture of houses and low-rise flats. And even then that principle is complicated by the minority of residents who need to park vans and business vehicles that are both bulky and unsightly.

Turning to the question of the need to use a car, the guidance on sustainability incorporated into documents such as the Housing Corporation's *Housing Quality Indicators* and the 20 criteria listed under *Building for Life* issued by CABE make a direct link between car use and access to effective public transport. The need to have a car, as well as somewhere to park it, obviously reduces in proportion to the availability of alternatives in the form of trains and buses. Many keyworkers work unsociable hours but, in any case, most car journeys are not just getting to and from work, and for various reasons a large proportion of these are still difficult to make using public transport. Finding secure, affordable and manageable solutions when densities are increasing demands re-examination of all the options, especially those that have been in operation for some time, such as car clubs, convenient bike storage, green travel plans, etc.

### The physical options for parking

These become more complicated as densities increase, but they also vary according to the ratio of parking spaces per dwelling that is required. Working upwards from the lowest densities these are:

### The built-in or integral garage in terrace houses

These are exclusively related to low-density layouts involving houses rather than flats. Although invariably much prized by residents, the built-in garage has generally been regarded as something of a scourge in terms of streetscape, leading to soulless frontages dominated by metal 'up-and-over' doors and with hardly any opportunity for the occupants of houses to monitor what is going on in the street. In addition, many residents of such houses choose to use their garage for storing anything but the car while the car itself sits on the hardstanding in front of it, or simply to use the hardstanding as parking for a second vehicle.

However, it may be that this well-deserved prejudice against built-in garages is largely a result of the invariably unattractive and ill-thought-out application of the principle in small, narrow-frontage houses. Suppose, for instance, that the inclusion of a garage or even an open carport on the street frontage resulted in houses with first-floor living rooms that had large overhanging bay windows

Well-detailed street parking at Coin Street, Southwark, London. Architect Haworth Tompkins.

urveying the street, and that access to the ear garden, refuse and other storage could e gained via the garage. Although this could nly be provided in houses with frontages in xcess of 6 metres, it would remove unsightly ars from the street and provide real quality-f-life benefits for residents.

**arking within the curtilage of terrace ouses** The provision of parking 'on street' r 'off street' is seldom a design decision for ne reasons explained below.

is a common and popular practice, almost vorldwide, to provide individual parking paces 'off street' in front of each house, ccupying what would otherwise have been art of the front garden. Estate layouts of mall houses combining homes for sale nd for affordable rent with in-curtilage arking in preference to street parking have een approved in great numbers simply s a means of reducing management costs - and satisfying consumer demand for a uaranteed space close to home. Many local uthorities will not adopt (that is, assume esponsibility for) estate roads that contain arking bays. Responsibility for roadway naintenance, long and short term, then falls n the owners of properties.

Once a decision has been made to choose n-curtilage parking, the results can vary oetween two extremes depending on the rontage and depth of the plot, as well as other issues to do with defensible space, enure and the upkeep of gardens. The irst solution is a satisfactory, if suburban, American-style layout in which a generous and continuous strip of carefully mown grass with no boundary fences separating one house from another is punctuated by concrete hardstandings for each house. The result is only successful where the collective service charge is sufficient to pay for effective day-to-day maintenance and where the proportion of soft landscape is much greater than the concrete hardstandings. In most cases this means that the average terrace-house frontage would be quite sufficient to include a built-in garage as well.

The second and much less satisfactory application is where house frontages are so

narrow that there appears to be nothing but a continuous concrete strip from the back of the pavement up to the external front wall of the terrace, with endless crossovers to the footway. In this situation the front curtilage is neither part of the public realm nor the occupant's own private realm, and often becomes a dumping ground.

**Street parking** The alternative to parking off street and in curtilage is to provide planned parking on street as part of an access-road layout. From the narrow point of view that values having 'your own car parked on your own plot' this is obviously a much less popular option with most residents, but in terms of urban-design quality it has overwhelming advantages. The other significant advantage is flexibility. It allows for some households to park two or three cars and others to park none. However, street parking can also be a reason for the local authority to refuse adoption on the basis that they are prepared to adopt the road and the pavement but not the bit in between.

By laying out parking bays at right angles to the street as well as allowing space for street trees it is still possible to achieve space for nearly twice as many cars as can be achieved with the in-curtilage alternative. It also allows for properly laid out defensible space at the front of houses, marked out with low brick walls, combined with railings and a gate leading directly on to a footpath. Layouts at densities below 50 (or 75) dwellings per hectare and with a required parking ratio of 1:1 can normally achieve the number of parking spaces required 'on street'.

And there is an added community-safety argument to apply in favour of this alternative. If a car is normally parked in front of a house its absence is more noticeable, suggesting that its owners are away; cars parked in unmarked bays in the street are nothing like so noticeable.

**Parking courts**, invariably at the rear of dwellings, can be a successful way of dealing with a parking problem by hiding cars and allowing streets to be more intimate, or they can be disastrous. The normal arrangement is to provide a gap in a terrace between two houses or an archway leading to a rear 'courtyard', which is entirely surrounded by the rear gardens of the houses it serves.

Whether this arrangement succeeds or not largely depends on the quality of the immediate neighbourhood and the tenure of the housing it serves. In principle, rear parking courts provide beneficial access to back gardens, preferable to having to carry everything horticultural through the living room or kitchen. However, there may be serious obstacles in obtaining Secured by Design certification due to the vulnerability of houses that have become accessible from the rear.

There are some sure-fire rules to apply to design and layout when planning a parking court appears to be the only solution available:
• security is made worse if there is more than one way in and out. A single entrance with a gate installed as part of the design can be controlled by an electronic fob key if necessary. It is often difficult to tell what degree of security is going to be needed in a given situation: it is better to be safe than sorry as the funds needed to install a security gate are never available if they have not been included in the main package of works;
• cheap and insubstantial fencing degrades after only a few years and then becomes unsightly;
• opaque boundaries leave anyone on their own at night very vulnerable to crime. Better to have robust walls up to, say, 1200mm with transparent fencing or trellising above that. These boundaries need to allow householders the ability to see into the court while providing sufficient isolation for their own private open space;
• rear entrances to gardens should only be provided if gates are as robust as the rest of the boundary treatments;
• good lighting is essential;
• parking courts need constant maintenance. Detritus of any kind breeds more detritus and anything left broken, such as fencing, planting or lighting, encourages vandalism.

**Undercroft parking** So called because these are parking areas beneath flats, courtyards or raised podiums, but fundamentally above ground. The obvious advantages are that the parking area is naturally lit and ventilated and relatively easy to access; it is therefore cheaper to construct and less liable to be affected by crime or anti-social behaviour than full basement parking. The main disadvantage is that because the parking area is visible and therefore more secure from the street outside this can have a severely deadening effect on life at street level. The only way to provide any ground-floor residential space with direct, level access from the street is with outward-facing, single-aspect accommodation with the undercroft sandwiched behind it.

Parking undercrofts under residential structures with load-bearing cross walls determine the centres of those cross walls, which may not be economic without some form of concrete-framed transfer structure.

Certain sites are better suited to undercroft parking by taking advantage of natural slopes, so the undercroft might be at ground level on the access side but at basement level – and therefore mostly disguised – on the street frontage. This suggests the kind of 'cut-and-fill' cross section used by Victorian housebuilders with the street raised a half level above mean ground level and access to the undercroft half a level below.

**Underground parking** The combination of underground car parks and housing, mostly associated with local-authority developments from the 1960s and 1970s, has acquired a thoroughly deserved reputation for problems with security and crime. The mere mention of underground parking is normally sufficient to produce an adverse reaction in the minds of both developers/housing associations and residents, with instant visions of malfunctioning security, muggings and vandalism.

So why are underground car parks making a comeback? The principal reason is a product of the densities at which many large new mixed-tenure schemes now have to be developed, reflecting both housing demand and soaring land values. Mixed-tenure housing at densities of around 50 dwellings er hectare can usually accommodate ufficient surface parking to meet planning equirements while the developers of many igher-density schemes are encouraged to nake little or no provision for parking. Where here is a requirement for parking associated vith new housing at high densities, due either to low PTAL ratings or simply incoming consumer demand, going underground is the only option.

There are then several crucial issues that nay mean the difference between success or failure:
• security systems need to be able to prevent unauthorised access by pedestrians as well as vehicles;
• without taking security systems, both physical and electronic, to ridiculous extremes, for instance by adopting the nethods employed by the Home Office n secure establishments, the viability of underground car parks is extremely area sensitive. As the character of an area changes, particularly in terms of local teenage culture and drug use, the chances of success can also change. One large local-authority-owned car park in central London, beneath an extensive tenanted estate built in the early 1970s, used to be a byword for misuse of almost every kind imaginable – drug use, rough sleeping and vandalism – but has been re-established as a workable facility protected solely by fob-key-operated doors and roller shutters. Any determined miscreant could, however, easily obtain access for whatever purpose and the only possible explanation must be that 'low life' in the surrounding streets is not as low as it used to be;
• security systems that are overseen by CCTV linked to 24-hour concierge monitoring are far more effective than those that are not;
• 24-hour concierge services have a major impact on service-charge levels and affordability. To make them economic for tenants paying affordable rents, at least 200 dwellings need to be served by a single concierge system.

**Car-stacking systems and central multi-storey parking** Mechanical car stacking systems are mainly used in exceptionally

high-density housing schemes on the Continent, but the capital costs and the implications for service charges are likely to preclude their use in the UK except for high-value private housing in inner cities.

Central multi-storey car parks, a feature of many post-war local-authority estates, mostly long since abandoned or demolished, have staged a comeback on the Continent where car-free streets allow residents to drive up to their entrance doors in order to deposit shopping, children or the elderly on condition that their cars are then stored in a multi-storey car park close to the distributor street. But this, of course, only works where the community is sufficiently mature and residents feel confident about their own and their vehicle's safety (see Chapter 17, Solarsiedlung, Freiburg).

**Security systems for parking courts, undercrofts or underground car parks**
Electronic security systems can sometimes be essential but they are never foolproof and require enormous amounts of maintenance to remain effective. Systems such as barriers simply to control the movement of cars are prone to wanton damage and there are other more effective ways, such as clamping services, that achieve the same objective.

Electronic gates or shutters that control the movement of cars and pedestrians can be effective and even essential in high-risk areas. The key to success with any type of electronic system is whether or not it is linked to a 'manned' concierge system.

## Background + security, Chapter 8

The system developed for car parking is
entirely bound up with the general approach
to security. The topography of the site meant
that there was a difference of a whole floor
level between the access road and the canal
towpath. This allowed the construction
of almost invisible 'podiums' beneath the
two central eight-storey blocks to house
95 cars. The often prohibitive expense of
creating a full basement was avoided and
all flat entrances could be at street level – an
enormous advantage. It also means that all
parked cars can be concealed from the street
and that there is a single secure entrance and
exit to each block, which is closely monitored
by a full-time concierge.

The main pedestrian and vehicular entrances
are both from the same street. Cars descend
a central ramp and enter the two car parks
via controlled gates under the two eight-
storey blocks. Lifts in those blocks connect
directly with the parking level.

Site location plan. Parking
undercrofts extend beneath the
podium deck. These undercrofts are
protected by the 24-hour-concierge
system previously described (pages
134, 137) and do not impinge on
the quality of the open spaces.

**Above** Ramped entrance to parking
undercroft.
**Right** Fob-key security gate
monitored by concierge.

# The Bolonachi Building,
# Site D, Bermondsey,
# London SE1

**Background + layout, Chapter 4**

At these densities, 'off-street' car parking is difficult to achieve affordably even if, as in this case, the planning brief only required a ratio of 0.4 cars per dwelling. Underground car parks are notoriously as expensive to run as they are to build, so in a scheme with nearly 50 per cent of either shared ownership or affordable rent this was not an option. Excavation of basements would have been additionally complicated due to the high water table in this area of former Thames marshland. As a very rough average, an underground parking space in a basement garage adds approximately 30 per cent to the cost of building a 70-square-metre flat. If the parking space is provided in an undercroft beneath the building, but not underground, the additional cost is about half that much.

Instead, the design incorporates a car park at street level beneath the main amenity space, in the form of a raised courtyard enclosed by housing on all four sides. To disguise the car park from the street and to preserve the all-important 'live frontage' on to the surrounding streets, the design adopts a family maisonette type that has a single-aspect ground floor with its front door opening directly on to the street. This floor is backed against the car park but has a dual-aspect first floor with a rear patio at the same level as the main first-floor courtyard.

The courtyard is perforated with openings that have three functions: to provide natural light and ventilation; to make the parking level safer as it can be viewed from above; and to provide large species trees that are rooted at ground level, reaching up through the openings into the courtyard above; something that can only be achieved if planted at ground level due to their weight.

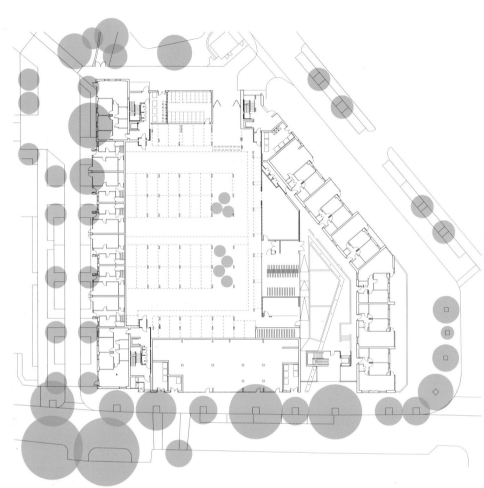

First-floor layout plan.                                    1:10

**Above** Cut-away perspective showing another variant on the parking undercroft whereby the car park is completely disguised from the street by the lower single-aspect storey of outward-facing maisonettes. The car park is ventilated naturally through large openings in the podium above, through which trees – planted in the ground – grow.

**Right** Aerial view of completed development from the north-west.

In 2000 the London Borough of Hounslow was faced with massive repair and improvement costs on its estate at Page Road. Unable to fund them, it decided to consult residents over the possible transfer of ownership to a housing association.

After a competitive selection process, Catalyst Housing Group and a national housebuilder were selected by residents to redevelop the whole estate in stages, based on a design by Pollard Thomas Edwards. This increased the overall number of dwellings by 167, from 153 to 320, in a mixed tenure development of which 30 per cent is for outright sale. A large proportion of the new dwellings are terrace houses.

After the housebuilder withdrew from the scheme, Catalyst decided to assume the role of developer and to work within its highly successful partnering framework with the contractor Inspace and Pollard Thomas Edwards.

The brief required a 1:1 parking ratio overall: at 87 dwellings per hectare this is not easy to achieve with all surface parking. However, although the new Page Road development contains a large number of single-family terrace houses, the architects resisted demands for in-curtilage parking, and managed to achieve the parking requirement in on-street bays at right angles to the adopted streets, interspersed with generous amounts of tree planting.

**Architects** Pollard Thomas Edwards Architects
**Developer** Catalyst Housing Group
**Site** 3.672 hectares
**Number of dwellings** 320
**Density** 87 dwellings/hectare (276 Hr/ hectare)
**Mix** 99 x 1B + 153 x 2B + 58 x 3B + 10 x 4B
**Affordable** 70 per cent rental and shared ownership
**Parking spaces per dwelling** 1

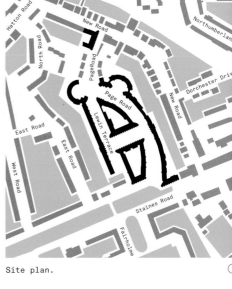

Site plan.

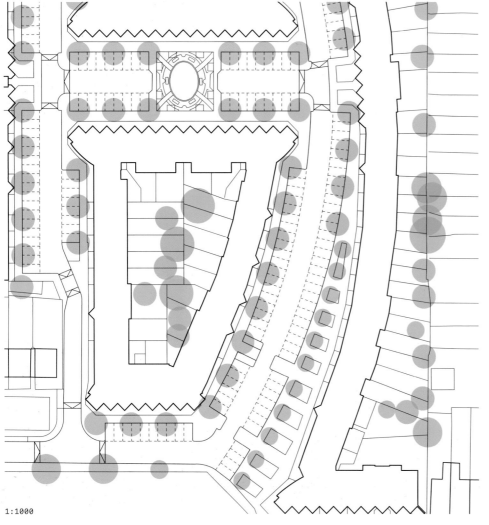

1:1000

Masterplan. This is an example of a well-ordered surface parking arrangement with cars parked at right angles to the roadway, interspersed with trees and shrub planting between the roadway and the pavement. This is much preferable to the alternative of in-curtilage parking, being tidier, clearly defining the public/private realms, and also accommodating more cars.

Three different arrangements
for car parking and planting.

In liberal social terms the most successful streets are those you can walk down without knowing or caring about the social background or financial circumstances of the people who live there. The fact that such streets exist at all, and they are mostly restricted to eighteenth- and nineteenth-century inner-city locations, is largely due to the process of gentrification that has been taking place in these areas since the 1960s.

## Mixed tenure

In a liberal society the most successful streets are those you can walk down without knowing or caring about the social background or financial circumstances of the people who live there. The fact that such streets exist at all, and they are mostly restricted to eighteenth- and nineteenth-century inner-city locations, is largely due to the process of gentrification that has been taking place in these areas since the 1960s.

Until then, most inner-city houses were owned by private landlords who had been mismanaging their property portfolios for decades. Eventually the buildings had become so undercapitalised that any surplus from rental incomes barely scratched the surface of what was needed to put them back into decent repair. Over the succeeding 20 years or so many of these properties were bought and refurbished by young pioneering middle-class families, by local authorities or by grant-aided housing associations. This soon led to a massive increase in the value of this kind of property when the better-off decided it was now safe to buy into areas that had previously been dismissed as slums. Large terrace houses with gardens within easy reach of work in the city centres could now be regarded confidently as good family homes and highly mortgageable investments, and the gentrification process spiralled.

Well before the end of the last century these same local authorities and housing associations had become victims of their own success. It was no longer financially feasible for them to buy more properties in the areas they had earlier helped to gentrify and that were now changing hands at prices nearly a hundred times greater than they had paid for them 40 years earlier.

Although mixed-tenure streets had only been made possible by gentrification, their value in social terms has been widely recognised. The challenge has now become that of creating the condition of integrated and flexible tenure in entirely new developments.

Mixing homes of different tenures in new developments of all kinds and densities has been a preoccupation for social-housing providers for more than a decade. Making all the different tenures look the same is an accepted principle, but quite how far to take the physical integration of households from different social and financial backgrounds is still a subject for constant speculation, no single solution seeming entirely satisfactory. As the proportion of affordable homes in every scheme increases, due in part to UDP-enforced Section 106 agreements, and the funding of affordable rented housing is more and more dependent on cross-subsidy from the sale of private homes, the degree of integration, mixed streets, mixed blocks, mixed cores and/or mixed amenity space is under constant review.

## Flexible tenure

The stock of traditional terrace houses has proved remarkably adaptable, being transformed at various stages from large single-family homes into several small flats and maisonettes, and now sometimes back into single-family homes. Although garden access for upper-floor flats has been difficult to resolve satisfactorily and the existing structures have not lent themselves to providing good standards of sound or fire insulation between tenancies, flats in street properties are still the housing of choice for most tenants and most owner-occupiers.

In relation to new housing, the question often arises, why make a distinction between houses or flats built for affordable rent and those built for sale? If flats and two-to-three-bedroom houses for affordable rent have generally been built to more generous (Parker Morris) space standards than those for sale, why not build one size to fit all?

The answer turns out to have very little to do with the actual space but much more to do with occupancy, layout and facilities. The question of merging minimum space standards across the board is addressed in Chapter 5. But apart from the actual space requirements across the tenure spectrum there can be considerable differences in lifestyle.

In general terms, owner-occupiers:
• under-occupy the space they buy and tend

Street and rear views of City Wharf, Islington, London, by Pollard Thomas Edwards, a development of mixed-tenure flats. Each tenure has its own lift and stair core, but the external appearance is indistinguishable.

# Mixing tenures and flexible tenures

move house when they need more space;
tend to enjoy higher levels of employment
and therefore spend less time at home;
keep bedrooms spare for visitors or to use
as workrooms;
can afford luxuries such as en-suite
bathrooms;
prefer open-plan living as their lifestyles
involve more entertaining and fewer
competing noises and activities than those
of less well-off families with several teenage
children;
can afford to spend more on planting and
maintaining their gardens and on tidy storage
arrangements for bulky items;
can afford a higher level of caretaking and
day-to-day expenditure on the maintenance
of common circulation and shared areas of
planting and grass, especially around the
front curtilage of houses or flats;
can afford to spend more time away in
the sunshine elsewhere, if their homes
and/or gardens turn out to be sunless or
overshadowed;
have a vested (financial) interest in buying
the biggest house they can afford in the
almost certain knowledge that in the long
term its value will increase, especially if it is
well-maintained.

By contrast, tenants in affordable housing:
are allocated homes that meet their precise
needs at that point; moving to somewhere
larger is usually difficult except in cases of
chronic overcrowding;
need bedrooms that are large enough,
properly lit and ventilated to meet the
requirements of teenagers who spend a lot of
time there and should not have to share with
siblings;
need enough living spaces for different
members of the household to pursue different
activities at the same time;
need a private open space, a balcony in
the case of a flat or a garden in the case of a
house, that is large enough for all the family
to use at once, that gets sunlight at some time
of the day and where they can dry washing
without becoming conspicuous;
need as few shared facilities as possible
in order to reduce service charges to a
minimum. These include common circulation
and shared areas of planting and grass,

especially around the front curtilage of
houses and flats.

Some of the elements in these lists have
design implications. The challenge for
designers and developers is to build
new housing that is, as far as possible,
flexible enough to satisfy the lifestyle
differences indicated by these contrasting
lists of aspirations, and to find common
denominators that will fit both owners and
tenants without causing service charges to
be unaffordable for the less well-off.

**Alternative plans for same-size two-bedroom flats in different tenures**

These layouts are based on a typical 70-square-metre shell, 7.1 x 9.85 metres. They illustrate the probable difference in living patterns between a household paying an affordable rent and a household in owner-occupation of the same size flat. They also show the potential for altering the internal layout during the lifecycle of the whole structure.

The layouts are based on assumptions about the principal living pattern differences between the two types of household:
• occupancy of the affordable flat is likely to be one or two adults plus at least one but possibly two children. Space and the possibility of 'separateness' between generations is therefore at a premium;
• occupancy of the owner-occupied flat is likely to be one or two adults sharing but not cohabiting – or one or two adults cohabiting with at least one working from home – or one or two adults cohabiting and able to afford a spare guest bedroom;
• the affordable flat has a kitchen/dining area that is separate from the living room. The washing machine is in the kitchen;
• the affordable flat has a larger second bedroom to take twin beds;
• the owner-occupied flat has a second en-suite bathroom;
• the owner-occupied flat has open-plan living/dining/cooking space with the added possibility of uniting the second bedroom with the living space; the washing machine is in a separate cupboard;
• the owner-occupied flat has built-in wardrobes to both bedrooms;
• both flats have one bathroom to Lifetime Homes standards;
• both flats have balconies of the same size, large enough to use to eat meals outside in summer.

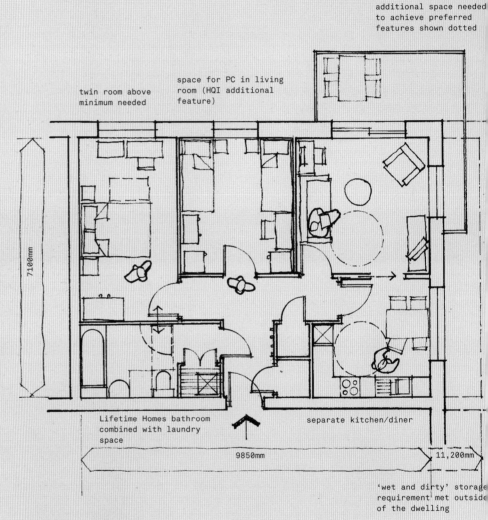

twin room above minimum needed

space for PC in living room (HQI additional feature)

additional space needed to achieve preferred features shown dotted

7100mm

Lifetime Homes bathroom combined with laundry space

separate kitchen/diner

9850mm                    11,200mm

'wet and dirty' storage requirement met outside of the dwelling

**Two-bed, four-person affordable layout at 70 square metres** to Lifetime Homes standard.

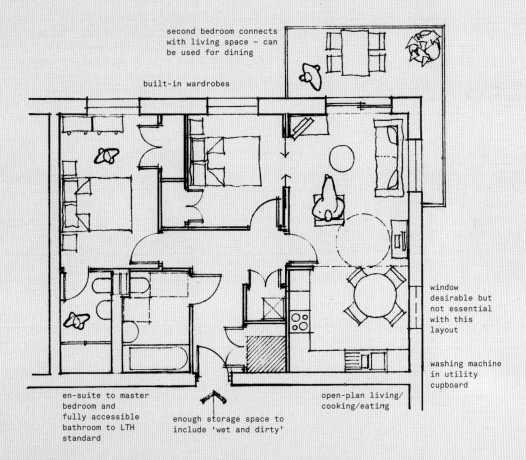

second bedroom connects
with living space – can
be used for dining

built-in wardrobes

window
desirable but
not essential
with this
layout

washing machine
in utility
cupboard

en-suite to master
bedroom and
fully accessible
bathroom to LTH
standard

enough storage space to
include 'wet and dirty'

open-plan living/
cooking/eating

**Two-bed, four-person private flat at
70 square metres** to Lifetime Homes
standard.

# Adastral, Barnet,
# London NW9

Adastral may well prove to have been at the start of a seismic shift away from the perceived position that having affordable tenants as your next-door neighbours must inevitably devalue your property.

The site, one of several that together made up the old Hendon RAF base, forms part of what is one of the largest regeneration areas in London. The base closed down after World War 2 and the site had already been redeveloped for housing during the 1960s. Its grim low-rise, all affordable rented flats had developed terminal social problems largely derived from the poor, impermeable layout that cut off any idea of integration with the wider neighbourhood.

Conceived in 1999, Adastral South is the first site to be redeveloped and is intended to provide a model for wider regeneration. It aims to dissolve estate boundaries and reconnect the area to the rest of Barnet while tripling the number of dwellings on the site. An illegible maze of walkways, cul-de-sacs and subways has been demolished to make way for a thoroughly permeable layout connected to the surrounding suburbs with a comprehensive network of 'streets', pedestrian routes and existing greenways.

Considering the very large proportion of terrace houses integrated with small and domestic-scale blocks of three- and four-storey flats, the layout is able to provide a significant central open space; this also contains the existing mature trees and the community centre. The flats are either at the corners and ends of terraces or lining the principal pedestrian routes and the main distributor road to the north of the site.

Apart from creating a new neighbourhood of crescent-shaped streets, a circus and three short 'mews', the two developers, led by Notting Hill Housing, have pioneered the integration of different tenures. As an example, the three 'mews' are lined with two-storey houses on both sides with a vehicle entrance at one end and a footpath at the other. Alternate houses are either for rent or for sale and it takes a keen eye to detect any difference between the two. In fact, as the plans show, the two house types vary in

width and size, with the rented version being the larger. This difference reflects the fact that, given the same number of bedrooms, houses for affordable rent need to be larger than houses for sale on the basis that tenants, once housed, are less able to move if they need more space and occupy their homes to the fullest extent – that is they are allocated their home on the basis of need, which inevitably means full occupancy of both bedrooms – while developers are unwilling to build larger houses for sale than those of their competitors, because they claim they are unable to recover the extra cost of construction through the sale price.

That argument certainly prevailed in 1999. Ten years later there are signs that, given all the different kinds of tenancy now available – from affordable rent to intermediate rent, moving into shared ownership and finally to full ownership – more flexibility is needed. A house built to be occupied under an affordable tenancy may well become owner-occupied, or vice versa.

Notting Hill Housing took the innovative step of setting up a resident management company covering all three tenures at Adastral – affordable rent, shared ownership and outright ownership. Its ultimate objective is that the resident management company will evolve to take full control of all the housing, its landscape and facilities. Each household has one share in the company and the right to vote. Directors are appointed from among the resident community and contractors are appointed by the company, with powers to hire and fire. The company also has some control over the service-charge budget. Early signs are that both this structure and the nursery provision in the community centre are important catalysts in breaking down barriers between residents who are owners, shared owners and tenants.

**Architect** Pollard Thomas Edwards Architects
**Developer** Notting Hill Housing Group with Bellway Homes (North London) Limited
**Site** 4.6 hectares
**Number of dwellings** 320
**Density** 70 dwellings/hectare
**Mix** 2 x 5B + 7 x 4B + 72 x 3B + 169 x 2B + 70 x 1B
**Affordable** 46 per cent
**Parking spaces per dwelling** 1
**Non-housing uses** community centre

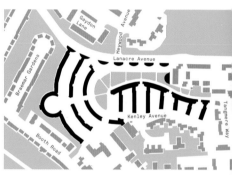

Site plan.

ws houses in terraces where
nted and shared-ownership houses
ternate with one another. The
nted houses are larger than
ose for shared ownership but
herwise they look identical. A
re example of genuine 'pepper
tting' mixed tenures.

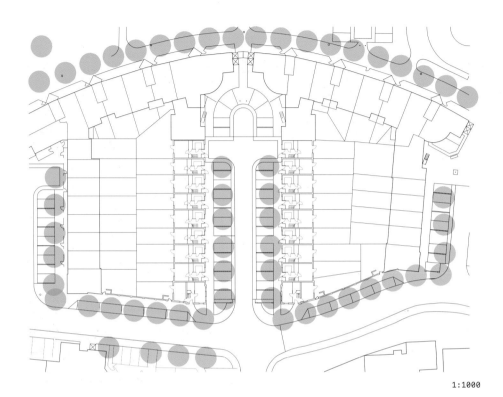

1:1000

Typical plan of mews development
in which alternate houses are of
a different tenure with a larger
rented house at the end of each
terrace.

Two-bedroom house types for
different tenures; the different
floor areas are a reflection of
construction costs and therefore
the sale price of the shared-
ownership houses. The larger
rented houses have more storage
space, while neither now has
enough space for separate
recycling bins.

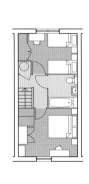
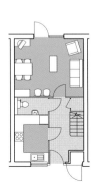
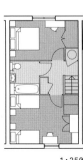

1:250

**Top** The mews are in effect short
cul-de-sacs but with a pedestrian
passageway at the far end leading
out to the main road and to the park
on the other side of the road.
**Above and right** This is deliberate
mixing of tenures. The layout has
been designed so that owners and
tenants live next door to each
other; each mews house – externally
identical – differs in size and
tenure from its neighbour.

**Background + layout, Chapter 4**

From the earliest days of consultation with the Aylesbury Estate in the 1990s it was evident that the tenants believed Southwark Council's unwritten agenda was to reduce the number of council homes and sell off the best bits to the private sector. That the council's aim for the regeneration of the area was to create a mixed-tenure environment is undeniable. Whatever the political complexion of the council has happened to be – and this is likely to change several times over the lifespan of such an enormous project – the only question was how to achieve a social mix without significantly reducing the number of council tenancies and allowing private developers to insist on developing the areas with the highest land values. This meant that the existing density had to be increased overall without resorting to building high.

The initial phase for redevelopment therefore had to be a demonstration of good intentions and the fulfilling of promises. And it shows how far private-sector developers – in this case London & Quadrant Housing Trust acting as its own developer for sale as well as rent – have moved towards establishing mixed-tenure communities over a 20-year period. The question still is, how far can UK society go towards the kind of integration through which households of completely different social backgrounds and income levels can choose to live, literally, next door to each other?

Choice is a major factor. Housing developers are not going to take reckless investment decisions over mixing tenures if these are likely to threaten sales. The ten years between 1998 and 2008 were a period of unmet demand in the private sector. It was this shortage of housing for sale, particularly of flats in urban areas, that allowed developers, encouraged by the policies of social integration adopted by most local authorities, to assume the burden of risk and successfully to integrate private sale with affordable housing on a scale never previously envisaged. Even so, there were still examples of major housebuilders insisting that affordable flats should be built

without balconies, because the tendency of some tenants to use them to store anything from cycles to unwanted furniture would affect sales of private flats!

As can be seen in examples of developments involving houses rather than flats, there is less likelihood of tensions developing between neighbours from different social backgrounds if the only shared space is the street, rather than a common hallway, lift or staircase. Social anonymity becomes easier as densities increase and the most acceptable compromise as far as flats are concerned, adopted for the early phases of the Aylesbury regeneration, is to separate the extreme opposite ends of the social spectrum so they do not share entrances, lifts and staircases but to place blocks of different tenures next to each other, more or less at random, in the same street.

The diagrams show the disposition of tenures within each street and each block. The three different forms of tenure – outright sale, shared ownership and affordable rent – are indistinguishable from one another in external appearance.

**Above and right** Diagrams showing tenure breakdown. The central core serving the largest number of units is for both private and shared ownership while the cores serving the smallest number of units is for affordable rent. Ground- and first-floor maisonettes are for affordable rent and have their own street-door entrances. **Top right** CGI perspective of completed scheme.

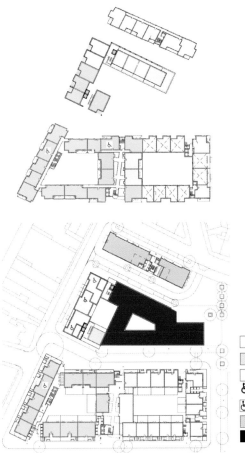

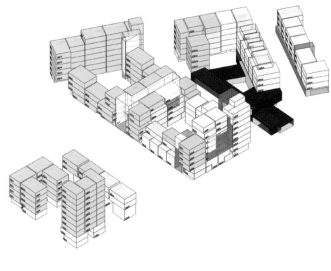

☐ Affordable

▨ Private

☐ Shared ownership

♿ Wheelchair unit

♿ Wheelchair-accessible unit

▨ Retail

■ Day centre

# Kenworthy Road, Hackney, London E9

The 14–16 Kenworthy Road scheme involves redevelopment of a site currently housing redundant bedsit accommodation and a nursery. The scheme will rehouse the nursery and provide 119 new mixed-tenure family and one- and two-bed homes. Integrated with the scale of the surrounding buildings, the massing of the scheme responds to the scale of Homerton Hospital to the north and to the five-storey Cardinal Pole RC School to the east.

This is a sensitive location, adjacent to a mental-health unit. The new scheme addresses overlooking issues of the existing residential accommodation along the west boundary where openings are kept to a minimum. The opportunity to reinvigorate the western edge of Kenworthy Road has been exploited with an active street frontage through the introduction of family maisonettes at ground level with own-door access from the street and defensible garden spaces defined by low walls and railings.

The public outdoor space is organised in two interlinked courtyards as raised home-zone areas to calm traffic. The southern courtyard is mews-like, with planting defining the primary route through the site. In the north courtyard, private gardens are arranged around the perimeter for the family maisonettes while the heart of the courtyard mixes planted areas, a children's playground and further car parking. All apartments have generous balconies. The urban landscape is softened by hedging and ornamental planting, together with street and feature trees throughout the scheme.

Residential accommodation is spread across three blocks grouped around two linked courtyards. The rear block is lower rise and contains primarily single-aspect units to maintain privacy for the mental-health unit beyond. The nursery is located in one corner of the scheme, enlivening the junction of the access road for the mental-health unit and Kenworthy Road. It is smaller in scale, both to respect the existence of the rights of light of the terrace opposite but also to reinvigorate a previously neglected corner of the site. The more domestic quality of the nursery architecture is enlivened with brightly coloured panels and timber screens. A large corner opening and more generous street frontage give the new building a special civic presence.

All flats are designed to Lifetime Homes standards with 10 per cent wheelchair-adaptable units. Large areas of south-facing glazing are incorporated to exploit the benefits of passive solar energy. A green roof to the lower-rise section of Block C aids water attenuation and provides a habitat for urban wildlife while PV solar panels will ensure that 10 per cent of the scheme's energy demands are met with power generated from renewable sources.

With the accommodation neatly split at planning stage – 50 per cent private sale, 25 per cent intermediate rent/shared ownership and 25 per cent affordable rent – the developer, itself a not-for-profit housing association group in an uncertain market, needs flexibility in making its marketing decisions. Its decision, therefore, to adopt a single range of space standards for one-, two- and three-bedroom flats has been shown to be particularly adroit as decisions over which tenure to adopt can be made at the point of disposal according to demand.

In a location like Hackney the income and social differentials between potential outright purchasers, shared owners and intermediate rent tenants are much smaller than they would be in higher-value parts of London. Kenworthy Road may therefore prove to be an interesting trail-blazer for flexible tenure with important implications for service charges and management methods – and for the design of communal areas.

**Architect** Levitt Bernstein Associates
**Developer** Network Housing Group
**Site** 0.64 hectares
**Number of dwellings** 123
**Density** 186 dwellings/hectare
**Mix** 2 x 5B + 8 x 4B + 25 x 3B + 58 x 2B + 30 x 1B
**Affordable** 50 per cent affordable and intermediate rent
**Parking spaces per dwelling** 0.27
**Non-housing uses** nursery

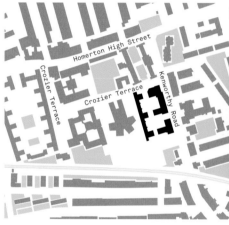

Site plan.

Another mixed-tenure scheme of
flats and maisonettes but in this
case the developer has chosen to
unify space standards between the
different tenures with the aim
of making decisions over whether
to rent or sell at the time of
completion.

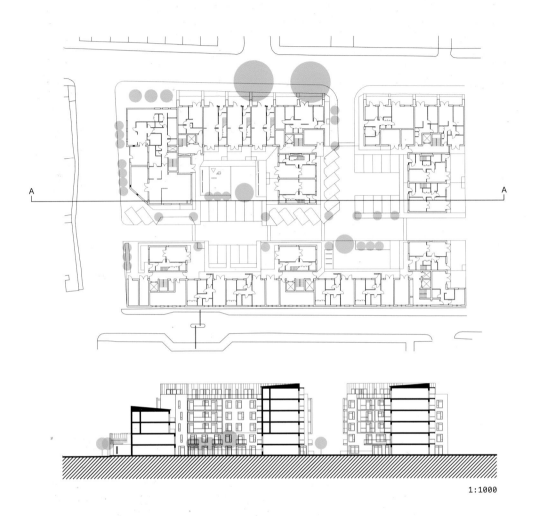

1:1000

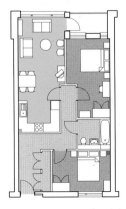

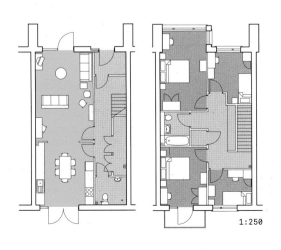

1:250

**Above left** Layout plan and section A–A of a dense central courtyard development in which all types of tenure are sharing the same external spaces. Six cores of lifts and stairs serve the upper-floor flats in order to reduce the length of access galleries, while all the flats adjacent to the boundary with the mental-health unit have a single aspect facing into the courtyard.
**Bottom left** Typical dual-aspect two-bedroom flat.
**Bottom right** Dual-aspect four-bedroom maisonette.

| Ground floor | First floor | Second floor |
| --- | --- | --- |

| Fourth floor | Fourth floor | Fifth floor |
| --- | --- | --- |

**Above** CGI perspective of completed scheme.
**Right** Tenure distribution diagrams: with affordable rented shown in purple, intermediate housing in pale blue, and shared ownership in green.

Donnybrook, East London, by
Peter Barber Architects for
Circle Anglia Housing Group.
This was a competition-winning
scheme in which the architect
aimed to recapture the spirit
of traditional life in the East
End of London, where neighbours
interacted because of the intimacy
and small scale of the spaces
between buildings.

Architects incline towards the view that the ideal client is one who produces a flexible brief and who encourages and funds their particular brand of innovation. This chapter is about patronage; how and when good patronage produces good housing.

Of all the choices we make in our lives, those about where and how we live are among the most important and, for those who have options, certainly the most personal. The degree of choice that individuals can exercise obviously depends on their means. At one end of the scale, tenants paying an affordable rent have very little choice. Is this perhaps why so many tenants of affordable housing from the 1960s through to the end of the 1980s reacted negatively to what they were given by social landlords and architects who 'knew what was good for them'?

Architects and corporate-housing clients often have an uneasy relationship. The former complain of their clients' apparent unconcern about architectural quality, and the latter bemoan architects' lack of understanding about what clients perceive as real issues. Social housing is geared towards achieving uniformity rather than individuality because consistency and homogeneity are actually quite helpful when allocating and maintaining rented homes. In contrast, superficial differences seem to help sell houses on the open market. In either case, bespoke design of individual homes is inappropriate and the process is depersonalised. With all types of tenure there is an understandable but usually regrettable desire on the part of the third-party client to use standard house and flat plans, as long as the overall design and layout make the most of the site; this is the very opposite to the priorities for a commissioned house. Housing developers, whether in the social or private sectors, are virtually 'proxy' clients. The battleground between architects and the developers usually revolves around which of them has the best understanding of what choices the eventual occupant would make, if only that occupant was there to exercise choice at the design stage.

The seeds of unease go back at least a century when the large-scale proxy client first began to emerge. Before that, the ability to choose where and how one was to live ranged from those with sufficient wealth to commission their own purpose-built houses to those without any means at all who were expected to accept gratefully whatever they were given. In Britain from the seventeenth century onwards this system simultaneously produced fine terraces and squares of enduring quality, and the most squalid slums. By the end of World War 1 in 1918 public conscience dictated that the worst slum dwellings should be replaced, and this programme accelerated after World War 2.

The patrons of these programmes were either local authorities building estates of houses and flats for rent on the sites of the worst slums, or speculative builders who, in the main, built semi-detached houses for sale in ribbon developments. Tenures were then less polarised in terms of internal space and amenity but, arguably, differentiated more by typology and style. Architects were instinctively drawn towards involvement in the design of social housing simply because they felt they had a freer hand with 'clients' who did not really have a say, and the opportunities for dramatic and imaginative architecture were much greater.

With inherent imagination and encouraged by training, architects possess the ability and aptitude regularly to analyse and reconfigure conventional approaches to housing design and to make radical proposals. But these proposals can only be properly tested through genuine client choice. Choice over what kind of 'home' people want can of course be expressed in several ways, the single bespoke house being the most straightforward – a direct collaboration in which the client initially selects an architect and then exercises choice over the design as it develops. Where a third party, a developer, is involved in commissioning designs for homes for which choice is ultimately to be exercised by either purchaser or tenant, there is ample room for disagreement, architects invariably believing that the client is preventing them from best satisfying the needs of the eventual occupant. For almost a century some of the most ambitious and gifted architects, faced with the choice of focusing their efforts on either the developers of private housing or on public social housing, have concentrated on the latter as it has been seen to offer more

scope for innovation, looser briefing and available funding – altogether a softer target. While the developer of private homes was largely avoided on the basis of being too conservative, his public-sector equivalent was seen as more open to radical ideas.

Disregarding the many examples of poorly designed high-density estates that still litter UK cities, it is worth looking at what happened when all the most talented designers of a generation were let loose on commissions for social housing, with clients who were not themselves likely ever to live in any of the homes produced.

From the 1950s to the 1970s many celebrated architects, including Denys Lasdun, James Stirling, Alison and Peter Smithson, Erno Goldfinger, Neave Brown, Benson & Forsyth, Darbourne & Darke, Chamberlin Powell & Bon, Ivor Smith, and Patrick Hodgkinson, completed major publicly funded housing schemes that were more architecturally ambitious than anything produced in the private sector in the same period. Only some of these have survived, and those that have owe their survival more to location than to an ability to please successive generations of tenants. Lasdun's 'cluster block' in London's Bethnal Green, based on cutting-edge sociological theories developed in the 1950s, only survived after the client group for whom it was designed moved out en masse and the building was successfully refurbished for white-collar middle-class owner-occupiers working in the City of London. James Stirling's dramatic neo-Corbusian scheme at Southgate in Runcorn, near Liverpool, was summarily demolished in the architect's own lifetime. The same fate may yet overtake the Smithsons' Robin Hood Gardens on the edge of London's Docklands.

If further proof of the unsuitability of over-sophisticated design for social housing is needed, Darbourne & Darke had two major public-housing schemes in London, one in an up-market part of the City of Westminster and another on the borders of Islington and Hackney. The former is now a Grade 2 listed historic building, very sought after for owner-occupation, while its Islington counterpart has been partially demolished

Housing at Runcorn New Town by James Stirling, 1967, now demolished.

and the remainder fundamentally altered in order to cure chronic security problems and anti-social behaviour.

A lesson to be drawn from these examples must be that the brightest architectural brains of a generation trained their sights on an apparently unrepresented and inaccessible client group whose real aspirations were either ignored or never understood by the local-authority 'developers' who were building in their name. Fortunately, one unintended consequence of the 'right to buy' introduced by the Thatcher government in the 1980s has been an infiltration of leaseholders who greatly appreciate the inherent qualities of many of these estates. This evident appreciation has proved to be a turning point in their popularity.

Perhaps because some of the early Modernist urban architecture had achieved an iconic place in city dwellers' affections, or perhaps because even the general public had grown tired of the sterile Postmodernism of the 1980s and 1990s, the last decade has seen a rapid transformation of the urban-housing scene: for the first time, architects have found perfect outlets for their imagination in all the big UK cities as well as some of the smaller ones. Research by the larger firms of surveyors identified a market of youngish, reasonably affluent, competitive, much less conservative and much more style-conscious purchasers, particularly in big cities such as London and Manchester.

If there is a now a general assumption that the Postmodern or contextual design solutions to building flats in inner-city locations, much favoured until the end of the 1990s, have successfully been replaced by a radical Modernist approach across all tenures, no such assumption can be said to cover the efforts of the house-building industry in the design of house types for low-density (50 dwellings per hectare) suburban locations.

In responding to popular demand, and in most locations, developers still claim to – and undoubtedly do – encounter much more conservative purchasers, especially from the buying public, when providing new family

homes at suburban densities. However, like an echo of the infamous demise of the British motorcycle industry in the face of Japanese competition, the philosopher Alain de Botton showed contemporary Dutch examples to prospective volume purchasers and asked whether they would like to swap. Almost all replied that if a better design option were available they would take it.

And there are successful built examples that contradict the dominant view of the average UK purchaser of new houses as someone with a clear preference for the tried and tested – in terms of planning, layout and design. These exceptions seem to occur in areas where developers have set out to create an entirely new market, such as at Newhall in Harlow, Essex, or Accordia in Cambridge, both by the same developer. Appealing to an admittedly more sophisticated purchaser, these schemes break the traditional mould by a combination of skilful marketing and exceptional design. The lesson for architects who seriously want to engage in this process of mould-breaking is to search out and to collaborate much more closely with prospective housebuilders/developers in selling ideas for an entirely different way of living, including the added value of addressing climate change.

The move towards more mixed and better-integrated tenures, unthinkable to housebuilders only a very few years ago, means that one option – that of carrying out any more bold experiments in solely publicly funded housing – is now virtually closed. Although there are, and will continue to be subtle differences between homes for affordable rent and private sale, it almost goes without saying that if the idea of mixing households from different income groups in the same street is to succeed, these differences should not be recognisable from the outside. By and large the style preferences of tenants, particularly those who depend on subsidy of one kind or another, are based on the kind of house they would buy if they were in a position to do so; it is therefore the style of the private-sale component of any new housing that determines the design of the whole. People are travelling more and getting used

seeing other types of housing on TV,
magazines and from retailers like Ikea
nd Habitat who promote fresh styles at
ffordable prices.

o the architect, even the architect of social/
ffordable housing, can now address the
ustomer more directly. Customer focus
the name of the game and architects
hould no longer have to rely solely on the
rchitectural press and the approval of their
eers for endorsement of a much more
adical approach to the design of twenty-first-
entury housing.

**Background + sense of place, Chapter 1; privacy,
Chapter 9**

Although the Royal Free won several major
awards – including Civic Trust and Europa
Nostra awards – when it was completed,
it has never been described as 'architects'
architecture'. Were it to be designed now the
approach to architectural style, even by the
same design team, would be very different,
and it is important to determine why this
should be.

The 1980s were years of retrenchment in
housing design after a backlash to the
uncompromising Modernism of the 1970s.
Many non-architects, led trenchantly by the
then prime minister, Margaret Thatcher and
enthusiastically supported by the Prince of
Wales, complained that a whole generation of
council tenants had been experimented
upon, without being given an opportunity to
decide what kind of housing they would live
in if they were allowed to choose for
themselves. Several major schemes by
distinguished and very creative architects
had become difficult to manage and
unpopular with tenants by the early 1980s
and were in the process of demolition after
less than 15 years of life. Meanwhile, much of
the architectural profession had taken refuge
from the storm by switching into
Postmodernism. This was the period of
Prince Charles's infamous 'monstrous
carbuncle' speech, damning Ahrends Burton
Koralek's competition-winning Modernist
design for the National Gallery extension.

Like so many of the well-known post-war
estates, the Royal Free Square development
is 100 per cent social housing with no
prospect of any resident being able to
exercise the 'right to buy'. The challenge was
therefore to design the new social housing in
a high-value location that would not acquire a
'social housing' stigma.

Whoever writes the definitive history of
social housing in the latter part of the
twentieth century will point out that some
of the most successful examples are to be
found in buildings converted from another
use – sometimes a different form of housing
but sometimes not housing at all. And this
is because, following the Modernist stamp
imposed on most social housing from 1949 to
1979, combined with the fact that 'gentrified'
Georgian or Victorian terrace houses had
become the home of choice for many urban
middle-class families, a style of architecture
belonging to an earlier era does not
stigmatise or pigeonhole the inhabitants as
belonging to any particular class or income
bracket. By adopting a style similar to the
existing Victorian hospital buildings, the new
housing in Old Royal Free Square freed the
residents from social categorisation.

**Right** Entrance door to a three-
bedroom terrace house for
affordable rent in Old Royal Free
Square. Some features of the
design closely follow the details
of the existing nineteenth-century
hospital buildings to which they
are attached. Conceived in the
middle of the 1980s, during a
decade in which public opinion
strongly associated Modernism in
housing design with 'council'
estates and social deprivation,
the aim was to build 'classless'
housing and prevent any social
stigma being attached to residents
on account of the design of their
homes.

# Cremer Street, Hackney, London E2

This development by the Peabody Trust has its origins in the same early 1990s' initiative by the London Borough of Hackney as Nile Street (see Chapter 9). The aim was to use the borough's various landholdings to generate shared-ownership flats for keyworkers. The scheme was developed without public subsidy.

When it became apparent that land at below full market value would not be sufficient subsidy on its own, the Peabody Trust designated 27 of the 69 flats for outright sale. These are in a seven-storey block nearest to the street. This block includes a lift, whereas the other, four-storey, blocks have five separate cores with staircase access only. The trust retains a 25 per cent stake in each of the flats for shared equity, so purchasers only have to raise mortgages for 75 per cent of the cost.

Car parking in an overlooked rear courtyard is shared by both tenures and is protected by a fob-key-controlled steel gate. All the flats have balconies.

This area of London contains a very large percentage of local-authority-owned social housing, much of it in post-war four-storey blocks of 'walk-up' flats that are now mostly in poor condition. In searching for an economical building form for the affordable flats at Cremer Street, the Peabody Trust chose a simple layout principle that is not dissimilar from much of the surrounding council housing. This is based on a terrace with five separate stair cores, each of which has only two flats per floor, making eight flats in all for each core. There are no lifts serving the affordable shared-ownership flats, since a lift serving only eight flats is basically uneconomic and linking stair cores together would have meant either internal corridors or external access galleries, both of which can create security problems.

While the configuration of the flats has a strong resemblance to much of the municipal housing in the area, the architecture is quite different, and is especially distinct from any of the surrounding municipal housing of the 1960s and 1970s. For any potential shared owner nervous at the prospect of living in another uncompromisingly modern building there is ample reassurance in the form of 27 flats, identical in appearance, at one end of the terrace; these sold outright to private purchasers, each of whom presumably had exercised choice over the home they were looking for and what it looked like.

In London and other UK cities the private market has led the design revolution away from the stultifying efforts of the Postmodernism of the 1980s or the neo-vernacular, towards an environment for an altogether more stimulating lifestyle. This is encouraging residents in affordable housing to follow suit.

**Architects** Levitt Bernstein Associate
**Developer** Peabody Trust
**Site** 0.4 hectares
**Number of dwellings** 69
**Density** 173 dwellings/hectare
**Mix** 2 x 3B + 57 x 2B + 10 x 1B
**Affordable** 61 per cent
**Parking spaces per dwelling** 0.73

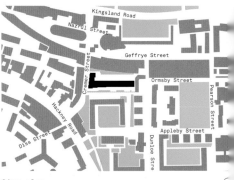

Site plan.

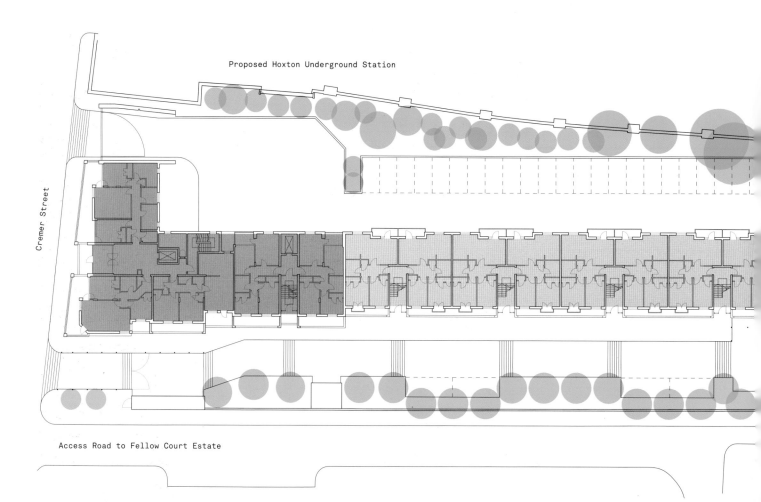

Proposed Hoxton Underground Station

Cremer Street

Access Road to Fellow Court Estate

1:50

Layout plan. The flats for private
sale (dark grey) are in one group
at the south end of the site on
six floors with a lift. Those for
shared ownership (pale grey) have
no lift and are on four storeys,
with two flats per floor. There
is a single rear parking court,
protected by a fob-key-controlled
security gate and half the parked
cars are in an undercroft beneath
the lowest floor of flats.

**Above and below** The external walls are finished with STO render, which is protected from the effects of weather by the broad overhang to the roofs.

**Below right** Entrances to flats and stair cores are protected by mechanical door-entry systems but the risk of anti-social activities taking place is much reduced with only eight flats per entrance.

Apart from price and the quality of the place itself, most people thinking about buying a new house or flat – and this doesn't just apply in city or town centres – look at three over-riding factors. These are: what is the neighbourhood like; what are the neighbours like; and will the investment go up in value over time?

Most purchasers want to be surrounded by other people like themselves, neither substantially richer nor substantially poorer. A perception that poorer neighbours will ultimately affect investment value, and therefore the decision to purchase, has haunted developers for decades. It was pressure to provide more affordable housing, spread evenly throughout each neighbourhood in London and the south of England, that began to force developers seriously to consider how they were going to meet the conditions imposed on them by planning authorities. Eventually, schemes began to emerge which showed that what had been considered impossible was not impossible after all. Although the sudden shortage of houses or flats for sale may have influenced purchasers to consider having tenants in social housing as near neighbours, the taboo has now been broken with the help of good design: the concept of socially integrated and interdependent communities has become a reality.

The design of Tabard Square is an excellent illustration of the way private sale and affordable rented housing can be successfully combined in a dense urban setting. The scheme originated in 2001 with developer Berkeley Homes commissioning a very high-density mixed-tenure scheme on brownfield land that responded to the demand for affordable homes as well as homes for sale close to Borough High Street on the southern fringes of the City of London.

As a scheme of more than 150 dwellings per hectare, Tabard Square falls within the definition of 'superdensity'. Over and above the density of 206 dwellings per hectare there is a considerable amount of retail and community space at street level. Undoubtedly its central location, the availability of public transport and

the presence of viable commercial uses, including a small supermarket and a crèche in the square, contribute greatly to the sense of place and a feeling of being 'somewhere', as opposed to being 'anywhere'.

But important as these considerations are, the developer's decision to treat all the different tenures in one bold unified style has made it difficult to distinguish one from another. Unlike some examples from the 1960s, where social housing for families was squeezed into crude towers while the owner-occupier families spread themselves in town houses around their base, at Tabard Square the tower is designed as small flats for sale with the social housing much closer to the ground.

Security at Tabard Square is well covered. There is a 24-hour concierge who controls access to all flats and the underground parking by means of CCTV; gates to the square are closed between midnight and 6 in the morning, and each lift and stair core to the affordable flats block serves a maximum of 14 flats.

The residential tower in the north-west corner of the square provides a landmark for the development and a beacon for regeneration in the Borough area. The concept for the tower was based on creating a base unit on plan, which is then rotated through 90 degrees, providing north-, east-, south- and west-facing orientations. The public areas of the apartments maximise views over the City with full-height glazing, while the private zones are expressed as solid components. As the tower climbs, an elegant spiralling profile is formed as the building terminates against the skyline. At the very top is a light beacon, linked to a barometer that changes colour with fluctuations in atmospheric pressure.

**Architect** Rolfe Judd
**Developer** Berkeley Homes (North East London) Limited
**Site** 2.77 hectares
**Number of dwellings** 572
**Density** 206 dwellings/hectare
**Mix** 45 x studio + 321 x 1B + 178 x 2B + 28 x 3B
**Affordable** 37 per cent
**Parking spaces per dwelling** 0.42
**Non-housing uses** supermarket, 1550 square metres + other retail, 2441 square metres

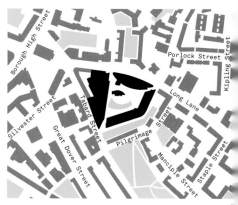

Site plan.

**Right** Tabard Square on Borough Road, just south of London Bridge, is an area of increasingly high value sought after by City workers. This is reflected in the ambitious design and layout with a tower for private-sale flats. The open space has a nursery and community facilities in the centre and the whole complex – including the underground car park – is monitored by a 24-hour concierge.

Second-floor layout plan.

1:1000

Access to the central ground-floor space is controlled at three separate points but the majority of space at this level is devoted to retail and business use. This necessarily restricts the number of lift and stair cores to the flats above. Identifying the 37 per cent affordable housing from the outside is difficult.

Like 'sustainability', 'flexibility' is one of those words we use very lightly but usually manage to avoid building into our designs on the grounds that it costs too much, is too long term and doesn't sell as an idea. Past attempts to incorporate flexibility into the planning of new homes have almost always resulted in uneconomical solutions. In the early 1970s at least one scheme of experimental flexible housing was built in London using a system developed by the Danish architect N. John Habraken: this permitted dwellings to be subdivided, adjoining dwellings to be combined, enlarged or reduced, or subdivisions within dwellings to be altered. The fact that this was an experiment that has not been repeated speaks for itself although, as a social-housing scheme built by the soon to be defunct GLC, there was unlikely to be much demand for the type of change that the system allowed.

By contrast, the traditional English terrace house, which was never intended to be at all flexible, has proved capable of the most astonishing transformations in spite of inherent problems with poorly designed foundations, the practice of building structural timbers into brick external walls so they rot and cause instability, and the lack of an effective method to prevent rising damp. Houses built before 1918 have provided, and continue to provide, flexible solutions to the needs of different household sizes.

Two overwhelming qualities account for the terrace house's continued life, even after two hundred years. The first of these qualities lies in the economy of street layout. Most eighteenth- and nineteenth-century urban houses were built in terrace form for reasons of economy both in land use and cost of construction. Most were also planned either with short gardens or with no garden at all between the house and the street. This creates good streets with a secure feeling of enclosure. At the same time, except in the infamous northern back-to-back layouts, they were usually provided with generous gardens at the rear.

The second quality was accidental and derives from the type of construction used in Britain ever since the Great Fire of London of 1666. Although timber was the material of choice, regulations introduced as far back as the seventeenth century required houses to be separated from each other with solid brick walls. The result was a hybrid construction that had timber internal partitions and floors supported by brick walls around the outside to prevent the spread of fire. As far as flexibility is concerned, the key has proved to be the use of lime mortar as the chief ingredient for brickwork, rather than Portland cement, which has been used in the construction of all housing since around 1918. This has meant that the original brick structures can be altered or have openings cut into them at will, as can the simple timber load-bearing internal structures.

One disadvantage of assuming that these simple structures are capable of a more or less infinite number of variations in their lifetimes is that they sometimes get crudely hacked about before the evidence is concealed under finishes. This is particularly true in relation to the installation of mechanical services. Ultimately, structural integrity is affected and just occasionally the most spectacular collapse occurs.

Various lessons can be learned from all this experience and applied to a future that does not involve using current, and by now almost traditional, methods of brick and block construction. Brick and block external walls with timber intermediate floors and trussed rafter roofs are already unsustainable for a whole variety of reasons: being too labour intensive and slow; involving too much wastage of material on site; containing too much embodied energy, and not easily achieving the requisite energy performance. Roof spaces constructed with lightweight timber trussed rafters can not be converted into attic rooms.

It is too early to forecast which of the bewildering array of construction methods now being tried out will emerge as worth replicating on a large scale, but certain general principles should apply to them all, of which the following are important:

**Clear spans between party walls** In the face of the inevitable pressure to reduce frontages of both houses and flats, in order to optimise densities and thus reduce costs per dwelling, there is little doubt that the flexibility in the use of space within a dwelling also reduces. Circulation routes begin to impinge on the functional space within rooms and the proportion of space given over to circulation also often increases as dwelling plans become narrower and deeper. In houses with timber intermediate floors the current economic maximum internal span is 5.4 metres (for complete flexibility in the positioning of partitions and assuming these are also of lightweight construction, the spans would have to be reduced by 10 per cent). In flats with hollow-core concrete slabs – the most common form of concrete floor construction in housing – spans of up to 15 metres can be achieved, but with an overall structural depth excluding screed of 400mm. Solid pre-stressed plank floors can span up to 7 metres with a thickness of only 100mm excluding screed.

Even when it is impossible to achieve the economic maximum, bedroom frontages in family homes should not be narrower than 5 metres, which is the minimum for a double bedroom to be converted into two single bedrooms side by side.

In houses with gardens that are larger than a basic patio (with depth that is no greater than the frontage) access to the garden that doesn't go through a living room or kitchen is highly desirable. In family homes with gardens (as opposed to patios) a through hall giving access is highly desirable.

**Replaceable services** Too little effort is expended at the design stage in planning sensible routes for internal services, and how they can eventually be renewed without rehousing residents while the work is done.

Regulations controlling the layout of internal waste and soil pipes have become increasingly less onerous, especially the regulations covering the venting of small-diameter waste pipes from baths, sinks and washing machines, with the result that assumptions are now made about positioning these fittings almost anywhere to suit the internal plan without having any regard for

the services installations or future access to them. Designers are too often denied responsibility for working out service routes. This often results in unsightly boxing-in, which can compromise furniture layouts or wheelchair turning circles, or unsightly external terminals and intakes on otherwise well-considered elevations.

With the increasing complexity of mechanical services, due partly to the introduction of the Code for Sustainable Homes, specialist engineering consultancy should relieve the architect of the burden of finding accessible routes for heating, drainage and ventilation services. In practice very little technical advice is available at the design stage as the mechanical and electrical design is made the responsibility of subcontractors who are only appointed much later, and also partly because qualified assessors are required under the Code for Sustainable Homes. The Code deals extensively with saving water and energy and has added to the list of specialist consultancy services now required for the design of housing, but the appointment of assessors tends to blur areas of responsibility.

The same goes for electrical services, which must be renewed from time to time in the lifecycle of the average residential building. New housing should allow for the addition of renewables as the eventual goal of 'carbon neutral' homes becomes a reality.

**Renewing external weathering surfaces**
External wall surfaces can be divided into two types: those that may improve with time and weathering and those that do not. By and large the appearance of most external brickwork improves as it weathers and so it is important that its lifespan is not affected by lack of frost resistance, by pattern staining, or by having built-in components, such as artificial stone, that are less permanent than the brick itself. Structural external brickwork is now a rare commodity. This was not always so and certain brick structures, especially those in soft red brick built around the end of the nineteenth century and now listed, must one day become a huge conservation issue.

Apart from brick, few external surfaces, such as render, tiling, timber and all other forms of cladding, can not eventually be replaced. But many of these suffer the disadvantage that they appear at their best only when new and deteriorate slowly thereafter, until they eventually need to be replaced altogether. Render and timber can be successfully painted or treated periodically but most other forms of synthetic-resin-based or coated-metal surfaces can only be restored by periodic washing, provided their joints and fastenings don't deteriorate faster than the surface itself.

Roofs need to be treated in the same way. Those with steep pitches and that are therefore highly visible are usually clad in traditional materials such as slate and tile but, whereas slate generally retains its original surface, tiles either weather well or, like almost all concrete tiles, their appearance suffers increasingly with age.

Flat roofs using new and better materials and details are making a comeback after the disastrous and well-documented material failures of the1960s and 1970s. Increasing numbers of non-trafficable flat roofs are being designed as green roofs but, whether this is the case or not, designers should remember that after the first few years non-trafficable flat roofs present a very gloomy prospect to the flats looking down on them1.

**Adaptable structures** Given the bewildering targets for the numbers of new homes needed, and the drive towards leaner, quicker methods of construction, it is most unlikely that structures will ever again have anything like the built-in spare capacity of their Victorian and Edwardian predecessors, which allowed holes to be punched through walls or ceilings in a variety of different situations. A highly engineered lightweight steel frame based on structural steel sections no more than a millimetre thick, or any kind of stressed-skin construction, is unlikely to score highly by comparison with structural timber stud-frame construction.

**Lifetime Homes** The original concept of Lifetime Homes came from a piece of research commissioned, published and

promoted as *Meeting Part M and Designing Lifetime Homes* by the Joseph Rowntree Foundation. The research was originally based largely on the idea of providing flexibility for household members who might suffer from temporary disablement, or age-related inability to move around a two-storey house. The idea caught on and, since the launch of the London Plan, it is now a requirement for new housing of all tenures within the GLA. The government is also promoting the concept in relation to its strategy for dealing with Britain's ageing society, and Lifetime Homes will become mandatory for housing receiving public subsidy by 2011, with a target to extend to all new housing by 2013.

Many of the issues raised in Lifetime Homes are about flexibility. It offers guidance on a whole variety of issues that can be roughly divided between those affecting the design and layout and those that are a matter of additional specification. They range from access to homes, including the approach from designated car-parking areas, to circulation areas both within common parts and inside individual dwellings and manoeuvring space in rooms themselves. Many of these imply some additional floor space over the basic minimum, but the important principle is to make appropriate provision for future adaptation from the outset, as complete retrofitting can be difficult, if not impossible, to achieve. Care also needs to be taken to ensure that there is enough space for ramps to accommodate changes in level, as well as provision in the plan of each house or maisonette to fit a stairlift and a 'through the floor' lift should either become necessary.

All of this is detailed in DD 266:2007, a draft code of practice, which is considering Lifetime Homes as a key component of a new generation of more accessible housing. DD 266:2007 also covers the specification of items such as the provision for additional electrics, things that are relatively cheap at construction stage but infinitely more complicated to have installed at a later date.

Consultation is currently taking place on the extended proposals contained in

D 266:2007. The introduction outlines the eed for greater flexibility: 'The Draft for evelopment explains how, by following the rinciples of inclusive design, general needs ousing can be made sufficiently flexible and onvenient to meet the existing and changing eeds of most households, and so give isabled and older people more choice over here they live.'

art of an initiative led by the DCLG, it icludes a long overdue widening of the cope of Lifetime Homes to reflect the nuch broader range of dwelling types urrently being built and those likely to e constructed in the future. It also takes ccount of contemporary solutions to veryday practicalities by considering issues ke underground parking, access to shared menity space and current construction echniques.

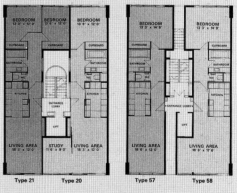

Flexible plans at the Barbican
in the City of London. These
photographs and plans show that
in the 1960s Chamberlin Powell &
Bon designed some flexibility into
the flat plans, creating a study/
guest-bedroom space off the living
room of a one-bedroom flat. The
photographs show this device still
very much in use today.

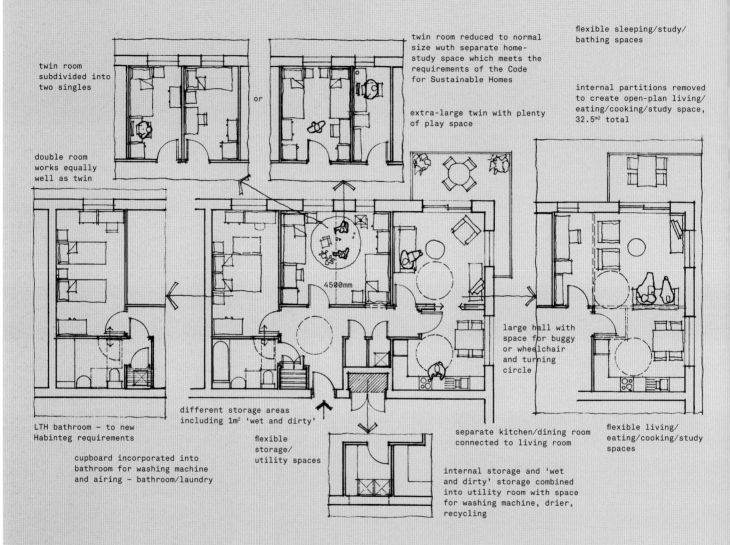

twin room
subdivided into
two singles

or

twin room reduced to normal
size wuth separate home-
study space which meets the
requirements of the Code
for Sustainable Homes

extra-large twin with plenty
of play space

flexible sleeping/study/
bathing spaces

internal partitions removed
to create open-plan living/
eating/cooking/study space,
32.5m² total

double room
works equally
well as twin

4500mm

large hall with
space for buggy
or wheelchair
and turning
circle

LTH bathroom – to new
Habinteg requirements

cupboard incorporated into
bathroom for washing machine
and airing – bathroom/laundry

different storage areas
including 1m² 'wet and dirty'

flexible
storage/
utility spaces

separate kitchen/dining room
connected to living room

flexible living/
eating/cooking/study
spaces

internal storage and 'wet
and dirty' storage combined
into utility room with space
for washing machine, drier,
recycling

**Alternative internal arrangements to Lifetime Homes
standards for a two-bedroom, four-person flat over different
stages of its lifecycle**

This layout is based on a typical rectangular
plan shell of just under 80 square metres.
It illustrates some of the possible plan
variations that offer choice at the design
stage or that can be carried out over the
life of the building provided there are no
structural walls within the plan itself. In
all cases the changes can be made without
reducing occupancy.

Particular features of the plan include:
• a large twin bedroom capable of being
divided either into two single bedrooms or a
smaller shared bedroom plus a separate study/
workroom or play space;
• living space that can be opened up to include
the kitchen/dining room and, potentially, the
study too;
• different options for storage/utility space
– either two internal stores with separate
external provision for 'wet and dirty' storage,
or a single, large utility area;
• an accessible bathroom that can also function
as laundry room by incorporating the airing
cupboard and washing machine, or accommodate a
walk-in shower in the same space;
• a double bedroom that can be furnished as a
twin and can connect directly with the bathroom
to provide an en-suite option.

# Designing in flexibility

**The main features of Lifetime Homes as applied to a typical two-bedroom, two-storey house**

1 Parking space capable of being widened to 3300mm.
2 Distance between house entrance and car parking kept to a minimum.
3 Level or gently sloping approach to the house.
4 Accessible threshold covered and lit.
5 Living or family room at the entrance level.
6 Space identified for temporary entrance-level bed.
7 Walls able to take adaptations.
8 Low window sills.
9 Space identified for future platform lift to bedroom.
10 Provision for future stair lift.
11 Bathroom planned to allow side access to WC and bath.
12 Easy route for a hoist from bedroom to bathroom.
13 Sockets, controls, etc., at convenient heights.
14 Accessible entrance-level WC (opportunity for shower to be fitted later in three-bed or larger homes).
15 Width of doors and hall allow wheelchair access.
16 Turning circles for a wheelchair in ground-floor living rooms.

For a full list of criteria, see www.lifetimehome.org.uk.

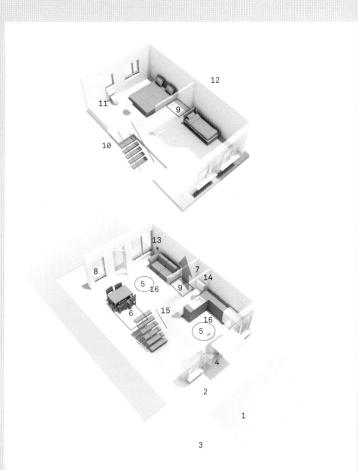

In 1997 the Joseph Rowntree Foundation began an initiative examining ways of funding affordable housing for single people without recourse to public subsidy. CASPAR, as it became known – Citycentre Apartments for Single People at Affordable Rents – was a demonstration project to persuade City investors that a revived private rented sector building high-quality, properly organised homes could produce a return equal to the types of investment usually chosen by pension funds or their equivalents. The foundation developed a financial model, working back from the outturn rents it wished to charge to arrive at an 'all-in' combined construction and land cost. It then promoted two competitive demonstration projects, one in Birmingham and one in Leeds.

Both competitions were designed to eliminate the trap confronting promoters of many architectural competitions in which the estimated cost of the winning schemes proves over-optimistic, and the end result achieves the design objectives but at an unaffordable price. In both cases competitors were asked to set up design and construction teams in order to submit contractor-led, fully costed schemes and to implement them.

The Leeds project as submitted was ambitious, seeking to 'tick a number of boxes' in addition to those the original competition brief included. As well as aiming to develop well-designed small and affordable apartments, it sought to demonstrate the advantages of off-site manufacture, low maintenance, ultra-efficient energy performance and flexible internal planning to Lifetime Homes standards, all within a very tight timescale.

The location was a sloping site formed by the curve of a slip road to an urban motorway. The construction method chosen was timber frame with the kitchen, entrance hall and bathroom made in a factory in Cambridgeshire as a single 'volumetric' unit. The rest of each apartment was assembled on-site using prefabricated 'flat-pack' floor and wall panels. Rising from three storeys at the upper to five at the lower end of the site, the timber structure was capped by a projecting steel-framed, stainless-steel sheet roof. Each flat had a balcony suspended from small-diameter steel rods from the supporting steel frame of this roof at the lower end of the slope while the whole access balcony system was supported in the same way at the rear.

Conforming to the spirit of Lifetime Homes, there were three lift and stair cores so all apartments were fully accessible. Internal layouts were to Lifetime Homes standards. Each had two principal rooms with the addition of a third room, designed to perform three possible functions – extra bedroom, dining space or study – according to the needs of particular households. The overall area of each flat was only 51 square metres, which provided a considerable degree of internal flexibility with a minimum of space devoted solely to circulation.

The form of timber-frame construction employed allowed walls to be economically superinsulated and all windows were triple glazed. The energy and noise-control strategy was devised by Max Fordham and Partners. The external fabric adopted had U-values of: walls 0.24 W/m²K; door 0.50 W/m²K; roof 0.20 W/m²K; ground floor 0.20 W/m²K; and windows 1.40 W/m²K.

The fabric heat loss for a typical flat is 485W (based on 20°C inside and −1°C outside). Warming from solar gain, lighting, appliances, cooking and occupants amounts to around 450W. The high levels of thermal insulation meant that the fabric heat losses were substantially offset by internal heat gains. If the flats were naturally ventilated by trickle vents this would result in a total flat heat loss of 1145W. Allowing for the heat gain this represents a heat demand of 695W.

In order to overcome the problem of noise intrusion into the flats, mechanical ventilation was adopted. This played a key role in the choice of heating system. The fresh-air supply was heated to offset heat losses from flats. By running the fresh and exhaust air past each other in a sealed heat exchanger, half the outgoing heat could be reclaimed and this gave a total heating demand for a flat of 542W. This is 22 per cent less than if the flats were naturally ventilated.

**Architects** Levitt Bernstein Associates
**Developer** Joseph Rowntree Housing Trust
**Number of dwellings** 45
**Mix** 45 x 1/2B flats
**Affordable** 100 per cent
**Parking spaces per dwelling** 1

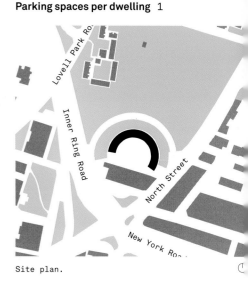

Site plan.

**Right** Exterior showing the red-stained external screen/cladding to the short access galleries off each lift and stair core. The cladding to the volumetric units themselves was grey-stained feather-edged boarding while the access galleries were designed to be suspended from the cantilevered ends of the transverse steel roof beams.

The combination boiler provided hot water and heat to a water-to-air heat exchanger within the heat-reclaim unit. A room thermostat in the living room started the boiler when there was a demand for heat.

The design rate of one-half an air change per hour was achieved by cycling the fans at normal speed: half an hour on, then half an hour off. When heat was needed the fans ran continuously at normal speed. When cooking or running a bath, a manual boost switch ran the fans at twice normal speed, automatically reverting after 2 hours.

Traditional warm-air heating systems have a reputation for problems of low humidity resulting from the fact that the airflow rate is based on the heating requirement rather than ventilation. In the case of a leaky building, with high-infiltration heat loss, the introduction of large volumes of dry external air reduces the humidity in the space. In the CASPAR II system the low heat losses and airtight construction minimised the airflow rate so the humidity within the flat was no worse than that of a naturally ventilated dwelling with radiators.

Fundamental to the heat-reclamation system and acoustic performance is the need to minimise infiltration through gaps in the construction. The heating system was designed on the basis of an airtightness of 2ac/h and the flats were tested to ensure that this was achieved. Specifying a maximum air-change rate has little effect unless all potential air-leakage paths are identified and overcome through careful detailing. The pod units were wrapped in a waterproof membrane at the factory. Windows were detailed to minimise infiltration and letter-boxes were located at ground level to avoid penetrating the front door.

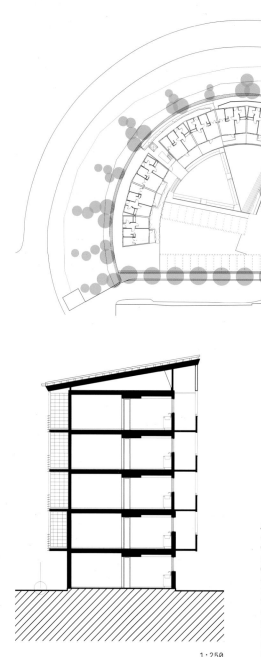

1:100

1:250

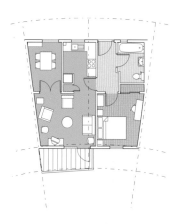

1:250

**Above** Layout plan. A single controlled entrance leads into a central courtyard with parking for 45 cars – an excessive parking requirement imposed by Leeds City Planning Department. Due to the considerable slope across the site the landscape was stepped in triangular terraces of mown grass. At the upper end of the site there are only three storeys, which increase to five storeys at the lower end. The three lift and stair cores serve short access galleries at the rear, which only have to bypass one flat to reach the front door of the furthest flat at the end of each access gallery.

**Left** Section shows the modular volumetric pods at the rear of each flat (shown in transit on the opposite page) and the transverse steel roof beams, from both ends of which are suspended private balconies on the inside and access galleries on the outside.

**Bottom left** Flat plan. The modular volumetric units include the (wheelchair-accessible) bathroom, hallway, kitchen and flexible study/second bedroom. The living room and main bedroom are constructed from 'flat-pack' prefabricated timber wall and floor panels.

**Above right** External view at night. Coloured lighting around the blind arcading beneath the roof was the product of an arts project – the colour changed every 4 minutes.

**Right** Internal view of the courtyard.

**Far right** Construction sequence.

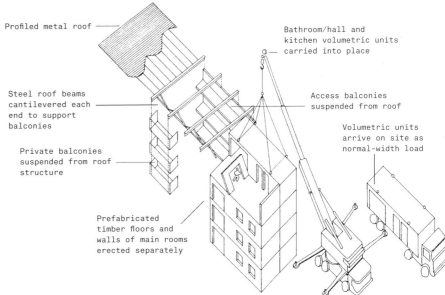

Profiled metal roof

Bathroom/hall and kitchen volumetric units carried into place

Steel roof beams cantilevered each end to support balconies

Access balconies suspended from roof

Private balconies suspended from roof structure

Volumetric units arrive on site as normal-width load

Prefabricated timber floors and walls of main rooms erected separately

# Modular houses at South Chase, Newhall, Harlow, Essex

**Background + layout, Chapter 3**

The principles behind the modular terrace housing at Newhall have already been described. As applied in terrace form, the simplest of these houses is a two-storey, two-bedroom house of 78 square metres, which fits into a plot with a frontage of 4.45 metres.

Where achieving a high suburban density is not the priority that it was at Newhall, and plot widths can be wider, there are several options for extending the two-bedroom house as the demand for extra space increases over the lifecycle of a family. To an initial development of two-bedroom houses in pairs on plots with frontages that are wide enough, several options for side extensions can be added. The first of these is a two-storey side extension containing additional living space with a third bedroom above. A fourth bedroom can also be added to this, with either a carport or a workspace on the ground floor. Finally, as the diagram shows, the space between these two extensions can be roofed over to provide additional double-height living space.

Arguments over the importance of flexibility in the design of both houses and flats have rumbled on for years. Many people have no objection to moving home, downsizing or upsizing as their needs change. Others, having become emotionally attached to their homes and neighbourhoods, rue the day they chose to live in a house that was incapable of accommodating even a loft extension. Given these two positions, there is clearly no such thing as one correct answer: officialdom encourages those underoccupying their homes to move to somewhere smaller, while the principle behind Lifetime Homes is to make it easier for people to stay put in later life.

For those who wish to put down roots for their adult life in one place, the idea behind these modular houses by Proctor and Matthews provides a practical and attractive solution.

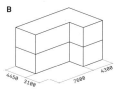
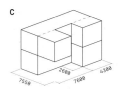
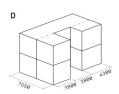
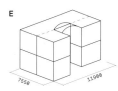
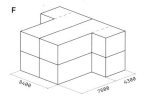

**Top** The covered courtyard.
**Above and left** Diagrams showing:
**A** basic two-bedroom house module; **B** two-bedroom house extended to three-bedroom house; **C** three-bedroom house extended to four-bedroom house; **D** four-bedroom house with car port filled in to provide an office space; **E** four-bedroom house with covered internal courtyard; **F** pair of semi-detached three-bedroom houses.
**Right** Internal view of corridor and staircase.

# Part 3_Technical issues_

The decade after World War 2 produced opportunities for a generation of radical architects, fired by the ideals inherent in rebuilding a better Europe. Taking ideas that had originated in prewar Germany, Scandinavia and the Netherlands and influenced by Le Corbusier's published work, designers were basing the form of their housing designs on functional issues.

The decade after World War 2 produced opportunities for a generation of radical architects, fired by the ideals inherent in rebuilding a better Europe. Taking ideas that had originated in prewar Germany, Scandinavia and the Netherlands and influenced by Le Corbusier's published work, designers were basing the form of their housing designs on functional issues such as separating cars from pedestrians, increasing densities, building flats and maisonettes instead of houses, including large areas of shared open space, and providing access to sunlight for all dwellings, district heating, etc. All these ideas constituted fertile ground for radical design solutions and in this heady situation the conventional approach to urban design and street-based layouts, which were felt to have either been based on irrelevant suburban densities or the nineteenth-century street, were brushed aside.

For younger architects involved in housing, 1968 was some kind of turning point, as it was in many other fields. Radical architecture began to give way to social concerns, so that around 1973, the year of the first oil crisis and when difficulties facing some of the new generation of public-sector housing estates were becoming evident, there was a 180-degree turn in thinking. Designers acquired a whole new set of concerns about defensible space and privacy, conventional street frontages, a return to the 'vernacular' and, above all, the question of security.

While there is now no question of abandoning the hard-won lessons about layouts based on the principal of the street and the paramount need for security, if targets for carbon-neutral housing are to be met by 2015 new design solutions for internal planning and site layouts have to be found that combine all the best features of apparently contradictory approaches.

Attempts to 'sell' renewable forms of energy as being in the interest of long-term domestic economy, rather than simply appealing to householders to reduce their carbon footprint, are in their infancy and sustainability in all its forms is a hard thing to promote on ethical grounds alone. But remorseless rises in the cost of fossil fuels, reductions in the availability of water and the eventual need to recycle almost everything will eventually change all that, and new housing needs to be capable of responding to innovations as they become imperative or economically viable.

Leaving aside wider issues to do with neighbourhood and facilities such as public transport, employment, schools, childcare, healthcare, shopping and leisure, built form and urban design must respond to the increasing demands brought about by climate change. Some of these measures are simply a matter of laying on the appropriate infrastructure while others can have a fundamental effect on the built form.

**Maximising passive solar gain through building orientation** Architects and urban designers have in the past used the orientation of new housing as a major determinant in its layout, often with the disastrous results that only come about when uncompromising emphasis is loaded on one particular feature. Organising plans so that every flat or house receives direct sunlight into one of its principal living spaces at some time of the day is always possible, except in north-facing single-aspect dwellings, which should be avoided in any case. But that is different from planning all dwellings with their principal living space facing due south to take advantage of passive solar heating, as this means effectively that conventional street layouts, lined on both sides with houses, are impossible to achieve.

It may therefore be worth concluding that orientating houses and flats specifically to take maximum advantage of passive solar gain is less important than other factors in street layout.

**Solar collectors and photovoltaics** Solar collectors for domestic hot water are now regularly installed in new housing, providing a third of hot water needs. Some solar collectors can be installed on flat roofs, but for maximum effect on pitched roofs both solar collectors and photovoltaic arrays need to be orientated to within 90 degrees of due south – though efficency obviously reduces considerably towards the extremes.

As the goal of achieving zero energy by 2016 approaches it is important to future-proof all new housing by ensuring that both options can be retrofitted without altering roof structures. This provides interesting opportunities for designers in terms of the profile of roof slopes, which need to vary according to whether streets are running north–south or east–west.

**Heat recovery and whole-house ventilation**
As architects mourn the passing of the traditional chimney as an important design element and component in roofscapes, the 'chimney' in revised form is making a comeback. Next to thermal insulation and airtightness, whole-house ventilation with heat recovery is becoming an essential component in reducing the energy required for space heating and to provide the necessary minimum number of air changes. The twenty-first-century chimney is most unlikely to be constructed of brick or any other form of masonry, and its function is akin to a modern ship's funnel in providing a casing to house all the ventilation needs of a single house or block of flats.

**Storage for twenty-first-century lifestyles** Being able to store conveniently all the kinds of possessions that we acquire at various stages in our lives, from cycles to buggies, let alone all the different items for recycling, becomes more challenging as densities increase, and a shed in the rear garden without direct access to the street is no solution. In this respect the design of urban housing has progressed very little from the Victorian and Edwardian model in spite of a recognition that we all own much, much more and that it can't be stored just inside the front door or, worse still, in the front garden.

It is noticeable that people living in sought-after locations are prepared to put up with the lack of storage in their highly prized flats or houses, and use all manner of ingenious means to compensate. But as densities inevitably increase in locations that are not all that sought-after, a terrace house or flat must incorporate convenient storage into the basic design if it is to be sustainable in the long term. (Some of these issues have been dealt with in Chapters 5 and 6.)

### Background + private open space, Chapter 6

This is replacement housing for part of the unloved 1970s' South Kilburn Estate. To make it possible for residents to move once from their existing homes straight into their new homes, avoiding an interim move away from the neighbourhood, the new scheme had to fit on a tight and irregularly shaped piece of 'leftover land'. It also involved negotiating the challenges of fitting in liveable dwellings at high density while minimising impact on neighbours and the environment.

The scheme does this by innovatively adapting the historic precedent of the narrow gaps often found between Victorian terraces – characteristically seen in the adjoining conservation area as well as many others around the city – into more generous 'urban breaks'. This simple re-establishment of the traditional street pattern, a contemporary reinterpretation of a typical Georgian or Victorian terrace, not only breaks the rhythm of the roofline and the façades, but most importantly allows the sun to penetrate into the (communal) gardens behind. It also allows each dwelling to enjoy high levels of daylight, reflected sunlight and good natural ventilation.

Sunlight and daylight are both reflected by having the flank walls and recesses of the building breaks finished in rendered white panels. A similar strategy has been used for the rear façades in order to reflect daylight into the open spaces but also to minimise any visual impact or loss of light to the existing dwellings surrounding the development. The pattern of the random brick slips to the front façades has been taken from the mottled effect of buildings originally built using London stock bricks that have now weathered unevenly.

The second environmentally sustainable urban-design principle was to turn the potential negative loss of shared open space into a positive gain. A substantial portion of Granville New Homes is built on a patch of land that was low-quality and unused, but open space nonetheless, the loss of which is always a potentially sensitive issue. The intention behind the layout and massing is to

create a hierarchy of open spaces at different scales and levels in the new buildings, from window boxes on balconies and roof terraces to extensive green roofs. There are also front and back gardens to family units as well as shared gardens and a 'pocket park'. Roofs take on a particularly important role for both residents and wildlife, and they provide positive overlooking to both the street and the communal gardens.

Repetition is further avoided by the positioning of generous cantilevered balconies that also provide shading to prevent excessive solar gain. Additional shading to large windows without balconies above them is provided by projecting canopies designed in a similar language to the balconies.

Sedum roofs play a significant role in water retention by delaying run-off and reducing localised flash floods. Rainwater is collected and stored underground with a pumped system for irrigation. At higher levels, the roofs have solar evacuated tubes mounted horizontally, designed to provide a total of 30 per cent of the estimated heat energy needs (water and space) and around 15 per cent of all energy demand.

Although the architects moved the building line back to accommodate mature trees along Granville Road, during site clearance it became obvious that several trees could not be retained during construction, and they were replaced with similar mature species.

Granville New Homes was built as a result of a limited architectural competition. This winning entry proposed many innovations (as the diagram opposite shows), not all of which have been included in the built scheme. After much consultation with residents, ideas such as the inclusion of allotments in the communal gardens were not thought to be practicable by the residents' steering group and were omitted from the later proposals.

External view showing community facility built into the street corner.

**Above** Rear shared garden.
**Below left** Evacuated-tube solar panels.
**Below** Original diagram from the competition entry showing the environmental principles built into the design in a form that could be easily explained to residents.

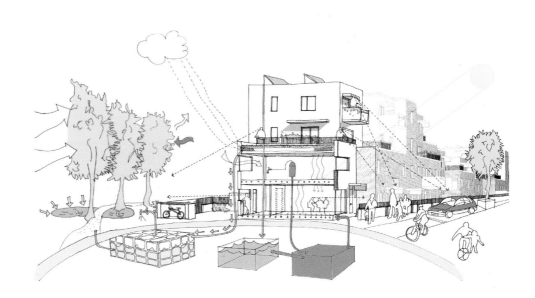

# Midsummer Cottages, Milton Keynes



In 1994 the new city of Milton Keynes, unarguably the most successful of the UK's postwar new towns, promoted and made land available for an international exhibition, 'Futureworld'. The aim was to demonstrate 'the latest in house designs, building techniques and materials, energy efficency and environmental control'. In addition to the various housebuilding companies that participated, a local housing association secured a site to construct five houses with the aim of fulfilling all of those objectives.

In detail, the solution offered included:

**energy efficency**

1 highly insulated external envelope (U-values: walls 0.2, roofs 0.15, floors 0.25);
2 triple-glazed windows;
3 low external air leakage (<3ac/h at 50 Pa);
4 high thermal mass to store solar energy and other heat surpluses;
5 gas-fired condensing combination boilers;
6 mechanical ventilation and heat recovery (1ac/h) controlled by humidity sensors;
7 summer cooling/winter warming of incoming air using 'earth tubes';
8 low-energy compact fluorescent lighting;
9 water economy using rainwater butts.

**elimination of hazardous materials**

10 low embodied energy of materials and components;
11 sustainably sourced materials;
12 four-compartment refuse and recycling store;
13 no CFCs or HCFCs in materials and finishes.

**low skill content in construction**

14 solid masonry external-wall construction to encourage low-skill labour training;
15 construction to exploit simple on-site technology.

**anticipation of lifestyle changes**

16 no load-bearing internal walls;
17 'knock-out' floor panel for future wheelchair lift.

In January 2009, 15 years after the houses were first occupied, two of the five current owners were interviewed with the aim of trying to find out how the houses were performing, particularly in respect of the energy-efficency measures originally installed. All occupants are shared owners and neither of the interviewees had been in their houses for more than five or six years. It was clear that the houses are popular and considered to be well planned and comfortable. Both households, particularly the houseowner with small children who had only turned on her central heating once (in 2009) in the six years since she moved in, expressed strong satisfaction with the thermal performance of their homes.

If the above-average thermal performance can be attributed to the first four passive measures built into the houses – 1–4 in the list – virtually nothing can be attributed to the active measures – 6, 7 and 8. The low-energy lighting did not survive the original sales team in 1994 who thought the houses would sell better without it! Some progress has indeed been made since then.

Neither interviewee was aware of the central ventilation and heat-recovery system, nor the summer cooling/winter warming effect of the earth tubes, as the humidity-based control sensors had long since been removed. Both owners recalled seeing these sensors when they moved in but, in the absence of any briefing from their housing association, they either removed the sensors themselves or had them removed by local tradesmen, who did not know what they were either!

If there is a lesson to learn from Midsummer Cottages it is that the inclusion of any equipment to generate renewable energy in individual dwellings – photovoltaics, solar panels, heat-recovery systems, heat pumps, biomass boilers, domestic CHP, etc. – is only viable where occupants are committed to their upkeep and to seeing a financial return on the additional capital expended on their installation. This probably rules out virtually all affordable housing. However, the additional passive measures, such as higher standards of insulation, thermally super-efficient glazing and airtightness, are the only cost-effective ways to 'future-proof' all new homes for rent and shared ownership unless responsible landlords can afford to provide constant training and monitoring.

**Architect** Levitt Bernstein Associates
**Developer** Midsummer Housing Association with URBED + Joseph Rowntree Foundation
**Site** not applicable
**Number of dwellings** 5
**Density** not applicable
**Mix** 1 x 2B + 2 x 3B + 2 x 4B
**Affordable** 100 per cent shared ownership
**Parking spaces per dwelling** 1

**Right** The front elevation in 2009. By contrast with the photograph on page 210, this shows overgrown front 'gardens' and poor attention to the timber cladding.

**Right** The front elevation
on completion in 1994. The
houses, set well back from the
road with parking spaces in
curtilage, would always have
needed constant care, as would
the timber cladding.
**Below** Plans of all five houses.

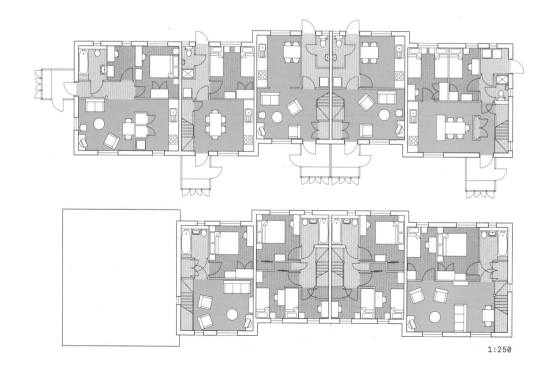

1:250

**Above** The group of five houses as first completed, designed to operate with a whole-house ventilation system.
**Below** House fronts in 2009, no longer distinguishable as a single composition due partly to the differing approaches to gardening.

RuralZED is the brainchild of architect Bill Dunster and his ZEDfactory. It is intended as a practical demonstration of the application of the principles of building truly sustainable housing in a rural context, suitable for the 70 per cent of the UK that is built or planned at densities up to and including 55 homes per hectare. RuralZED is a town-building product and programme that uses the initial community construction process to create the infrastructure and skills to generate a permanent legacy of income-generating local business – effectively future-proofed by delivering the highest standards of the Code for Sustainable Homes rather than importing bulky and expensive components.

The plan – designed around the central idea of a community of people committed to combating climate change – has more than a touch of idealism about it. In a tough area with the usual problems brought about by social and economic deprivation, the local crime-prevention officer would have much to say about some of the security aspects of things such as houses that can be accessed from both front and back. And there would need to be serious commitment from all residents to maintain the 'public realm', especially the 'pocket parks', the green-finger allotments, etc.

As with so many measures designed to address and ameliorate the effects of climate change, this is a plan that might need to be administered through a very local collective management structure in which all members of the community would have a financial stake regardless of their tenure.

There is much more to the idea of ruralZED than the physical fabric of the housing itself. In very general terms ZEDfactory aims to solve the funding gap cited by UK housebuilders as the reason they are unable to market the idea of zero-carbon housing in this sector of the market. The ruralZED house could be initially built and marketed as a Code level 4 home but with a Code level 6 building fabric (HLP 0.8W/m$^2$/K). The purchaser would then retrofit the renewables using two sources of funding, the first of which would be the stamp duty relief attracted by a Code level 6 house and

the second an energy mortgage, the monthly payments of which would be balanced by savings on utility bills.

In explaining their proposals, ZEDfactory writes: 'The ruralZED system is constructed from a relatively small number of prefabricated components that are delivered to a construction site in flat-pack form, numbered and packed in the correct sequence to facilitate fast erection on site, with maximum weather protection and security. This strategy saves transporting the large volumes of air usually associated with prefinished prefabricated pod and room systems.

'For larger schemes requiring a minimum of 250 units per year with a wide variety of home types and sizes, it would be possible to set up an on-site computer-controlled laminated-timber machining plant – locating a permanent industry within the community that might go on to export home kits to other smaller sites after the original construction programme has been built.

'It should take about a day to drive a cluster of short-bore prefabricated GGBS concrete mini-pile foundations – creating no drilling spoil, and potentially saving 80 per cent of the embodied $CO_2$ compared to a conventional mass concrete strip foundation with concrete block and beam ground-floor slab. The piles have simply adjusted stainless caps that allow accurate direct connection to the ruralZED laminated-timber frame absorbing tolerance in both plan position and height. Prefabricated incoming services sleeves and access chambers can then be laid in place in precision-dug trenches – allowing future connection to centralised site-wide services.

'A simple demountable rainproofed shelter housing an electrically powered overhead crane rail allows premachined laminated timber columns and beams to be bolted together in self-aligning jigs in dry working conditions – with an all-terrain forklift delivering the assembled portals to each plot and hoisting them into position. This strategy of predrilling and prefabricating all connections enables a typical two-storey three-bedroom structure – including

High density

Low density

Pocket park

Pocket park

Pocket park

Pocket park

Pocket park

Pocket park

Pocket park

Village green

Community hall & barrow market

Landark community

bees hives

lake

Layout plan for a rural settlement suitable for an eco-town. Note the allotments in prominent locations at the rear of houses and on footpath routes. Although the density varies from one end of the site to the other, the number of shared spaces, long front gardens and footpaths suggest a community that would need to work together in order to minimise service charges and to ensure that the public realm does not become unkempt.

dovetailed floor joists and cladding rails –
to be erected in one day by the fitting team.

'A weatherproof breathable membrane
mechanically fixed to the walls, floor and roof
with clamping batons protects the frame from
wind and rain, and a simple airtightness test
is undertaken before adding any external
cladding or internal finishes. This greatly
facilitates any remedial work, needed to
demonstrate compliance with the onerous
airtightness standards required by the new
Code for Sustainable Homes. This test is
repeated after the prefabricated, prepainted
and preglazed timber windows, doors and
rooflights have been installed – making it
easier to identify any air leakages that may
occur under pressure and ensuring the
thermal efficiency of the completed near-zero
heating specification home. Internal walls
and ceilings are then lined with thermally
massive prefabricated polished eco-concrete
wall and floor slabs, or vaulted extruded
terracotta ceiling bricks designed to fit
between exposed timber joists.

'A range of external wall-cladding options –
from durable thermally treated timber to lime
render and locally sourced weatherboarding
or extruded terracotta mathematical tiles
– allows the finishes to vary to suit local
preference. Roofs can be sedum or zinc
or aluminium standing seam or clay tile,
depending on pitch and planning constraints.

'A ZEDfabric zero-carbon thermal
services kit – comprising a windcowl with
passive heat recovery and ductwork kit,
prefabricated external woodpellet boiler
and pellet store with DIY-ESCO community
software, heat-metering hot-water cylinder
controls and pump set, and solar thermal
collectors with roof-mounting kit – is included
as the base specification in every ruralZED
build, and can be easily adopted by most
local plumbers without requiring specialist
training in renewable-energy components
or design. By integrating all electrical and
control elements within the intelligent hot-
water cylinder, it is as easy to install as any
other basic tank, with complex solar-specific
elements already within the component.

'If Code level 6 is required, a simple

renewable electric package is included in
the ruralZED kit of parts, using special bulk-
purchased fit-and-forget mono-crystalline
PV panels, which clip on to the south-facing
slopes of the pitched roof-surfaces. It is
critical that the masterplan is designed
to optimise the output of solar-electricity
generation, with careful attention to
overshading and sunlight rights to individual
households.

'A low-embodied-$CO_2$ kitchen option made
from remanufactured salvaged kitchens is
offered. However, most customers wish to
choose their own components.

'A ruralZED garden kit has also been
developed with Garden Organic at Ryton
(part of the Henry Doubleday Research
Association) to maximise the biodiversity of
the new home, garden and roof surfaces,
paying particular attention to maximising the
useful horticultural productivity of the double-
glazed sunspace (where seedlings, herbs
and citrus fruit can be grown out of season)
and vegetable production within raised
beds integrated within the plot boundary
fences. A communal herb-garden design and
communal fruit-orchard layout are available
for larger projects, completing the edible
public landscape concept. Local garden
centres will be able to supply the planting
list from stock, and only common indigenous
species have been specified.

'A detailed illustrated manual describing
each component, calling off the fixings and
relevant tools, demystifies the ruralZED
assembly process to enable almost any
motivated and competent individual
or self-builder to become expert after
witnessing and participating in a couple
of builds. The ruralZED team provides an
experienced project manager who assists
with technical queries, and inspects build
quality – certifying the quality of completed
constructions and providing the builder with
a photographic snagging survey to enable
the completed construction to meet ruralZED
standards of durability and environmental
performance. This simple process potentially
enables local erection jobs to be created
from a relatively unskilled but motivated
labour pool at any site larger than 24 units.'

Front and rear elevations of a
prototype three-bedroom house.

**Above** Perspective views of a ruralZED eco-settlement.
**Right** Floor plans of a typical three-bedroom house showing framed construction and two-storey sunspace.

  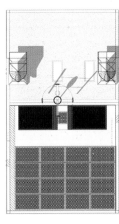

Chapter 13 covered aspects of the extraordinary legacy of the Victorian and Edwardian housebuilders, which has allowed their terrace housing and purpose-built flats to be so successfully adapted and converted for present-day lifestyles. But this legacy was very much an accident. The emphasis here is on current different forms of construction, some of which promise to be just as adaptable, and more scientifically engineered than their historic predecessors.

Most of the homes built before 1914 and still standing today were houses, some extremely large and subsequently converted into flats, but the majority were terrace houses of no more than four storeys. Now, as UK densities steadily increase, engineers are involved in the design of housing structures in two distinct ways: the first – for volume housebuilders – involves rolling out economical structures for two- and three-storey low-density houses and flats; in contrast, the second involves designing largely bespoke structures for high-density multi-storey flats and maisonettes. In the former the emphasis is on lean engineering to provide the most economical structural solutions with increasing amounts of off-site fabrication – a consequence of which is limited scope for subsequent adaptability. The latter relies on mainstream framed construction, which does provide greater scope for alteration in the future.

Leaving aside a low-risk approach to sustainability based on traditional forms and materials, commercial pressures and the lack of interest displayed by the buying public make it understandable that few volume housebuilders show much concern for the ultimate longevity of the homes they produce. On the other hand bespoke structures give their designers, and the teams of which they form part, more opportunity to consider a whole range of sustainability issues – from climate change to the future adaptability of homes based on demographic and lifestyle changes.

Given the urgent need for building new homes, the current emphasis has to be on speed and economy of construction. But a glance at the miniscule annual replacement rates of UK homes suggests a need for an almost infinite life for any new home and makes it worth analysing the non-traditional construction methods now being advocated.

Building on the principle that all successful housing goes through subtle changes of use during its lifecycle, this section examines the various types of construction employed, both now and over the past 40 years, to see what can be regarded as permanent (layout and infrastructure, foundations, superstructure, etc.) and what can be regarded as adaptable (external skin, mechanical services, internal space planning, etc.). The objective is to provide ways of going forward that will avoid the enormous waste involved in grinding up whole buildings into pieces the size of golf balls every couple of generations.

**Layout and infrastructure**
Since the wholesale spread of individual freeholds for newly built housing in the 1930s, usually on low-density suburban estates or, until 1939, lining all the main roads in and out of town, land assembly for the redevelopment of even poor and run-down houses has proved extremely difficult. It is hard to imagine decisions being taken to tear up established suburban roads with all the attendant problems of underground services and road closures now or at any time in the future. Such wasteful planning of semi-detached houses, or more recently detached houses only a couple of metres apart, lining roads to nowhere, needs to be replaced by layouts that provide the same advantages of lower densities – larger gardens in particular – without such profligate waste of space.

**Foundations**
If the Victorians handed us down a useful legacy of flexible structures it was not often built on firm foundations. The use of Portland cement instead of lime mortar was not widespread until after 1918. Until then foundations for houses were always too shallow and consisted of a few courses of spread brick footings that were incapable of resisting ground movement. Strictly speaking, no foundations are capable of resisting ground movement, which will occur under all foundations. However, the shallower

the foundations the more susceptible they are to significant movements. Major changes occurred in foundation depths after the hot summer of 1976 and there has been a very significant improvement in the performance of foundations built after that time.

Foundation methods in use now, covered by much more stringent Building Regulations, often involve concrete piling with ground beams on brownfield sites and deep strip concrete footings for buildings of not more than three storeys where ground conditions permit. Given that modern methods of construction are tending to produce lighter superstructures, it is possible to imagine the reuse of these later, better-engineered foundation systems – provided, of course, that the records of how they were built also survive.

### Superstructures

Conventional load-bearing 'brick and block' construction is likely to continue its decline in the scramble for leaner, quicker systems with increasing amounts of off-site fabrication. Systems to consider include those involving conventional steel frame, concrete frame, and various types of steel, timber or precast concrete-panel construction.

The last inevitably brings to mind the experiments in concrete construction of the 1960s and 1970s. But where these failed it was largely because of poor construction quality, inadequate seals, and short-life cladding materials that were combined with insufficient attention to issues of condensation, cold bridging, thermal insulation and ventilation – all factors that are now much better understood.

As superstructures become ever more specialised and highly engineered, the potential for adapting or reusing them depends largely on whether they are based on frames or load-bearing panels. Post-forming large openings in load-bearing wall panels, mostly used in the construction of two- and three-storey houses and flats, can be difficult to achieve. On the other hand, framed structures, either of hot-rolled

steel or concrete, which are uneconomical for buildings of less than five storeys, are inherently adaptable.

**Concrete-panel structures,** or in-situ 'tunnel form' concrete structures (which have high embodied energy anyway), don't take kindly to having holes punched in them. They score highly for their thermal-storage properties and work well in combination with houses or flats designed to make use of passive solar energy. Arguments abound on both sides as to whether 'heavy' structures cope better than 'light' structures in terms of general comfort in hot weather but there is plenty of evidence to suggest that solid masonry constructions do not heat up as quickly as lightweight structures in summer temperatures.

Some concrete systems endeavour to hide electrical services in conduit within walls and horizontal slabs. With the benefit of experience, this is surely a profound mistake: there are already too many examples of 40-year-old structures in need of new or upgraded electrics where the original conduit has proved impossible to rewire. A much better solution – and this will be a constant refrain – is a loose-fit design for the electrics and other services as a completely renewable package that does not affect the structure when it needs to be replaced.

**In-situ concrete frames** in combination with concrete floors are widely used for multi-storey flats at heights beyond the economic use of lightweight steel or timber frames. They are slower to erect than steel frames but perform well in terms of fire protection and the transfer of sound. The subsequent attachment of structures such as cantilevered balconies is a more complex operation than simply bolting on to a steel frame, but in every other respect they are equally adaptable.

**Cold-rolled lightweight steel-framed wall panel or steel volumetric construction** is now widely used for houses or flats, reaching heights up to eight storeys, which were unimaginable only a very few years ago. These are highly engineered structures mostly fabricated from thin-guage cold-rolled steel sections formed into framed load-bearing panels, usually with welded joints. There is therefore very little margin for error in terms of steel corrosion and it is imperative that these structural members are completely protected from exposure to external weathering and interstitial condensation for the whole course of their lives.

They are not structures designed to have much spare load-bearing capacity and although it would, in theory, no doubt be possible to make additional openings in floor or wall panels in 30 years' time, this would involve a thorough understanding of the structure, for which the original drawings and calculations are highly likely to have disappeared.

Due to their low thermal mass, these structures only work well in combating excessive passive solar gain if all other aspects are considered, including through ventilation to take advantage of night cooling.

**Hot-rolled structural steel frames** are also widely used in multi-storey flat construction at heights above the normal maximum for either lightweight steel or timber frame, or where larger internal spaces or more flexibility of layout are required. Compared to in-situ concrete frames, they are quick to construct and recyclable, but require careful measures to provide adequate fire protection and to prevent the transfer of sound via the frame itself. In most other respects they are eminently flexible but, having a lower thermal mass than concrete, suffer the same disadvantages as lightweight steel in dealing with overheating from passive solar gain.

**Structural timber frame**, by far the most common of all the non-traditional construction methods, is back in general use after being brought to an abrupt halt after the exposure of sloppy workmanship on national TV in the 1980s. This is a quality-control issue but, constructed correctly, there is no reason why a structural timber frame should not have an indefinite life. As with lightweight steel frames, the greatest risk is

from moisture ingress or from condensation, which is avoided by installing a breather membrane between the frame itself and whatever external skin is applied. These membranes are fragile and the greatest risk is from careless workmanship rather than faulty specification.

But structural, load-bearing timber frame is a highly engineered product normally based on storey-height vertical studs with similar section head and sole plates. It acquires rigidity by providing a plywood or OSB (oriented strand board) membrane on the external face. This effectively turns each frame into a rigid diaphragm that can only be altered or have openings made in it after a thorough engineering analysis.

Timber-frame structures are more tolerant of alterations to small-scale mechanical services such as domestic rewiring or local pipe runs than either concrete or lightweight steel-framed structures, but their inherent combustibility requires the structure itself to be protected to a half hour standard of fire resistance if less than 5 metres high and one hour if more than 5 metres.

**The external skin**
Provided no attempt is made to disguise the underlying construction by making the external skin appear to be structural through the use of what seems to be load-bearing brick, a huge range of materials are available. As with many other differences between 'urban' and 'suburban' or rural housing, there is still a public perception that equates the first with the use of contemporary mechanical surfaces that are not designed to weather, and suburban or rural with traditional materials that are designed precisely to become textured with age. Discounting natural stone as being beyond the means of most housing designers and their clients, two materials, brick and timber used as cladding or rainscreen, bridge that divide between urban and the suburban and rural. And both are capable, when carefully detailed, of weathering satisfactorily.

At some stage during the lifecycle of 'sustainable' housing structures, their external surfaces, if they aren't brick or

possibly timber, may need to be replaced.
Apart from surfaces applied wet, such as
render, the range of materials developed for
urban housing typologies – metals, coated
aluminium, glass, ceramics or composite
resin impregnated panels – are all intended
to remain pristine.

Generally the surfaces themselves have good
weathering characteristics but after, say, 30
years the joints and fastenings look tired and
pattern stained. Only timber and brick used
as cladding acquire the weathered patina
that can confer a feeling of permanence in an
otherwise constantly changing urban scene.

Whereas cladding to upper floors has to
provide little more than the properties of
a rainscreen and can therefore be chosen
from the range of lightweight materials, the
lowest floor needs to cope with surface wear,
splashing and even impact. The structure at
that level therefore needs protection using
heavier, more resistant materials such as
non-structural brick, concrete or tile. The
extra weight can be supported directly
from foundation level, while the lightweight
rainscreen above can be hung off the
structure at each floor level.

Another measure of 'sustainability' applies to
housing outside urban contexts. Residential
buildings in suburban or rural settings
need to form part of the unchanging natural
landscape, neighbourhood or street scene.
Surface texture therefore becomes much
more important, especially where the
external surface meets the ground and
provides support and a natural background
for planting.

Much has been written about this huge concrete-framed Modernist scheme in the decades since its completion in 1961 and much has happened to alter the national scene in terms of social housing. When Park Hill was conceived by Ivor Smith and Jack Lynn, entirely as social housing for rent, Sheffield was near to having full employment and architects were coming up with ambitious ways of satisfying the unmet need for affordable, that is social, housing.

The facts about Park Hill – now the largest listed structure in Britain – are astonishing: 985 flats in a single deck-access complex, owing much to the then pervasive influence of the ideas of Le Corbusier, whose Unité d'habitation in Marseille had been completed only ten years earlier. The architects' vision was to create 'streets in the sky', 3.5 metres wide, every third floor. Because of the topography of Sheffield these 2 miles (more than 3km) of 'streets' connect with existing streets at their southern end. And Park Hill was not only equipped with district heating but it also boasted the Garchey system of centralised refuse disposal.

Held in popular and critical esteem for 20 years, the prejudice against large scale, Modernist, concrete-faced, mono-tenure estates eventually caught up even with this internationally celebrated building. But while its popularity waned it was listed Grade 2* in 1998 and in 2004 a competition was held to determine its future. This was won by Urban Splash, which had established itself as a highly successful and innovative developer, with Hawkins\Brown and Studio Egret West as architects.

Since 1990 the policy for the southern half of England had been to persuade developers and their customers to accept the principle of mixing tenures as indistinguishably as possible. However, Urban Splash had built their reputation on developments containing very little affordable accommodation in the city centres of Manchester and Liverpool, where it was considered that there was already an imbalance in favour of affordable rented homes. At Park Hill, Urban Splash's proposals involved 'pepperpotting' a third of the new accommodation with homes

for affordable rent, stripping the original flats and maisonettes back to the concrete crosswall structure and replacing each cluster of four flats (consisting of a one-bed, two two-beds and a three-bed maisonette) with an ingenious five-flat cluster containing more small units. However, the recession of 2008–9 caused the developer to reconsider its original choice of apartment size, reverting to a mix more closely resembling the original but retaining the same division of tenures.

Another of the most contentious issues, that of managing mixed-tenure housing, is likely to be successfully overcome at Park Hill due to the incorporation of a 24-hour concierge. In the first phase there will be approximately 85 flats served off each of three cores and approximately this ratio will be maintained across later phases. Each core will have a secured lobby at ground level and a main 24-hour concierge will operate from the new stair and lift core adjacent to the four-storey 'cut' in the middle of the north block, which is likely to remain the principle concierge point for all of the phases. The concierge will monitor comings and goings from all cores and will also collect parcels and large deliveries adjacent to the main lobby. Letter post will be delivered to each front door, distributed traditionally along each street by the Post Office.

The proposals for Park Hill include the construction of a new multi-storey car park to increase the provision from 20 to 72 per cent and this will also be placed under the control of the concierge.

Apart from the concrete superstructure, what is being reused? It is intended to employ as much of the existing infrastructure as possible. The Sheffield District Heating System will continue to provide hot water to the whole of Park Hill and the existing service trench and risers will also be reused – the original planning of the building allows for efficient and fairly flexible reuse. New incoming and outgoing pipework will be needed, but the distribution will be the same.

Obviously this is a costly refurbishment given the requirements for the concrete frame to be repaired (in line with English Heritage's

**Architects** Hawkins\Brown and Studio Egret West
**Developers** Urban Splash Limited with Sheffield City Council
**Site** 13.29 hectares
**Number of dwellings** 985 (originally)
**Density** 69 dwellings/hectare
**Mix** not finalised
**Parking spaces per dwelling** 0.72 (originally 0.2)
**Non-housing uses** 6000 square metres of retail, community and medical facilities

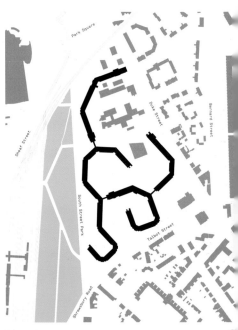

Site plan.

**Above** Photograph taken after
the original external skin and
non-structural partitions had
been stripped out in 2007-8, in
preparation for the entirely new
configuration of flats and insulated
outer skin to be fitted.
**Below** Aerial view taken in 1962.
Note the steep changes in level
that enabled the 'streets' at
every third floor level to connect
with the ground at some point.

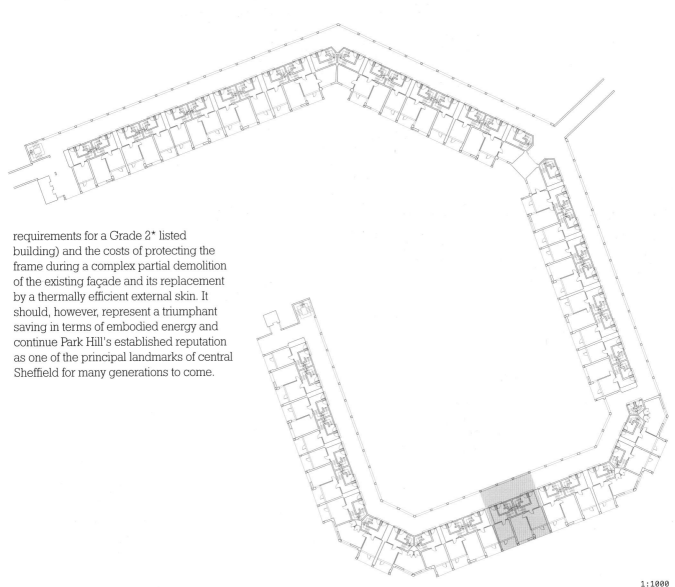

requirements for a Grade 2* listed building) and the costs of protecting the frame during a complex partial demolition of the existing façade and its replacement by a thermally efficient external skin. It should, however, represent a triumphant saving in terms of embodied energy and continue Park Hill's established reputation as one of the principal landmarks of central Sheffield for many generations to come.

1:1000

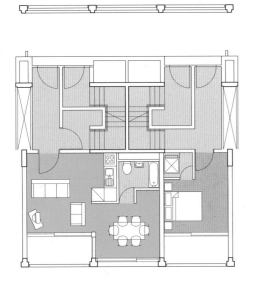
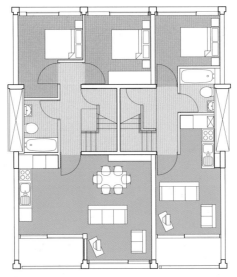
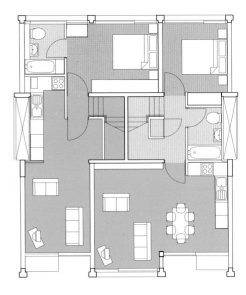

**Top** layout plan
**Above** Typical upper-floor configuration including new flat layouts.

1:250

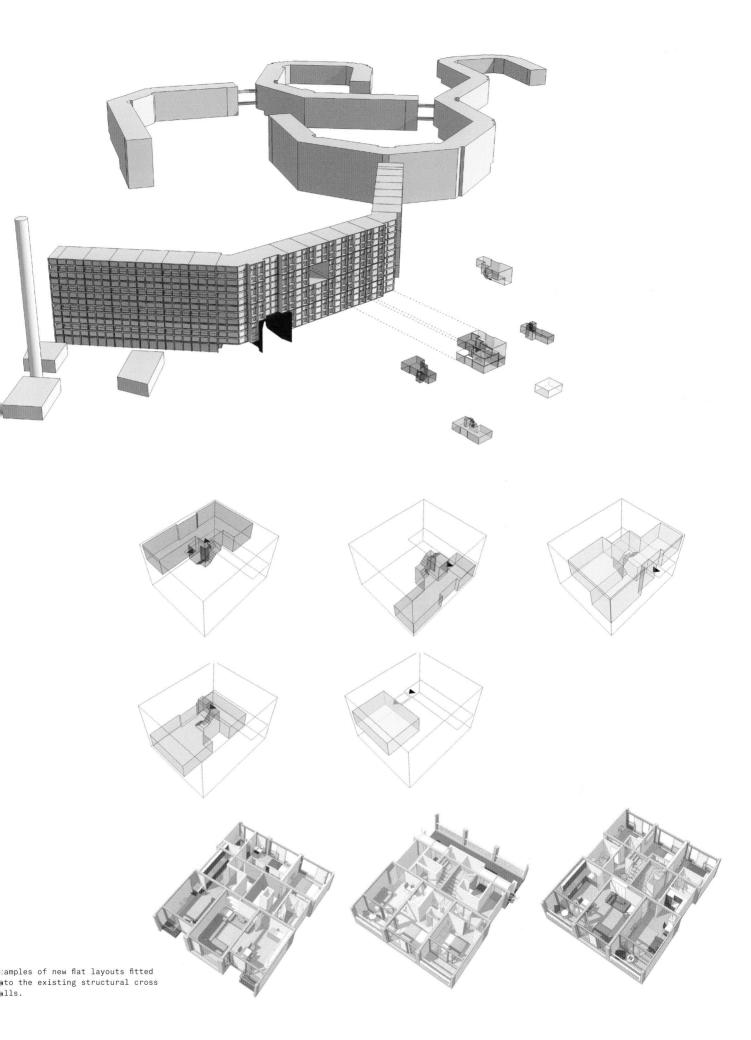

Examples of new flat layouts fitted
into the existing structural cross
walls.

Greengate House is a locally listed building in Plaistow, south of Stratford in East London. It dates from 1919, belonged to the local authority and was originally designed as a charitable hostel, even boasting a swimming pool. At the back, an outdoor recreation space with a tennis court and bowling green had degenerated into a car park. The building was subsequently adapted as a local-authority arts facility and then became completely disused.

Tower Homes, a specialist arm of the London & Quadrant Group, was searching for opportunities to provide flats for local keyworkers, following an initiative pioneered by the Joseph Rowntree Foundation in their CASPAR schemes in Leeds and Birmingham (see Chapter 13). The CASPAR principle was to build high-quality accommodation for key workers, without public subsidy and at affordable rents. Absence of subsidy when combined with the need for low rents always poses a challenge to developer and architect alike, and partly accounts in this case for the very high density in a largely suburban area.

The scheme has passed through two competition stages followed by a number of design stages. Several of these involved clearing the site altogether, as the existing building is of little intrinsic merit, apart from its sheer volume. However, partial retention of the existing concrete-framed structure and its façade has clearly helped to achieve a higher density than would otherwise have been possible. The design finally chosen is therefore a compromise that satisfies local concerns about removing a landmark, however incongruous.

The redeveloped site provides 64 units of affordable housing for key-worker groups. The retention and conversion of the front 6 metres of Greengate House enables the building's public presence to be maintained as a locally admired asset while the rest of the building is demolished to make way for a new wing of accommodation within the original footprint.

Beneath the original building was a full basement containing a swimming pool, and this space is now being reused as an underground car park, a benefit that would have been impossible had the basement not existed already.

The rear of the site, the former tennis court turned car park, supports two low-rise buildings, mews-like in scale, with a more suburban street frontage to the south. The new buildings on the north, east and west boundaries are grouped around a central landscaped courtyard to which all residents will have access. Gabion baskets filled with demolition rubble form the remaining boundaries. Green-roof and green-wall technology soften the new forms where they abut the adjoining gardens of two-storey houses, and are a key part of the sustainability agenda of the project.

The retained façade to Greengate Street has a number of discreet interventions to render it reusable and to signify the change of use. It also sets tall storey heights that are observed throughout the new structure behind it, allowing the deep plans to have better daylighting.

**Architect** Levitt Bernstein Associates
**Developer** Tower Homes, part of London & Quadrant Group
**Site** 0.373 hectares
**Number of dwellings** 64
**Density** 171 dwellings/hectare
**Mix** 29 x 2B + 35 x 1B
**Affordable** 40 per cent shared ownership, 60 per cent market rent
**Parking spaces per dwelling** 0.5

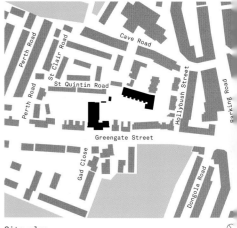

Site plan.

**Top** South facing elevation to the
new internal courtyard
**Below** The existing listed street
frontage determines the new higher
density overall building envelope
in an otherwise suburban setting

1:1000

**Top** Layout plan showing new
interlocking courtyards with a
mixture of flats and maisonettes for
various key worker groups.
**Left** Section A–A showing the reuse
of the basement for car parking
and the access gallery behind the
'green wall'; and section B–B
through the three-storey rear
block with cutaway roof to avoid
overshadowing.
**Bottom, left to right** One-bedroom flat
behind listed elevation to street;
ground-floor flat to rear three-
storey block; typical one-bedroom
flat in the main block; first- and
second-floor maisonettes in rear
three-storey block.

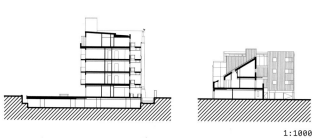

1:1000

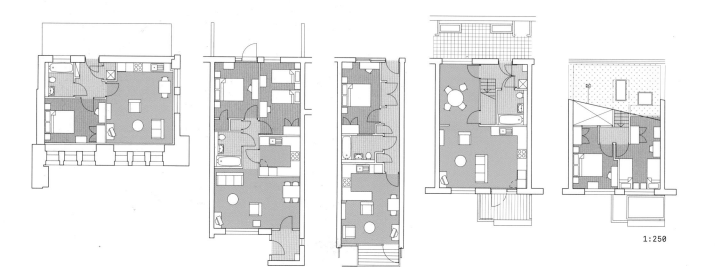

1:250

Top Shared rear courtyard
Below 'Green wall' on the north
side of access galleries to avoid
overlooking adjoining properties.

**Left and right** Weekend family house, Wiltshire, completed in 1964. The brief for this small house on a steeply sloping rural site was that it should be maintenance-free. The design was based on a single roof plane parallel to the slope of the land, with deep overhangs all the way round so that all rainwater was thrown clear of the external walls. The timber roof fascia is clad in zinc with an Eternit slate roof through which nothing projects. The external surfaces are either hard burnt brick, glass or unpainted Douglas fir. To date none of these surfaces has needed any maintenance, a record that can be attributed to the roof details and especially the overhangs on all four sides.

Architects are inventive people. When they embark on a new project they feel they have not given their best unless they can work a degree of originality into the design, believing that they will principally be judged on their ability to innovate. And the innovations can be about big things like planning, or small things like the materials used, or the way the parts of the building fit together.

Repeating what has been done before seldom wins awards. However, repetition of what has been done before, over and over again, is all around us, and much of it is based on tired and unimaginative thinking that does not meet the challenges of today, let alone the future. Small wonder that imaginative designers feel a strong impulse to strike out in new directions.

Housing can fail in a number of different ways. At its extremes it fails either because it was misconceived in the first place or because it was built in a way that made it unsustainable in the long term.
This chapter is not about individually commissioned, privately owned bespoke houses, many of which have lasted hundreds of years already and look set to last hundreds more. In the best of these the design of

the interior in every detail mirrors the architecture of the whole building. Examples of eighteenth- and nineteenth-century houses can be found in which the principal rooms with their plasterwork, joinery and fire surrounds are as timeless as the exteriors. Of course there are well-designed housing developments that continue to function satisfactorily after 60 or more years, even if they now need to be adapted to meet the impact of climate change or changes in household demography. But only exceptionally is internal design integrated with the overall architecture in the same way.

These examples of housing, especially flats and particularly the differences between one tenure and another, are worth studying as they contain lessons for architects, showing that good design is about applying good design judgement, understanding the building process and not making unrealistic assumptions about the end-user.

Fundamentally, buildings which in other respects fulfil their function satisfactorily can still ultimately fail in one or all of three ways: impractical detailing leading to water or damp penetration; poorly planned mechanical services; and failure to understand the expectations of the end-user.

At this point many architects engaged in the conceptual stages of housing design will protest that ultimate responsibility for keeping the rain out or making sure the pipes and wires can be maintained easily is often beyond their control; by the time that stage of design work is reached they have been replaced by another design team, often appointed by the contractor, which does not have the long-term interests of the building as its principal objective.

## The three causes of failure

**Detailing** Architects regard innovative detailing, the choice of materials and the ways they are used as important parts of their role as designers, but always and inevitably with an emphasis on their visual impact. In a conventional full-service contract the builder usually defers to the architect and, in doing so, ensures that he is responsible only for the quality of workmanship, not for the details themselves. Under a design/build method of procurement, it is the contractor who will make the ultimate decision over important details; the emphasis is more likely to be on economy and much less on visual impact.

This tension has roots going back at least to the nineteenth century, perhaps to the end of the Arts and Crafts movement, before

which the architect would produce typical details and the builder would then draw and apply them to every condition. Then, in the early days of the Modern Movement, experimentation in the use of new materials was led by the architect, with the contractor largely abdicating responsibility. If, for instance, the architect and the engineer between them specified a 150-mm solid fairfaced, painted reinforced-concrete external wall, all the contractor had to do was to make sure it was built as drawn, regardless of any problems that might develop later.

Over time this division has become more pronounced. Left on their own, builder/developers always repeat what has been built before. The details they employ are safe, conventional, usually bland and rely heavily on manufacturers' proprietary solutions. Failures are rare, but when they do occur they usually result from the selection of cheap materials. By contrast, architects of bespoke designs almost of necessity take an unconventional approach to external detailing, rather than tried and tested alternatives. Naturally, the plaudits, when they come, are earned for the immediate response they receive from their peers, the technical press and their clients, often in that

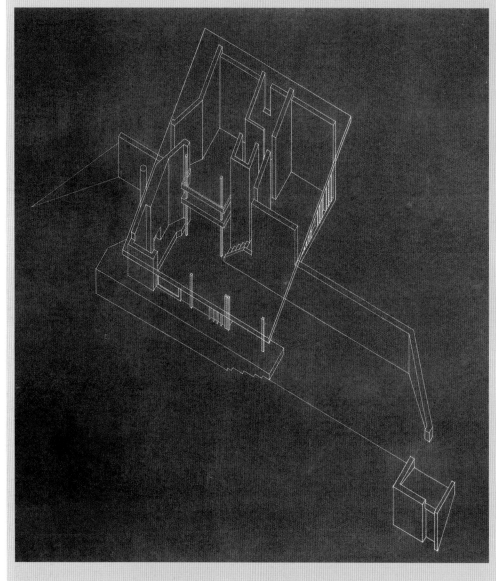

Weekend family house, Wiltshire, axonometric.

order of significance. Few architects base their reputations on the staying power of schemes they designed five, ten, or twenty years earlier, and they are encouraged by the attitude of many of their patrons, whose concerns for cost in use are strangely unscientific.

**The mechanical services dilemma** Apart from the interest generated by the impact of climate change on the field of mechanical engineering, the whole approach to its design in housing is curiously old-fashioned, given its over-riding importance to the function of 'home' in the twenty-first century. The way advice is obtained at the design stage is not encouraging, often a result of the client's desire to get design services cheaply by not employing an independent consultant engineer. Instead, the client relies on a 'free' service from a sub-contractor, usually only appointed when the building design has reached a relatively advanced stage.

In some building types – retail and offices come to mind – the routing of services and their replacement when they reach the end of their life can take place as part of each periodical refit, but in housing this is just not a practical option. Dismantling a large proportion of the interior of flats and houses in order to reach and replace the services can only be achieved by persuading the occupants to live somewhere else for the duration of the work, not a very likely scenario for those in social housing. At an early stage designers need advice on the optimum vertical and horizontal routes, combined with a strategy for replacing them – planned obsolescence – as they reach the end of their lives.

**Understanding the expectations and habits of the consumer** On the whole we (the collective we, not just architects) don't pay enough attention to the lifestyles of the people we design for, making some things over-robust and others not robust enough, hardly ever being encouraged to revisit the homes we design after 15 years of occupation to see whether the assumptions that were made in terms of design priorities were justified.

A perennial problem for 'developers' of housing designed for rent is that they don't know how the homes they produce are going to be treated by successive generations of tenants. Experience shows that if the design and fit-out is tough and basic there will be a reaction from tenants expecting something more sensitive – but these examples are likely to be far outnumbered by social landlords who have had to pick up the bill for flats and houses that have been used very harshly. In order to design responsibly it is important to know, for instance, whether bathrooms, showers and kitchens that sit on timber floors and are surrounded by lightweight partitioning can withstand the ill effects of careless use. These can be so fundamental that they cannot be remedied simply by the cyclical replacement of fittings.

Certain patterns have emerged from studying records of maintenance and replacement. The average lives of a kitchen, a bathroom and a central-heating system in rented housing have been recorded for years, although it would be interesting to know how the figures for rented housing might compare with owner-occupation or shared ownership of exactly the same standard of accommodation. The current discussion on producing 'tenure-neutral housing' tends to focus around the space requirements of one tenure compared with another, but maybe a robustness factor ought to be in there as well. Car-hire companies rent out the same kind of cars as those sold for personal use: do rented cars have a much shorter life on average?

Questions about the operation of heating and ventilation equipment and the use of housing designed with features to take advantage of passive heat and ventilation are covered in Chapter 17.

# Bradwell Common 2, Milton Keynes

In 1983 Milton Keynes Development Corporation completed three schemes that were similar in size, density and brief by well-known and highly respected architects: at Oldbrook by Colquhoun and Miller, at Bradwell Common by Edward Cullinan Architects and at Heelands by MacCormac, Jamieson and Prichard.

Although all were built without public consultation or participation they reflect the change then coming over the design of publicly funded housing, in strong contrast to the preceding 25 years of unrelenting Modernism. Choosing Bradwell 2 to illustrate the thought processes involved in designing with cost in use in mind does not imply that Oldbrook or Heelands were designed without taking this factor into account. Indeed, it is quite possible that the good sense employed by the designers at Bradwell was simply the result of working with an intuitive architectural language of frequently used details, which they employed to great effect in the massing and assembly of forms. In his critique of the three schemes (*The Architects' Journal*, 9 February 1983) Roger Stonehouse commented that 'there is no attempt to apply an arbitrary measure of complexity or ambiguity to make the forms artificially interesting, as is the present architectural trend in housing'.

How well has it survived? To answer this question you need to separate the design and what it has achieved from the management regime and what that is, in broad terms, not achieving.

Although Bradwell Common is still owned by the local authority, the Thatcher government's 'right to buy' legislation has ameliorated what would otherwise, by now, be homogenous 100 per cent occupancy by tenants on very low incomes. In most cases it is possible to pick out the houses that are owned rather than being rented, but the distinction is less marked than one might expect – many owners struggle to fund their mortgages, let alone pay for new fences at the back of their gardens. And of course it is highly likely that some houses are owned by private individuals who choose to live elsewhere, preferring to be irresponsible private landlords. The result is a public realm that is poorly maintained but just about survives. There are no boarded-up empty houses, no burnt-out or abandoned cars, and people do move to the Bradwell Common estate out of choice.

If challenged about why more effort and resources are not put into the maintenance of the public realm, and particularly the four potentially beautiful shared greens, the local authority would no doubt plead poverty resulting from the need to keep tenants' service charges affordable. But this would be an excuse rather than an attempt to find a solution, and it is not the purpose of this short critique to explore the future management of social housing.

What does stand out is the survival of the design, the architecture of the housing itself and the ideas behind the layout.

Basically, the whole scheme consists of simple timber-framed forms with shallow, front to back, concrete-tiled and pitched roofs with deep overhung eaves, elegantly rationalised rainwater downpipes, and timber-clad upper floors above a facing-brick lowest storey. The houses, mostly two-storey, face a simple grid of streets so that their private rear gardens open on to one of the four landscaped greens. The design is robust enough to withstand the inevitable replacement by the local authority of every window and doorframe using uPVC, and even the impact of tacky uPVC screens erected to enclose some of the original recessed front porches is reduced by the sheer variety of simple massing alternatives offered by the many single-storey lean-to roofs that project from almost every house, front and back.

The original choice of external materials – brick and timber – obviously had a lot to do with cost, but the brickwork to the houses as well as the robust perimeter brick walls defining the front curtilage of houses are surviving well. Even the timber cladding shows little sign of disintegration after 25 years, although what the current management regime may eventually replace it with induces a shudder.

**Architect** Edward Cullinan Architects
**Developer** Milton Keynes Development Corporation
**Site** 3.41 hectares
**Number of dwellings** 158
**Density** 46.3 dwellings/hectare
**Mix** 16 x 1B + 24 x 2B + 110 x 3B + 8 x 4B
**Affordable** initially 100 per cent
**Parking spaces per dwelling** 2

Rear view of houses around one
of the four communal greens.
Simple roof plans and details
have allowed these timber-framed
and timber-clad houses to weather
well in spite of insensitive uPVC
window replacements.

However, the lack of investment is most evident in things like the wooden fencing to the gardens leading out on to the green spaces, by now broken down. A collective effort of will is needed to renew it all in a uniform way.

Designing shared spaces at the rear of private gardens went out of fashion on security grounds in the 1980s, and the combination of lush vegetation and alleyways could almost have been designed as escape routes for burglars. But at Bradwell Common the overwhelming argument for creating such spaces can be seen. It's a green and peaceful environment and, properly managed, a good and safe place for children to grow up in. The simple forms, architectural vocabulary, and practical detailing of all the housing is an object lesson in designing with 'cost-in-use' in mind.

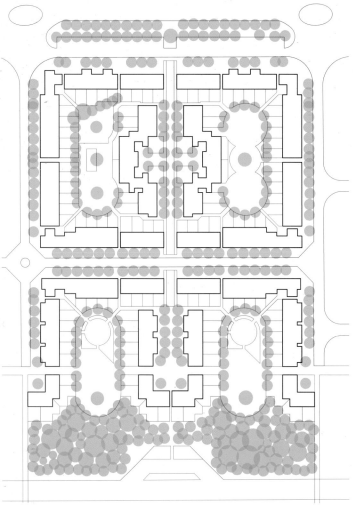

1:2500

Above Layout plan. A simple grid of streets lined with two- and three-storey terraces along the street frontages. Rather than lay the houses out with their gardens back to back they enclose four greens to which the houses have access via gates at the ends of their gardens. At the southern end a bund has been formed with intensive planting to eliminate noise from a main distributor road. Inevitably there are problems, not only with the upkeep of these spaces and the mature planting in them, but also the generosity of provision is fertile territory for some anti-social behaviour.
Right However, as the photographs show, the houses themselves, including a small number of flats, are standing up well.

Santa Monica, Los Angeles, California. An apartment block incorporating PV panels as external cladding on the south-facing elevation as part of the architecture.

### Designing with zero energy in mind

All new housing must be 'carbon neutral' by 2016 but so far developers and the buying public have shown little enthusiasm for paying the extra costs involved or accepting a different approach to design. Although the target of achieving carbon neutrality is clear and unequivocal, the means of achieving it are constantly changing, as measures that were thought to be impossibly uneconomic only a very few years ago suddenly become necessities. The problem for designers is to produce design solutions for homes that have to be adaptable enough – future proofed – to accommodate the changes that are bound to occur between now and 2016, and beyond. This is not made any easier by the technical experts and manufacturers, among whom there is only a certain measure of agreement on the best ways forward.

**Reducing the demand for heat** Fortunately, there are several absolute priorities on which practically everyone agrees – all new homes must be superinsulated to PassivHaus standards or the point at which, in combination with airtightness and whole-house ventilation with heat recovery, there is virtually no need for space heating of any

kind. At this point the heat produced from domestic appliances, lighting, computers, plasma TVs, etc., makes a significant contribution to meeting demand.

By combining these three factors the actual space-heating requirement is reduced to a minimum (and is delivered most efficiently by underfloor heating). However, achieving it has a considerable impact on the thickness of external walls and roofs and the amount of glazing, as the table opposite shows.

Comparing PassivHaus standards with The Code for Sustainable Homes' level 5 using the Energy Savings Trust's recommended U-values (walls an roofs 0.15; roofs 0.13; windows 1.3), Code level 5 standard is still not as high as the German PassivHaus standard, which requires 0.1 or better for all elements apart from windows (U-value of 1). The same goes for airtightness (UK Energy Savings Trust recommend 3:1 or better compared with PassivHaus 0.5:1). Effectively, this means that in the UK we aspire to achieve the PassivHaus standard, when in effect even the highest Code level would not perform as well as its German equivalent. Apart from some small differences in climate

## U-values and wall thicknesses

| | Building Regulations | Code level 3 | Code level 4 | Code level 5/6 |
|---|---|---|---|---|
| U-values | Maximum U-values walls 0.35 exposed floors 0.25 roofs 0.25 windows 2.2 external doors 2.2 | Maximum U-values[1] walls 0.25 exposed floors 0.20 roofs 0.13 windows 1.5 + BFRC C rating external doors 1.5 (glazed); 1(solid) | Maximum U-values[1] walls 0.20 exposed floors 0.20 roofs 0.13 windows 1.4 + BFRC B rating external doors 1.5 (glazed); 1(solid) | Maximum U-values walls 0.15 exposed floors 0.15 roofs 0.13 windows 1.3 + BFRC A rating external doors 1.5 (glazed); 1(solid) |
| External wall thickness brick/140mm concrete blockwork EPS insulation – value 0.035 | min. 335mm (min. 80mm EPS) | min. 375mm (min. 120mm EPS) | min. 405mm (min. 150mm EPS) | min. 465mm (min. 210mm EPS) |
| External wall thickness 100mm metal stud cladding or render + EPS insulation – value 0.035) | min. 215mm (min. 90mm EPS) | min. 255mm (min. 130mm EPS) | min. 295mm (min. 170mm EPS) | min. 345mm (min. 220mm EPS) |

[1] EST recommended

between the two countries, it is unclear why this should be and why the Code currently allows UK developers to meet level 5 or even level 6, supposedly 'zero carbon', when effectively the heat demand could be reduced still further.

**Energy from sustainable sources** As the superinsulation standard increases, the demand for electrical energy to assist in the provision of renewable heat becomes secondary to the demand for power to drive domestic electrical equipment. Nevertheless, with solutions for sources of renewable heat rapidly evolving, virtually all – including heat pumps and solar panels – need electrical input of some kind. Only solar space heating through a conservatory or sunspace or heat supplied from burning biomass in either an individual or a central boiler are truly carbon neutral. In any case, solar space heating is less useful as the thermal performance of a dwelling increases. The body heat of one person working from home is greater than the solar gain of a 2-square-metre window facing south throughout the year.

For water heating, solar panels can provide about 50 per cent of the average requirement

and biomass can provide the remainder – if the source of biomass is genuinely sustainable. While it would be possible to increase the capacity of solar panels to satisfy 100 per cent of the winter demand for hot water and space heating, this would require a giant array on the outside of the building, with significant cost implications, and would also mean excessive provision in summer temperatures. Most solar collectors are sized to provide 60–70 per cent of hot water demand with nothing left over for space heating. The water comes out of these arrays at >90 degrees C in the summer and at around 40 degrees C in the winter. In winter, water heated to 40 degrees C needs to be heated to 60 degrees C on a fairly regular basis to stop the *Legionella* bacterium building up.

Any solar thermal system must have a heat store and a capacity of 250 litres works well for dwellings. For a thermal store to be of sufficient capacity all the year round it would have to be very large and therefore not cost-effective.

Part of the issue is balancing the optimum angle at which panels are mounted for summer, spring and autumn with the steeper angles needed to get any kind of benefit in winter, which is why installers tend to use optimum angles for autumn and spring. In a combined underfloor and space-heating system, the underfloor component would probably only be augmented during spring and autumn, leaving most winter requirements to be met from elsewhere.

In energy terms the next step towards achieving zero-carbon homes therefore involves electricity, and here the situation is shifting rapidly. On the assumption that most sites are unsuitable for small-scale wind turbines able to meet total domestic demand, Combined Heat and Power (CHP) fuelled from a sustainable source, such as biomass, together with photovoltaic cells, is the most obvious solution. From large central systems serving whole neighbourhoods down to individual domestic installations, the scale and practicality of CHP is changing too frequently to be prescriptive here, as is the availability of biomass as a source of energy, but it seems unlikely that 100 per cent of electrical need will be supplied from photovoltaics for some time. As densities increase there is simply not enough roof area on blocks of flats to support an effective PV array. There are already examples of flats where the external, south-facing cladding is composed of PV panels. However, installing PVs vertically and facing south reduces their efficiency by 30 per cent compared to a south-facing pitched PV roof.

Grid electricity is more then twice as energy intensive ($0.43$ kg $CO_2$/kWh) as gas from the grid ($0.19$ kg $CO_2$/kWh). This means, for example, that heat from electrical radiators, when the power is supplied from the grid, is more than twice as polluting as standard radiators supplied by gas from the grid.

As long as the source of electrical power is free from $CO_2$ emissions – which, apart from nuclear energy, means supply from renewable sources – other options for generating low-temperature heat such as heat recovery, air-to-air or ground-sourced heat pumps, both significant consumers of electricity, become environmentally viable and preferred over gas sources.

## Off-site manufacture and achieving zero energy

For ten years designers and the construction industry have been experimenting with ways of reducing site time, overcoming labour shortages, improving supply-chain management, eliminating waste, improving the quality of finishes and tackling airtightness, through 'off-site' manufacture. No single technique has emerged that satisfies every situation but this section revisits several of them to see how they are standing up to wear.

Over the previous 60 years architects had been fascinated by the prospect of rolling out homes from a factory. The perennial problems have always been those of design standardisation and repetition and the need to guarantee sufficient quantities of the same product to get the cost down to affordable levels. Efforts to produce a range of standard house and flat types, applicable to many different locations in order to guarantee continuity of production, have not to date been successful. In contrast, there have been more successful hotel- and student-accommodation programmes or breakthroughs in the manufacture of completely fitted-out bathroom 'pods'. If off-site manufacture were to succeed, the volume housebuilders' ranges of loose-fit, low-density house types would surely be involved in the breakthrough.

Although an element of prefabrication is potentially a real answer in low-energy design, there is a limit to how far it can be taken. Taking as an example a development of houses on a tight urban site, the prefabrication of whole houses might actually result in lower environmental standards, simply because over-standardisation loses the opportunities offered by working within a particular site context and these are essential to low-energy design. For example, a living room should have different window openings and proportions depending on which direction it faces or where other buildings obstruct access to sunlight on particular parts of a site.

Prefabrication by volume builders has not yet happened on any scale. Nevertheless, slowly, almost imperceptibly, the manufacture of

Houses at Freiburg, Germany. The entire roof surface is made up of PV panels; these produce a considerable surplus of electrical power and have a capital payback period of only six years.

larger and more complex components off site is becoming commercially viable through the manufacture of bathroom 'pods', complete external wall panels and sometimes kitchens. By imposing few limitations on overall design flexibility, it is beginning to make commercial sense to prefabricate these labour-intensive components under factory conditions.

Ignoring for a moment the different materials used, off-site prefabrication falls into two categories: 'volumetric' and 'flat-pack' construction.

**Volumetric** manufacture exists in several different forms, employing either steel or timber as the basic structural material. As a system its most obvious advantage is the ability to supply completely fitted-out modules including all fittings, services and fixtures in sealed units, with very short on-site construction times. Its most obvious disadvantage is that, although there is little limitation on the maximum length of rooms, normal transport regulations mean that the internal width can be no more than 3.3 metres. Costs tend to be a shade higher than conventional construction but can be less overall if the time on site is taken fully into consideration. Possible storey heights become progressively more ambitious both for timber and steel but six storeys for timber and up to eight for steel is a reasonable rule of thumb.

**Flat-pack** construction using concrete, steel or timber is more versatile and less costly than volumetric. There is virtually no constraint on room sizes beyond the normal limitations of floor spans, and the labour needed on site in constructing wall panels, complete with windows and doors, and floors and roofs is considerably reduced.

In general terms, there are three alternative structural materials suitable for the off-site manufacture of housing: precast concrete, lightweight steel, and timber frame.

**Precast concrete** is probably the most challenging in terms of cost; economical precasting requires extensive repetition due to the investment required to make moulds, usually from steel. Concrete is a material that contains a significant amount of embodied energy due to the manufacturing process for Portland cement. Recent research has shown that concrete foundations are the biggest embodied-energy element of any new house; the more ecologically built the house, the higher is the embodied-energy proportion of the concrete foundations.

But concrete does have one distinct advantage over other off-site methods in environmental terms. Provided the concrete is kept on the inside of the external wall system, with the insulation and whatever is the preferred cladding on the outside, it acts as a thermal store, absorbing heat when the internal temperature rises and discharging stored heat when the building would otherwise be cooling down. Concrete walls and floors are ideal for houses and flats designed to absorb as much passive solar heat as possible by means of a sunspace or conservatory and this is an increasingly important factor as we move towards zero carbon for all new housing. Looking at long-term sustainability, it is inadvisable to introduce either electric or plumbing services into precast concrete wall and floor panels as they have invariably proved impossible to replace, even when run in conduit. This places limitations on lighting positions, switch drops and later adaptations/replacements, etc.

**Lightweight steel frame** There are several lightweight structural-steel-frame systems, all based on similar principles, some of which have been in use for up to ten years. The production method takes CAD data and fabricates rolled structural sections from thin (0.8–2.4mm) galvanised-steel strip, welded into rigid frames, some of which are then pre-insulated using rigid foam. Most applications to date use prefabricated wall panels to replace the traditional load-bearing inner skin of cavity-wall construction, assuming some form of masonry external skin or other rain screen.

Although the thermal properties of this type of lightweight steel construction are good and can be enhanced to achieve the highest required standard, there is very little thermal mass in either steel or timber construction and if passive solar gain is a built-in feature of the design high daytime internal temperature peaks can be expected in summer. Problems over interstitial condensation affecting lightweight steel frames have been reported from Canada; these echo the problems with Airey steel frames experienced in the UK after World War 2.

**Timber frame** Of the three most common structural materials, timber is the most frequently used, the cheapest and the most suitable for medium to small degrees of repetition. As with lightweight-steel frame panels, timber-frame wall panels, consisting of vertical studs with horizontal wall and sole plates braced on one face with a rigid OSB board, can be fabricated from CAD data, although obviously not in such an automated way. In their most common form, timber-frame panels are engineered to replace the inner load-bearing skin of a traditional cavity wall. Insulation fills the cavities within the thickness of the timber-frame panel and there is usually an inner lining of plasterboard. Since it has to be kept dry and free from condensation, the outer, boarded face has to be covered with an absolutely intact layer of breather membrane to which ties can be attached. These are then built into a masonry external skin or some form of lightweight cladding such as timber.

Allowance has to be made for timber frames to shrink after erection on site. If the building rises to five or even six floors the cumulative amount of shrinkage can be considerable; details have to allow it to take place without allowing any masonry external materials suddenly to become load-bearing. Of all the materials used in off-site manufacture, timber is the most receptive to the installation of electrical and plumbing services within the structure and to their replacement when they are worn out or obsolete.

## Making the most of passive solar
Obviously, all windows orientated anywhere in the sun's path will contribute towards solar gain inside a building, but only when the sun is out. The larger the glazed area the more temperatures rise when the sun shines – with the likelihood of too much heat gain – and fall when there is no sun at all and large glazed

areas are then contributing to overall heat loss. While external shading can be designed to reduce unwanted heat gain there is no useful means of capturing heat for use when temperatures drop.

Taking advantage of passive solar gain and capturing some of the heat is just one of many measures necessary to combat climate change, achieved via an unheated sunspace. Because they demand an understanding of how they can be used to best effect by the householder, opinions on their universal effectiveness and the measures needed to deal with overheating in summer are divided. To take full advantage, doors between inner living spaces and any kind of sunspace must remain closed when the sunspace temperatures are lower than the inside temperature and there is no sun, and opened only when the air temperature in the sunspace rises above that of the rest of the house. Heat gain through passive solar works most effectively in tandem with structures that have high thermal mass, absorbing solar energy when available for slow release when it is not, but high thermal mass does not feature strongly in many of the construction methods now being employed. Unwanted heat build-up in summer has to be reduced by a combination of external shading and passive ventilation.

We do build potentially thermally massive structures (inner concrete block and concrete floor slabs for example), but negate their effectiveness by covering them with plasterboard or suspended ceilings, immediately cancelling out the potential of thermal mass. Looking at the Energy Savings Trust's recommended U-values for masonry external walls for Code level 5 and 6 dwellings, the wall thickness goes up to at least 465mm, as opposed to 345mm for a metal-frame wall or 335mm for current Building Regulations. Building to PassivHaus standards with 0.1 U-values increases the thickness to at least 515mm.

## Using less water
As with renewable energy, the first steps towards using less water are relatively simple and inexpensive but become progressively

more expensive as we move towards the eventual goal of 80 litres per day, the government target, by 2016.

The first steps, changing to water-saving fittings, have an impact on specification but not on design. They are followed by arrangements for the storage of rainwater, usually underground, for use in flushing toilets, watering gardens and washing cars. Beyond that point further savings are only made by installing separate drainage for the waste water from baths and showers ('grey water'), as distinct from foul drainage ('black water'), so that this water can be processed and recycled for general domestic use, excluding washing and anything to do with washing. There are compact devices already on the market for capturing water from showers, basins and baths to flush WCs, with localised technology installed in each bathroom.

## Managing waste

There are two main strands to the issue of waste and buildings; waste during construction and eventual demolition, and the disposal of household waste during a building's lifecycle.

Reducing or eliminating waste during construction is a growing discipline but one which is extremely difficult to achieve. It should go without saying that, as housing forms the largest part of the national building programme, its importance as a source of waste should not be underestimated. Construction of properties in the UK produces 70 million tonnes of waste per annum – 17 per cent of the UK total – and the UK also produces 30 million tonnes of demolition building waste each year. As a general principle, off-site manufacture reduces the generation of waste. Otherwise there is little that can be done at the design stage to reduce waste during construction, which is down to the organisational skills of individual contractors. Again generally speaking, the less room there is on site for storage the greater the wastage through damage to unfixed materials. New regulations require all projects to have 'site waste-management plans' prepared for them.

Current strategies for reducing all kinds of domestic waste stem from climate change and the need to make drastic reductions in $CO_2$ emissions from landfill. Separating waste at source is much more efficient than bulk containerisation and the most basic approach to recycling involves separating dry from residual waste. More common than these two streams is the adoption of three: organics, dry waste and residuals, with separate storage for glass and hazardous items such as batteries.

The separation of domestic waste for recycling is having a considerable effect on planning the interior and exterior layouts of both houses and flats. Within the home it means having a single gathering point, usually in the kitchen. If built into the kitchen, separating waste at source internally usually involves compartmented below-worktop storage space: 1 x 600 mm floor units. More importantly, it involves much more storage outside the dwelling – that is, three bins of 60 litres internally – and a response to whatever system of collection is applied by the local authority, some of which have doorstep collections while others rely on householders depositing all their recyclables in Eurobins on the street. Much more centralised systems for collecting and storing rubbish are bound to follow, especially for new large-scale high-density schemes that have been provided with major infrastructure, such as the underground vacuum system at Hammarby in Stockholm (see pages 268–271).

All schemes for multi-storey flats must be provided with a store for bulky refuse (beds and mattresses are usually the largest objects) as well as separate spaces for the number of bins needed for different categories of recycling. These have to be provided inside the secure zone of the common circulation.

# Solarsiedlung, Freiburg, Germany

For a visitor from the UK the immediate impression of this development is such that it is difficult to understand why such a clearly stated demonstration, beautifully designed and engineered, is not being rolled out across every town and city in Europe.

It consists of 50 south-facing two- and three-storey houses in short terraces laid out on a 1.1-hectare site. The site is shielded from the main road by a three-storey building accommodating 5500 square metres of retail, commercial and office space, on top of which are nine two-storey apartments in pairs, very similar in form to the houses themselves.

The residential construction is modular timber frame, clad externally in stained timber and with triple-glazed windows. As the houses have south orientation the south elevations are almost entirely glazed and have a small external garden/patio. The roofs above have a deep overhang that is designed to cut out overheating in summer but to allow passive solar gain in winter.

The south-facing slope that accounts for about two-thirds of the total roof area is not merely covered with PV panels because these PV panels are the roof itself. They generate a considerable surplus of electrical energy, which is sold back into the local grid on a tariff that exceeds the price at which it is normally purchased. These houses are not simply zero energy – they are surplus energy, producing more than they use. While the householders obviously do consume energy, the net production of solar electrical power exceeds the net consumption of all energy. The actual surplus of an average house is 36kWh per square metre per year. The incentive to install PVs for individual house owners is an additional income stream that can repay the original capital investment in approximately six years.

To quote the architect: 'The investment (excluding the PV) is about 10 to 15 per cent higher than the same house would cost if built in accordance with current compulsory EnEV standards. For the average Solarsiedlung house, heating costs are about 150€ a year, as opposed to an estimated 3000€ a year for a conventional house.

This difference of 2850€ finances the extra investment. As for the extra capital investment for the PV itself, there is a subsidised credit from a state bank and after six years this investment is paid off. There is a feed-in guarantee over 20 years so that after the first six years the PV is adding to the household income. For an average house this would be about 3000€.'

Along the rear, north-facing wall of the latest houses are two core modules placed one above the other. These 'Power Boxes' contain the kitchen and bathroom, services control room, staircase, entrance lobby, cloakroom, utility room and downstairs WC – virtually all the complex parts of the house, which have been fitted out in the factory.

There are no affordable tenancies in this scheme. In the UK context it requires a degree of imagination to think of these houses, which embody a considerable additional investment in renewables, being occupied by affordable tenants without a strong commitment and interest on the part of the tenants and a great deal of support from their landlord. However, as the Solarsiedlung architect points out, predicted rises in energy costs suggest that this kind of prototype points the way for affordable housing in the very near future.

**Architect** Architekturbüro Rolf Disch
**Developer** Solarsiedlung GmbH
**Site** 1.1 hectares
**Number** of dwellings 59
**Density** 53 dwellings/hectare
**Mix** variable between 2, 3 and 4 bedrooms
**Affordable** none
**Parking spaces per dwelling** 0.4 + car club and remote multi-storey
**Non-housing uses** retail and commercial, 5500 square metres

l house and apartment roofs clad
th PV panels face due south. The
uth-facing elevation treatment
d the roof overhang are designed
r passive solar gain. In the
ckground is the three-storey
arrier' block of commercial and
tail fronting the main road with
row of two-storey maisonettes at
of level reached by a pair of
ft and stair cores.

1:1000

**Above** Solarsiedlung masterplan
showing plans of south-facing
houses, flats and maisonettes
together with the commercial
barrier block along the main road
frontage.

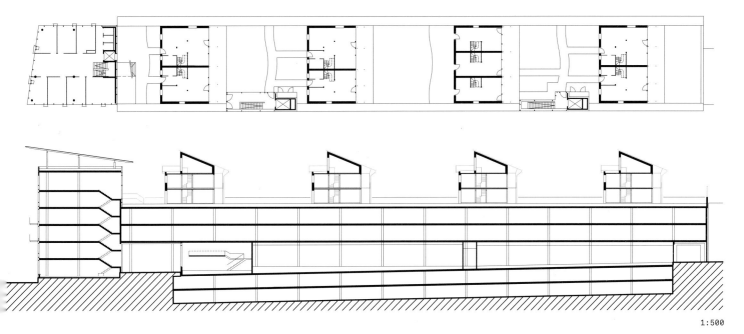

1:500

Above Plans and section of Solar
Ship.
Right Plans of two typical terrace
houses.

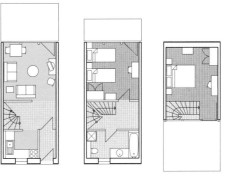

1:250

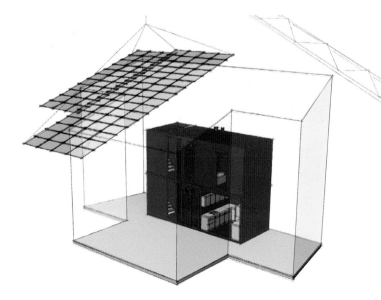

**Above** Rooftop view of the houses
from the south showing the huge
area of PV panels.
**Right** Diagram shower the volumetric
'Power Boxes' containing all the
mechanical components of the
houses.

**Top left** Houses from the rear.
With all houses facing south it
is inevitable that each has its
principal windows facing the rear
elevation of the house in front.
**Above** West elevation.
**Top right** The PV-panel roof viewed
from below.
**Left** View of apartments.
**Bottom right** Principal living room.

The designers and manufacturers of the Lighthouse claim that it is the UK's first net zero-carbon house that also meets the Code for Sustainable Homes level 6, the standard to which all new homes must be constructed by 2016. It is designed to encourage lifestyles that are inherently 'light' on the world's resources, balancing the practical needs of homeowners with a response to the climate change expected in the UK.

The project is the result of long-term collaboration between the developer Kingspan, architect Sheppard Robson, engineer Arup, construction consultant Davis Langdon and landscape architect McFarlane Wilder. The prototype was constructed at the Building Research Establishment in Watford in June 2008 and will remain on the site for four years while the building's performance is monitored.

The design and construction of the house proves that a carbon-free house is achievable but it places responsibility on both the technologies and the user. It is a living experience that relies on occupants adapting their lifestyles.

## Design
The heart of the design concept for the Lighthouse, the prototype of which is a 93-square-metre, two-and-a-half-storey two-bedroom house, is an ambition to create homes that are attractive, adaptable spaces designed for modern living, intuitively integrating sustainability. The environmental systems and construction methods should not compromise the quality of the occupant's life but add to it. It has also been designed in line with Lifetime Homes standards.

**Structure** The Lighthouse has a simple barnlike form, derived from a 40-degree roof accommodating a PV array. The sweeping roof envelops the central space – a generous, open-plan, top-lit, double-height living area, with the sleeping accommodation at ground level. The living space uses a timber-portal structure so floors can be slotted between the frames or left open.

Stability is achieved through the moment connections at first-floor and ceiling level. At ground level a timber-frame structural layout carries the vertical loads of the open-plan frames above and provides stability to the load-bearing shear walls. It is constructed using Kingspan Off-Site's TEK Building System, a high-performance SIPS (structurally insulated panel-based system) that provides high levels of thermal insulation and performance – U-values of $0.11W/m^2K$ and air-tightness of less than $1.0m^3/hr/m^2$ at 50Pa – potentially reducing the heat loss of a standard house by two-thirds.

The foundations are offsite timber floor cassettes on a ring beam of timber beams supported off the ground level by screw-fast pile heads. The piles involve minimal disturbance to the ground and provide suitable supports for domestic-scale dwellings. When the building reaches the end of its useful lifespan, the fast foundation support point can be removed.

## Technical design
The design of the Lighthouse embodies a response to predicted increases in temperature due to climate change, achieved through a combination of design techniques and systems.

**Solar gain and shading** At level 6 there is a mandatory heat-loss parameter that demands high U-values for the building fabric – 0.8 watts/$m^2K$ for the windows and 0.11 watts/$m^2K$ for the walls. As a result the ratio of glazing to wall in the Lighthouse is 18 per cent rather than the 25–30 per cent of traditional houses. This drove the decision to locate the living space on the first floor, enabling daylight and volume to be maximised with a top-lit double-height living space. Shading to the west elevation is provided by retractable shutters restricting direct sunlight and minimising heat gain in summer. Although future temperatures in the UK may reach levels similar to southern Europe, the sun angle will remain low.

**Selective thermal mass** Phase-changing material in ceilings absorbs the room heat by changing from solid to liquid within microscopic capsules embedded in the board. This process is reversed when the room is cooled with night air, working with the passive system of the wind-catcher.

**Architect** Sheppard Robson
**Developer** Kingspan

Right Prototype of the Lighthouse exhibited at the BRE in Watford.

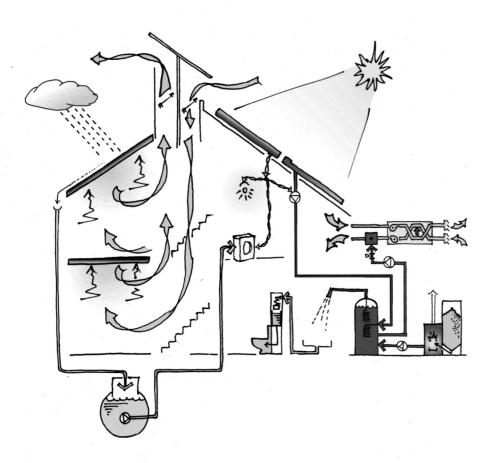

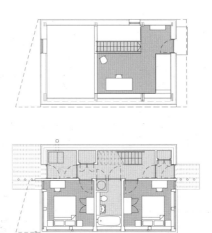

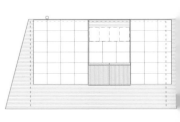

**Above** Diagram illustrating all
sustainability measures to achieve
a Code level 6, zero-carbon house.
**Right** Floor plans indicating the
timber-frame system.

1:250

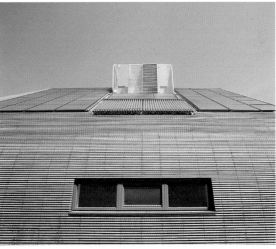

The prototype house showing
internal and external details,
including the glulam principal
structure.

Developer Urban Splash, with ShedKM as its architect, set out its proposals for the Britannia Basin site in Castlefield in line with the recommendations of Sir John Egan's report on rationalising the construction process. The scheme consists of 102 apartments in various sizes and types. These are based on a modular steel-framed, factory-produced, prefabricated residential unit. With a series of additional clip-on components including balconies, dining pods and a further bedroom, they provide high-quality compact accommodation for outright sale and rent.

The scheme forms part of a second phase of a development by Urban Splash, extending the regeneration of the Britannia Basin area, offering further types of accommodation in addition to those already provided by the earlier Timber Wharf and the Box Works. The proposals for Moho (modular housing) work within the overall masterplan for an area that includes Timber Wharf, also by Urban Splash with Glen Howells as architect, based around a new pedestrian street. The Moho site forms half of the city block with frontages on the new pedestrian street, Ellesmere Street, and Arundel Street. These all contain new commercial space to activate the street frontages at ground-floor level, below six floors of residential accommodation arranged around a central courtyard.

The plan is based on single-aspect flats with either an east, west or south orientation and views out either on to the street frontages or on to the private internal garden courtyard.

The Ellesmere Street elevation contains the main entrance to the scheme, which allows views from the street into the courtyard, part of which is a raised garden planted with mature trees. This provides space below it for residents' storage and cycles, as well as the ventilation plant for the two levels of basement parking. Access to the flats is either through the garden or the central lift and stair core linking the parking and the entrance to the floors above.

Moho develops the application of prefabrication already successfully used in mixed-tenure housing, and transfers it to the private sector. In most previous applications the units have been arranged with a narrow frontage – a product of the maximum 3.6-metre module width transportable by road without an escort – and deep plans. To create a mixture of accommodation sizes two such units then have to be placed side by side. But by rotating the module through 90 degrees, the window frontage of a room is no longer limited to 3.6 metres and the base module can be extended in length to accommodate an extra bedroom, the governing transportation dimension being the width and not the length.

Once the modules have been installed, stacked on top of each other, an external framework is constructed into which a series of supplementary prefabricated elements is fixed. This louvred framework provides shading from the summer sun, while allowing the lower angle of the winter sun to provide passive solar gain. Balconies, dining pods, louvred screens and balustrades infilling the framework all give a layered appearance to the elevation, adding further diversity to the three basic apartment types: 39 one-bed (38 square metres); 39 one bed plus (42 square metres); and 24 two-bed (54 square metres).

The developer's brief identified the fact that a significant number of city-centre apartments were outside the price range of many first-time purchasers and key workers within the city. Moho was designed to respond to this, building on prototypes such as Murray Grove in the London Borough of Hackney, questioning every aspect of construction and reinterpreting it to provide homes that positively and outwardly celebrate the aesthetic and technology of prefabrication.

Obtaining mortgage finance for modular construction was an obstacle that had to be overcome before the scheme could go ahead, and this was eventually achieved. Construction started in February 2004 and the first units were occupied in April 2005.

**Architect** ShedKM
**Developer** Urban Splash
**Site** 0.219 hectares
**Number of dwellings** 102
**Density** 465 dwellings/hectare
**Mix** 39 x 1B + 39 x 1B plus + 24 x 2
**Affordable** 40 per cent
**Parking spaces per dwelling** 1
**Non-housing uses** ground-floor retail

**Right** External street view.

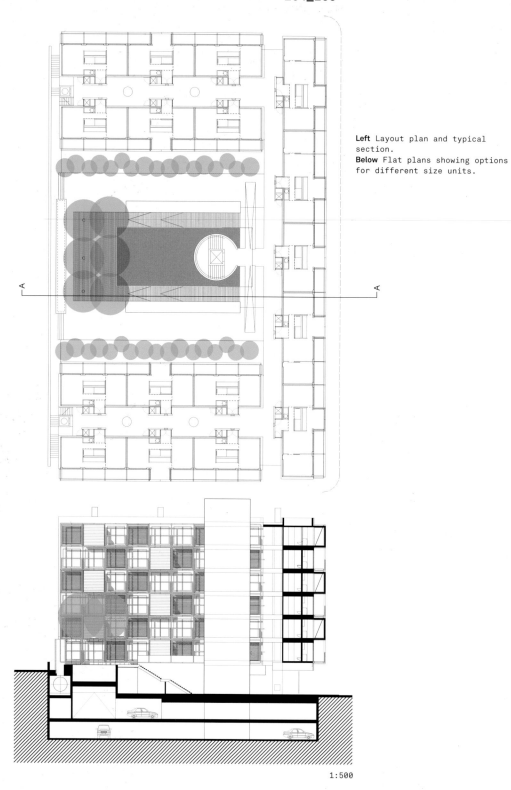

**Left** Layout plan and typical section.
**Below** Flat plans showing options for different size units.

1:500

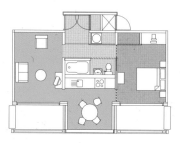

Moho:Moho Flat Types                                    1:250

Top External elevation showing the
self-supporting balcony screen
wall.
Below Construction principles
diagram.
Below right Internal view of
courtyard and circulation core.

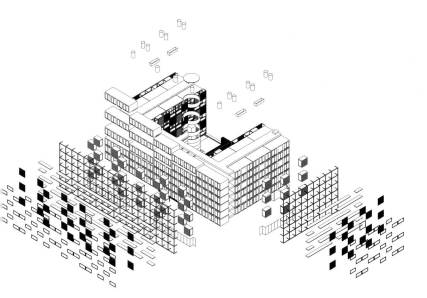

The Oxley Woods development grew out of the UK government's 'Design for Manufacture' competition, launched in 2005 with the aim of getting architects and house builders to collaborate in building high-quality homes at a construction cost of £60,000.

RSHP's response was to develop a generic house type capable of fitting into any location at suburban densities, using modern methods of construction. The combined team claimed two main threads to the design: timber-panel construction, and an energy-saving system they call 'EcoHat'. They settled on a practical way to cut construction costs on site by fabricating timber frames for walls, ceilings and floors in a factory-controlled environment with a high degree of airtightness. Considerable emphasis was placed on using materials from sustainable and managed sources with:
• recycled paper insulation;
• softwood cladding from renewable sources with no wastage;
• no superstructure skips on site;
• no wet construction beyond foundations.

Each house has two distinct zones: a 'service zone' combining bathrooms, utility space, boilers, kitchen and staircase, and a 'living zone' comprising living rooms, bedrooms and dining space.

The house shell was designed to exceed Building Regulations by 20 per cent but the construction team claim to have exceeded that target, achieving:
• airtightness $2.5m^3/(hrm^2)$ (Building Regulations 10);
• thermal insulation 0.22 U-value (Building Regulations 0.35);
• acoustic insulation 75dB (Building Regulations 55).

The EcoHat combines a whole-house filtered ventilation system with solar hot-water heating. Being virtually a stand-alone unit with a solar collector that is small in area, it has the advantage of being able to face south whatever the orientation of the house it is attached to. Attaching a sufficient area of PV panels would not be so easy but there is no intention of installing any form of electricity generation – the developer's aim is for the house to rely on locally generated electricity.

The developer claims that the fabric of the houses enjoy a 27 per cent reduction in $CO_2$ emissions compared with conventional new houses of the same size. With the inclusion of the EcoHat this rises to 40 per cent, and to 50 per cent if the EcoHat is fitted with solar collectors for hot water.

This Wimpey/RSHP system makes an interesting contrast with ZEDfactory's proposals for ruralZED and the completely different approach taken for the houses at Freiburg. Most notably, while ruralZED depends on thermal mass to achieve even temperatures through the summer/ winter cycle, Oxley Woods relies on the whole-house ventilation system. The houses at Freiburg rely on renewable electricity generation together with solar panels for hot water to achieve both heating and cooling.

**Architect** Rogers Stirk Harbour and Partners
**Developer** George Wimpey UK
**Site** 3 hectares
**Number of dwellings** 145
**Density** 48 dwellings/hectare
**Mix** 9 x 1B + 20 x 2B + 76 x 3B + 20 x 3/4B + 14 x 4B + 6 x 5B
**Affordable** 30 per cent
**Parking spaces per dwelling** 2

**Right** Typical view – street elevations.

1:2500

1:250

**Left** Layout plan, a mixture of
detached and terraced houses.
**Above** Two-bedroom house plans.

**Top** Two-bedroom houses in terrace
form.
**Centre** Typical street layout.
**Below left** Larger house type with
car port and room over.
**Below right** Interior views.

# New housing in Bourbon Lane, Shepherds Bush, London W12

This project was the result of an international competition to encourage Anglo-French collaboration and to demonstrate best practice combined with new thinking in the design of affordable housing. The competition was promoted by CABE and won by Cartwright Pickard in partnership with the French practice B+C Architectes. In recognition of the French theme the scheme has been named Bourbon Lane and the four mews are named after French duchies: Burgundy, Gascony, Normandy and Savoy.

The site was a challenging run-down piece of brownfield between the blank four-storey rear wall of the massive new £1 billion retail development at Shepherds Bush, and a mixture of traditional Victorian, Edwardian and later terrace housing, some of it listed. Eight timber-clad blocks rising to five storeys are set at right angles to the rear wall of the shopping centre. The decision to avoid lifts meant it was possible to have a greater number of separate stair cores, each of which serves only two apartments on each floor.

Family dwellings are created by the familiar device of placing one two-storey maisonette above another. Importantly, this allows all dwellings to have dual aspect, with the consequent advantages of access to daylight, sunlight and through ventilation. At second- and third-floor levels the structures are cut back to form roof terraces for the upper units. And the last bay to the ground floor is cut away entirely, by cantilevering the floors above over the access road to form a dramatic entrance to the common stair core at the end of each block.

Four of the spaces between the eight blocks, roughly parallel to each other, become the back-to-back gardens for the ground-floor maisonettes while the others become landscaped pedestrian cul-de-sacs or mews. One of the French contributions to the layout was to reduce the space between blocks to just 15 metres, a more efficient use of the site without any severe drawbacks from the point of view of privacy. All dwellings have either a garden, roof terrace or balcony.

The new Bourbon Lane is categorised as a 'home zone' with traffic-calming measures making the street and mews safe areas for children to play.

Each mews has its own sense of identity, clearly defining public from private space, and an informal car-parking layout is set between tall trees and native planting.

Unusually for buildings of this height, the primary structure is a steel frame, combined with external walls that are a prefabricated steel closed-panel cladding system providing a high degree of air-tightness. Walls are finished externally with a Siberian larch timber rainscreen. This is fixed horizontally with 12mm gaps between each board and promises to weather well. A fine-guage nylon mesh keeps out small birds.

Bourbon Lane boasts its own CHP plant, which supplies all space heating and hot water as well as satisfying a proportion of the electrical load. This is combined with whole-house ventilation including heat recovery, and U-values 20–25 per cent better than current Building Regulations. Energy costs should be very low, further encouraged by the installation of 'interface' units in each home that allow residents to see how much energy they are consuming. In terms of active mechanical services there is therefore much that is new to be tried out by residents and monitored by Octavia Housing and Care.

The number of innovative features at Bourbon Lane is entirely appropriate for a competition-winning scheme for a progressive housing association. All these features will, however, prove to be a distinct challenge for housing management and the association's maintenance team in the years to come. The history of collaboration between those responsible for development within most housing associations and those responsible for maintenance is an inglorious one. If developments such as Bourbon Lane are part of the journey towards all new housing being carbon neutral by 2016 the monitoring, resident support and maintenance will need to be of a very high standard indeed.

**Architect** Cartwright Pickard Architects
**Developer** Octavia Housing and Care
**Site** 0.81 hectares
**Number of dwellings** 78
**Density** 95 dwellings/hectare
**Mix** 2 x 5B + 5 x 4B + 12 x 3B + 31 x 2B + 28 x 1B
**Affordable** 100 per cent (58 per cent rent, 42 per cent shared ownership)
**Parking spaces per dwelling** 0.3

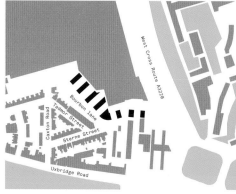

Site plan.

**Right** View of shared entrances to flats.

Layout plan — an almost impossible
site jammed up against the
monumental metal-clad wall of the
new Westfield shopping centre in
Shepherds Bush.

1:1000

**Right** External views showing cantilevered balconies and timber rainscreen fixed with gaps between each board, with a fine-gauge plastic net to exclude small animals.
**Below** Typical floor plans of one block.
**Bottom** Typical section showing a second-floor flat cantilevered over the shared entrance and with a roof terrace above it – a feat made possible by the steel-framed structure (see plans).
**Bottom right** View of shared circulation.

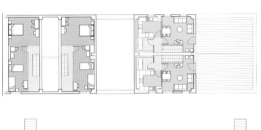

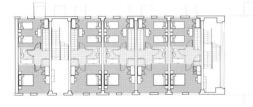

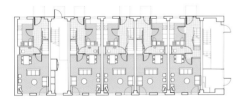

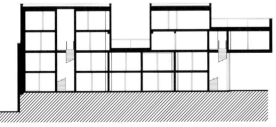

1:500

These 12 flats for keyworkers are part of a much larger regeneration project for the St Matthew's Estate. They are the result of a collaboration begun in 2003 between PRP Architects and Bill Dunster to produce an exemplar project, designed to put various low-energy initiatives into practice to reduce residents' heating costs, to be monitored over time. Costing 10 per cent more than constructing to current Building Regulations, the difference was covered by an additional grant from The Housing Corporation.

Apart from an emphasis on a combination of passive measures producing a building fabric with a highly efficient thermal performance and active measures such as solar collectors and a biomass boiler, this is an unusual scheme of flats in the way sunspaces have been integrated into the design. Each flat has a sunspace on the south side of the living room; this is constructed as part of a self-supporting steel-framed balcony structure, bolted on to the main masonry superstructure.

The building has a high thermal mass, absorbing surplus heat on warm days and evening out its distribution on cool days. This determined the choice of conventional load-bearing concrete block for the main structure.

As well as high standards of air-tightness, superinsulation and triple glazing, each flat is centrally ventilated with a built-in heat-recovery system. When solar collectors for domestic hot water and a central biomass fuel boiler are added, energy bills for each tenancy were expected to be £98 per year at the time of completion in 2003.

As built, the expected levels of $CO_2$ produced were 18.08kg/m²/year, which is only slightly above the government's initial target of a 60 per cent reduction (to 14.06kg/m²/year) by 2050. The design anticipates a future upgrade to include 130 square metres of photovoltaics mounted at roof level.

Apart from the determined attempt to address the issue of passive solar gain, this pilot project is also an exercise in 'future proofing'. It is, however, far from clear where housing associations will raise the necessary capital to add the renewables for which provision has been made. On the other hand it is a sensible objective. Renewable features such as photovoltaics will steadily reduce in relative cost as energy costs increase over time.

The combination of superinsulation and high standards of airtightness is the most important basic element, together with the central ventilation system. Keeping mechanical systems working effectively, especially in rented flats with a relatively frequent turnover of tenancies, is a new challenge to which designers can contribute by anticipating as far as possible the access that will be needed.

**Architects** PRP Architects with ZEDfactory
**Developer** Presentation Housing Association
**Site** 0.0752 hectares
**Number of dwellings** 12
**Density** 160 dwellings/hectare[1]
**Mix** 6 x 1B + 6 x 2B
**Affordable** 100 per cent
**Parking spaces per dwelling** none
[1] notional density: the development forms part of a large estate and the site has ill-defined boundaries

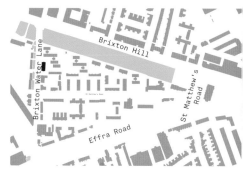

Site plan.

**Right** External sunspaces and self-supporting balconies on the street elevation.

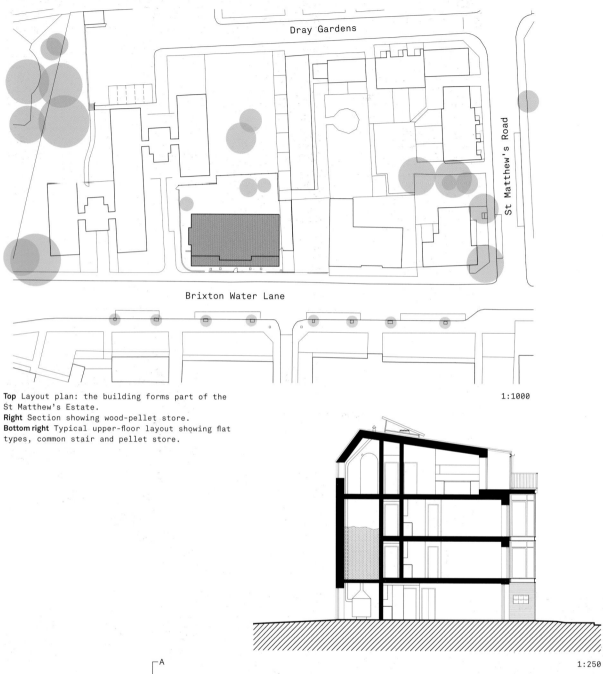

Dray Gardens

St Matthew's Road

Brixton Water Lane

**Top** Layout plan: the building forms part of the St Matthew's Estate.
**Right** Section showing wood-pellet store.
**Bottom right** Typical upper-floor layout showing flat types, common stair and pellet store.

1:1000

1:250

A

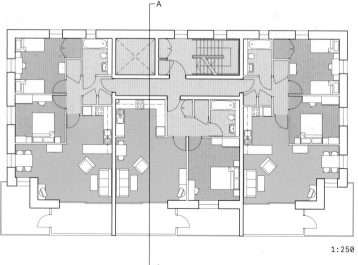

A

1:250

Top Exterior view.
Below The bio-mass boiler house.
Bottom right Passive solar sunspaces.

# Wembley City: large-scale waste management by Envac

Since World War 2 several different technical solutions have been tried for large-scale waste management in the UK. These include the Garchey system, which originated in France and was installed in a number of large new high-density developments for local authorities as far back as Quarry Hill, Sheffield, in 1939, and later at the Barbican in the City of London. This was a water-borne system for the removal of kitchen waste, to which every household in large blocks of flats had access from beneath the kitchen sink. What could be disposed of via a 100mm-diameter pipe was necessarily limited and a combination of abuse by householders and the enormous growth in the volume of packaging finally resulted in the system being taken out of service.

The Envac system, developed in Sweden from 1961, has been installed worldwide in 600 locations, serving private and social housing as well as commercial applications. It was selected as the central waste-management system for a new urban extension at Hammarby in Stockholm, where it has proved highly successful (Hammarby will eventually comprise 10,000 dwellings). Wembley City, the first Envac installation in the UK, will contain 4200 dwellings as part of a total residential and commercial development of 929,000 square metres. Obviously, the Envac installation has to be laid down along with the water supply, cabling, gas, electricity and drainage, as part of the urban infrastructure of a new neighbourhood consisting of at least 500 dwellings. Once the infrastructure is in place, as at Wembley, the phases of development can be attached to the Envac network as each comes on-stream.

Unlike earlier systems such as Garchey, Envac involves residents sorting their household waste and placing it in above-ground hoppers (the number varying according to the particular development's waste strategy) located in the street nearest to the block in which they live. Twice a day the waste accumulated beneath each hopper is drawn by a vacuum process to a central collection station. As the manufacturer's diagrams show, the advantages in terms of efficient and comprehensive recycling are enormous. At Hammarby the domestic by-products, waste and water are all recycled for electrical generation, biogas and space heating.

The impact of Envac on the design and layout of housing depends on the scale and density of development. Viable incorporation of the Envac system is much more an urban-design challenge than something that affects the design of buildings themselves – the underground installation is entirely external. It is hard to imagine the system being economic in developments at densities of less than 100–150 dwellings per hectare.

**Masterplanner** Rogers Stirk Harbour and Partners
**Architect** phase 1 PRP Architects
**Developers** Quintain Estates and Development plc + Genesis with Family Mosaic housing associations
**Site** 34.5 hectares
**Number of dwellings** 4200
**Density** 122 dwellings/hectare[1]
**Mix** 4 per cent x studios + 55 per cent x 1B + 35 per cent x 2B + 6 per cent x 3B
**Affordable** 47 per cent
**Parking spaces per dwelling** 0.46
**Non-housing uses** 929 square metres of development
[1] residential only covers a small part of the site. Within the area designated for housing the residential density is much higher than this

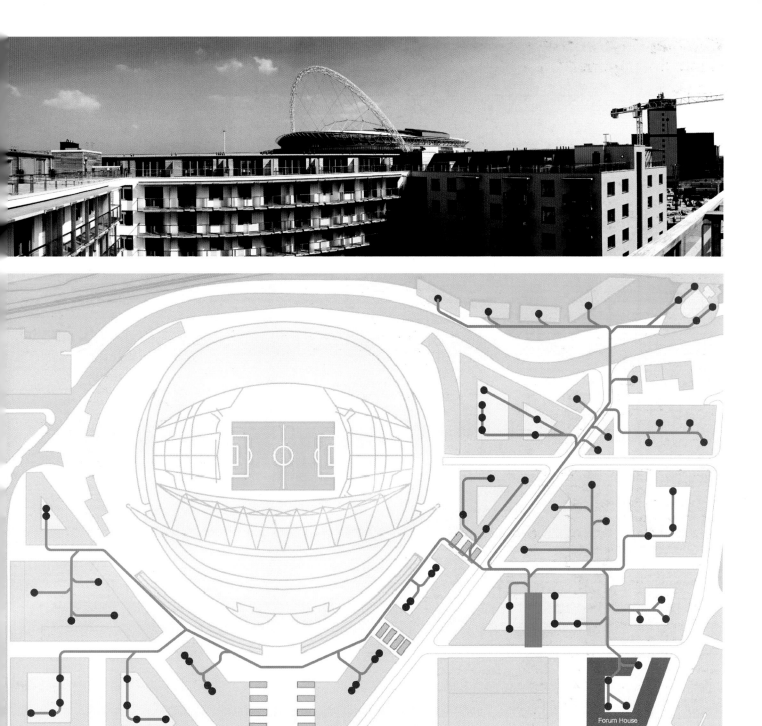

**Top** The first-phase flats complete.
**Above** Plan of the collection grid
of underground pipes at Wembley.

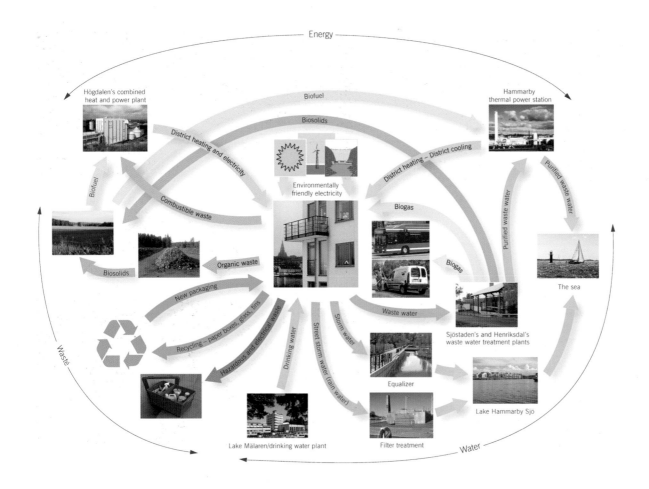

Energy

Högdalen's combined heat and power plant

Biofuel

Biosolids

Hammarby thermal power station

District heating and electricity

District heating – District cooling

Purified waste water

Biofuel

Environmentally friendly electricity

Combustible waste

Biogas

Purified waste water

Biosolids

Organic waste

Biogas

The sea

New packaging

Waste water

Sjöstaden's and Henriksdal's waste water treatment plants

Recycling – paper boxes, glass, tins

Hazardous and electrical waste

Drinking water

Street storm water (rain water)

Storm water

Waste

Equalizer

Lake Hammarby Sjö

Lake Mälaren/drinking water plant

Filter treatment

Water

**Top** The Hammarby model, showing all the processes in use there.
**Right** Envac hoppers at Hammarby, Stockholm.

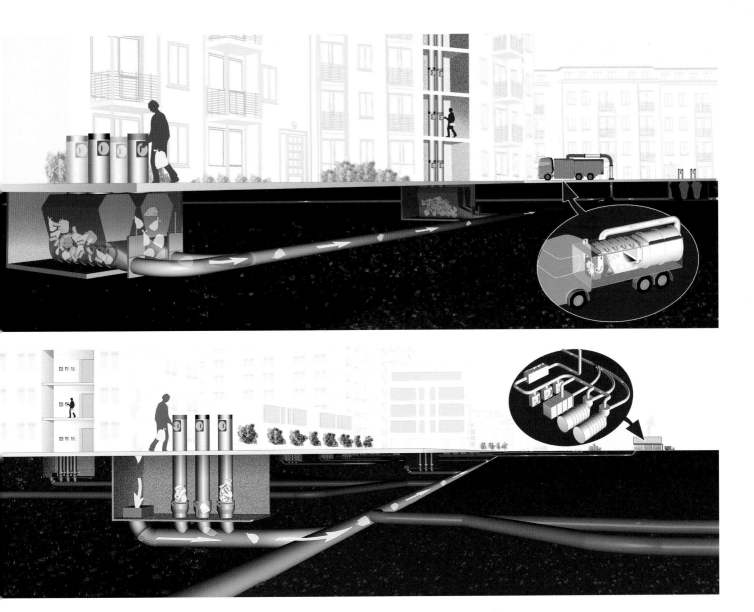

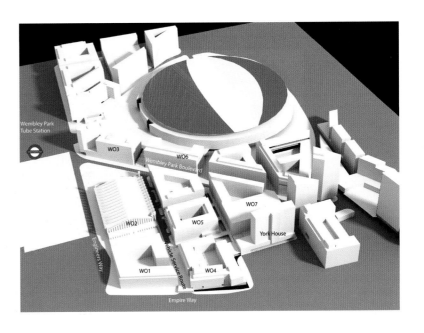

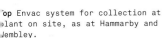

**Top** Envac system for collection at plant on site, as at Hammarby and Wembley.
**Centre** Envac system for on-site storage and subsequent removal by vehicle.
**Right** Aerial view of model showing high-density housing on a triangular site at the top of the image, above the stadium.

# The Hockerton Housing Project, Nottinghamshire

The original group of self-builders came together in 1993 and in 1996 obtained planning consent for five self-sufficient earth-sheltered houses on 10 hectares of agricultural land. The houses, designed by Brenda and Robert Vale with Nick Martin, who was also a project member, were designed to be self-sufficient in electrical energy, space and water heating and in the supply of water for all purposes. The aim was to achieve 'net zero' emissions.

The houses are designed without central heating but their high thermal mass – combined with superinsulation, central ventilation with heat recovery and conservatory/sunspaces – maintains them at an average 20 degrees C.

The autonomous water systems designed by David Leigh are divided into three separate parts – water for drinking, water for washing, bathing and flushing WCs, and water for irrigation – obviously with different degrees of filtration.

The entire supply of drinking water is collected from the glazed sunspace roofs and porches of the five houses and carried via copper gutters to concrete underground storage tanks. Each sunspace roof has an area of 66 square metres and this is sufficient to replenish the underground tanks, which have a total storage capacity of 25,000 litres. With average consumption of 20 litres per household per day there is sufficient supply for 250 days. The drinking water is pumped through a string filter, a carbon filter and a UV filter before being delivered to the houses.

Brenda and Robert Vale built a house for themselves which had a roof capable of collecting all the water they needed, but the area of more than 140 square metres is obviously not going to be achieved in the design of the average house. At Hockerton what is described as 'medium-grade' water is collected from rainwater run-off from the whole site, via swales at the side of the roads and the rear of the houses. It feeds into a sump at the lowest part of the site from where it is pumped into a reservoir of 25 x 3 x 2 metres deep, constructed at the highest level to store 150 cubic metres of

water. The filtration process consists of two 'slow sand' filters that remove solids and organic matter before the water passes into a holding tank to be pumped on demand to the point of use. The households estimate that their water consumption is only 25 per cent of a conventional home, but this is achieved through the general use of showers rather than baths, spray taps, water-efficient washing machines and low-flush WCs.

Due to the very low density of development and the surface-water catchment area there is no need for the Hockerton project to employ 'grey water' recycling. Grey water – waste water produced from domestic processes – accounts for about two-thirds of all household use. The other third is 'black water' used for flushing WCs; a number of proprietary systems are available that use bathing water for WC flushing or for garden irrigation. At Hockerton water for irrigating plants and vegetable cultivation is collected into a separate second pond and is untreated.

The water cycle is completed at Hockerton with its own sewage-treatment plant. This processes all water, including human waste, and finally delivers it into a lake that is suitable for swimming. There are two main components to this process. The effluent first passes for 10 to 15 days through a septic tank that allows solid matter to settle, and then into an elongated reed-bed system. The arrangement of suspended geotextile baffles in the reed bed ensures that liquid effluent spends up to three months being treated before passing through a gabion wall into the lake, having reached EU bathing quality standards. The design of the reed bed is extremely sophisticated , using both traditional and the latest scientific understanding of aquatic ecological processes, employing three types of reed floating on coir mats.

**Architects** Brenda and Robert Vale
**Developer** The Hockerton Housing Project
**Site** 10 hectares
**Number of dwellings** 5
**Density** 0.5 dwellings/hectare
**Mix** all single-storey family houses
**Affordable** none
**Parking spaces per dwelling** 1

**Top** General view of the five houses with the lake in the foreground.
**Above** Close-up view showing sunspaces and solar collectors with the reed bed for sewage processing at the head of the lake in the background.

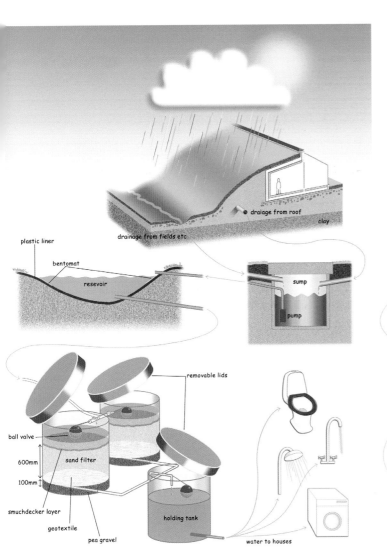

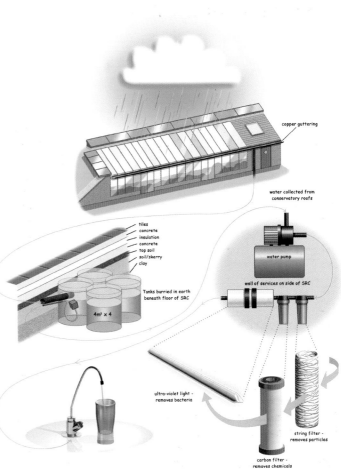

plastic liner
bentomat
resevoir

sump
pump

draiage from roof
drainage from fields etc
clay

removable lids
ball valve
600mm
100mm
sand filter
smuchdecker layer
geotextile
pea gravel
holding tank
water to houses

copper guttering
water collected from conservatory roofs
tiles
concrete
insulation
concrete
top soil
soil/skerry
clay
Tanks burried in earth beneath floor of SRC
4m³ x 4
water pump
wall of services on side of SRC
ultra-violet light - removes bacteria
string filter - removes particles
carbon filter - removes chemicals

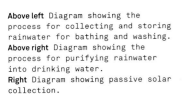

**Above left** Diagram showing the process for collecting and storing rainwater for bathing and washing.
**Above right** Diagram showing the process for purifying rainwater into drinking water.
**Right** Diagram showing passive solar collection.

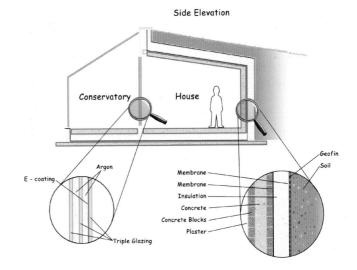

Side Elevation

Conservatory     House

E - coating
Argon
Triple Glazing

Geofin
Soil
Membrane
Membrane
Insulation
Concrete
Concrete Blocks
Plaster

**B** bedroom

**BRE Building Research Establishment** a trust providing research, consultancy and accreditation in many areas related to construction, including energy use and safety (www.bre.co.uk)

**CABE the Commission for Architecture and the Built Environment** (www.cabe. org.uk): a quango that advises government on architecture and urban design and is responsible (with the Home Builders Federation) for the Building for Life standards (www.buildingforlife.org)

**CHP Combined Heat and Power** (aka cogeneration): a technology that uses the surplus heat energy produced by electricity generation for space heating

**CGI computer graphic imagery** simulated pictures of buildings and projects, often reassuring, or even glamorous

**DCLG Department of Communities and Local Government** branded just as CLG, this is a government department, set up in 2001 and responsible for, among many other things, housing, planning and Building Regulations (www.communities.gov.uk)

**EnEV Energie-Einspar-Verordnung** the German federal energy-saving act. Covering all kinds of products and programmes, it prescribes, for example, the energy-effiency measures that are compulsory for new buildings. It defines the standards – progressive in UK terms – that must be met in order to qualify for state subsidies for construction or renovation

**EST Energy Saving Trust** a not-for-profit organisation providing free advice to businesses, communities and households, including information on achieving the energy criteria in the Code for Sustainable Homes (www.energysavingtrust.org.uk)

**GLA Greater London Authority** the strategic authority for the whole of London, set up in 1999 after a 13-year vacuum in the top tier of local government for the capital

**GLC Greater London Council** the strategic authority for the whole of London from 1965 (when it succeeded the London County Council) until 1986

**HBF the Home Builders Federation** represents and lobbies on behalf of the home-building industry (www.hbf.co.uk), and is jointly responsible (with CABE) for the Building for Life standards (www. buildingforlife.org)

**HCA the Homes and Communities Agency** a non-departmental public body sponsored by the DCLG. Its role in turn is to sponsor regeneration and communities throughout England (www.homesandcommunities. co.uk). Responsible for HQIs

**HQI Housing Quality Indicators** the HCA's system for assessing housing schemes (www.homesandcommunities.co.uk/hqi). HQIs incorporate the design standards that providers of affordable housing must meet if they receive NAHP funding

**HR habitable rooms** include living rooms, bedrooms, kitchens large enough to use for dining, etc.; exclude lobbies, bathrooms, etc.

**IMDA** internal minimum dwelling area

**LTH Lifetime Homes** a set of 16 design criteria intended to obviate the need to move home as families grow and change, and when infirmity sets in. The standards already apply in some areas and all publicly funded housing in England will have to be built to meet them from 2011. The private sector is supposed to follow in 2013 (www. lifetimehomes.org.uk)

**NAHP National Affordable Housing Programme** a government agency that funds new affordable housing and regulates housing associations. Despite the web address, it has already succeeded the Housing Corporation (www.housingcorp. gov.uk)

**NHF National Housing Federation** a body representing not-for-profit housing associations in England (www.housing. org.uk)

**P** person

**Pa pascal**, the SI unit of pressure, one newton per square metre

**PTAL** Public Transport Accessibility Level, a method of describing access to public transport that brings together frequency of, and distances from, transport services

**PV photovoltaics** the technology – emerging in the UK, emerged elsewhere – that converts light energy to electrical energy

**SAP Standard Assessment Procedure** the government's system for rating the energy performance of building. The procedure covers annual energy costs per unit of space and the predicted cost of water heating

**SBD Secured by Design** an initiative of the Association of Chief Police Officers, expressed in publications and online resources, that aims to baffle criminals by applying design criteria (www. securedbydesign.com/professionals/index. aspx)

**SIPS structural insulated panels** widely used in North America and Scandinavia and now being promoted in the UK as being environmentally friendly, flexible, light, etc.

**SLOAP** space left over after planning

**TMC** tenants management committee; **TMO** tenants management organisation

**UDP unitary development plan** a local authority's long-term strategy for land use and the policies and standards that will be used to make decisions on planning applications

# Sources of further information

...egulations and guidance change frequently. ...or up-to-date information go to http://www. ...outledge.com/9780415491501

## Accessibility
CABE: *Design and Access Statements: How to Write, Read and Use Them*. 2007. http://www.cabe.org.uk/AssetLibrary/8073.pdf

CABE: *The Principles of Inclusive Design. They Include You.)* 2006. http://www.cabe.org.uk/AssetLibrary/8853.pdf

GLA. *Wheelchair Accessible Housing: Best Practice Guidance* – consultation draft. March 2007. http://www.london.gov.uk/mayor/strategies/sds/docs/bpg-wheelchair-acc-housing.pdf

Habinteg Housing Association: *Lifetime Homes*. http://www.lifetimehomes.org.uk/

Habinteg Housing Association with Thorpe, S.: *The Wheelchair Housing Design Guide*. 2nd edition 2006. http://www.habinteg.org.uk/pages/whdg.html

National Disability Authority: *Building for Everyone*. 2002. http://www.nda.ie/cntmgmtnew.nsf/0/EBD4FB92816E8BB48025 6C830060F761/$File/Building_for_Everyone. pdf

*Older Persons' Housing Design: A European Good Practice Guide*. 2007. http://www.brighton-hove.gov.uk/index. cfm?request=c1163815

## Environment/sustainability
CABE: *Sustainable Design, Climate Change and the Built Environment*. http://www.cabe.org.uk/AssetLibrary/10661.pdf

DCLG: *Building a Greener Future: Policy Statement*. July 2007. http://www.communities.gov.uk/documents/planningandbuilding/pdf/building-greener.pdf

DCLG: *Code for Sustainable Homes: A Step-Change in Sustainable Home Building Practice*. December 2006. http://www.planningportal.gov.uk/uploads/code_for_sust_homes.pdf

DCLG: *Code for Sustainable Homes: Technical Guide*. May 2009. http://www.planningportal.gov.uk/uploads/code_for_sustainable_homes_techguide.pdf

DCLG: *Homes for the Future: More Affordable, More Sustainable*. Cm 7191. July 2007. http://www.communities.gov.uk/documents/housing/pdf/439986.pdf

English Partnerships: *A Climate of Change: English Partnerships' Response to the Environmental Agenda*. October 2006.

English Partnerships: *Carbon Challenge Standard Brief*. August 2007. http://www.englishpartnerships.co.uk/docdownload.aspx?doc=Carbon%20Challenge%20brief_0.pdf&pid=64241OphaK9K2AAJhl5lwMwRzZ4YhYXY

GLA with London Energy Partnership: website with on-line resources and toolkits at http://www.london.gov.uk/mayor/environment/energy/partnership-steering-group/index.jsp

Housing Corporation: *RuralZED: Affordable Sustainable Housing for Cornwall*. http://www.housingcorp.gov.uk/upload/pdf/CRHA_Rural_ZED_2005-07-29_FINAL_web72.pdf

## Health-related issues
CABE: *Physical Activity and the Built Environment*. 2006. http://www.cabe.org.uk/AssetLibrary/8954.pdf

Housing Corporation: Good Housing and Good Health? A Review and Recommendations for Housing and Health Practitioners. nd. http://www.housingcorp.gov.uk/upload/pdf/health_housing_20060816144328.pdf

## Housing quality including space standards
Building for Life standard: A Better Place to Live. November 2005. http://www.buildingforlife.org

Building for Life: *Delivering Great Places to Live* (includes BFL checklist). 2008. http://www.buildingforlife.org/AssetLibrary/9350.pdf

CABE: *Actions for Housing Growth: Creating a Legacy of Great Places*. February 2007. http://www.cabe.org.uk/files/Actions-for-housing-growth.pdf

CABE: *Buildings and Spaces: Why Design Matters*. March 2006. http://www.cabe.org.uk/files/buildings-and-spaces.pdf

CABE: *Creating Excellent Buildings: A Guide for Clients*. October 2003. http://www.cabe.org.uk/files/creating-excellent-buildings.pdf

CABE: *The Cost of Bad Design*. June 2006. http://www.cabe.org.uk/files/the-cost-of-bad-design.pdf

CABE: *Design Champions*. March 2006. http://www.cabe.org.uk/files/design-champions.pdf

CABE: *Design Review-ed* [sic] *Urban Housing: Lessons Learnt from Projects Reviewed by CABE's Expert Design Panel*. July 2004. http://www.cabe.org.uk/files/design-review-ed-urban-housing.pdf

CABE: *Housing: Raising Standards*. PowerPoint presentation. March 2007.

CABE: *What Home Buyers Want: Attitudes and Decision Making Among Consumers*. March 2005. http://www.cabe.org.uk/files/what-home-buyers-want.pdf

Carroll, Caitriona, Cowans, Julie and Darton, David (eds): *Meeting Part M and Designing Lifetime Homes*. Joseph Rowntree Foundation. 1999. http://www.jrf.org.uk/bookshop/eBooks/1859351441.pdf

DCLG: *Housing Quality Indicators*. http://www.communities.gov.uk/housingqualityindicators

DCLG: *Housing Quality Indicators: Housing Scheme Data Sheets*

DCLG. HQIs: Scoring spreadsheet

Drury, A. *Standards and Quality in Development: A Good Practice Guide*. 2nd edition. NHF. 2008

English Partnerships: *Quality Standards: Delivering Quality Places.* Revised November 2007. http://www.englishpartnerships.co.uk/qualityandinnovationpublications.htm

Housing Corporation: *Design and Quality Standards.* April 2007. http://www.housingcorp.gov.uk/upload/pdf/Design_quality_standards.pdf

Housing Corporation: *Design and Quality Strategy.* April 2007. http://www.housingcorp.gov.uk/upload/pdf/design_and_quality_strategy_20070501111140.pdf

Housing Corporation: *HQI: Housing Quality Indicators* (version 4). April 2007. http://www.housingcorp.gov.uk/upload/pdf/HQIFormv4_Apr_2007.pdf

Housing Corporation: *Plans That Meet the Standards.* http://www.housingcorp.gov.uk/server/show/conWebDoc.1058

HTA, LBA, PRP and PTE with Design for Homes: *Recommendations for Living at Superdensity.* NHBC, 2007. http://www.designforhomes.org/pdfs/Superdensity.pdf

London Housing Federation: *Higher Density Housing for Families: A Design and Specification Guide.* 2004. (Order from http://www.housing.org.uk/)

Office of the Deputy Prime Minister: *The Future for Design Codes: Further Information to Support Stakeholders Reading Draft PPS3.* December 2005. http://www.communities.gov.uk/documents/planningandbuilding/pdf/142898.pdf

**Modern methods of construction**
CABE: *Design and Modern Methods of Construction.* nd. http://www.housingcorp.gov.uk/upload/pdf/MMC_full_report.pdf

Housing Corporation: *Modern Talking: Building Better Value Homes Using Modern Approaches.* February 2007. http://www.housingcorp.gov.uk/upload/pdf/ModernTalking.pdf

**Planning policy**
DCLG: *Planning Policy Statement 1: Delivering Sustainable Development.* February 2005. http://www.communities.gov.uk/documents/planningandbuilding/pdf/planningpolicystatement1.pdf

DCLG: *Planning Policy Statement 3: Housing.* November 2006. http://www.communities.gov.uk/documents/planningandbuilding/pdf/planningpolicystatement3.pdf

DCLG: *Planning Policy Statement 7: Sustainable Development in Rural Areas.* August 2004. http://www.communities.gov.uk/documents/planningandbuilding/pdf/147402.pdf

DCLG: *Planning Policy Statement 22: Renewable Energy* (includes a companion guide). November 2006. http://www.communities.gov.uk/documents/planningandbuilding/pdf/147444.pdf

DCLG: *Housing: Overview of Policy for Housing Demand and Supply* (web links to the Barker Review and other related resources). http://www.communities.gov.uk/housing/housingsupply/overviewpolicy/
DCLG: *Planning Policy Statement 25: Development and Flood Risk.* November 2006. http://www.communities.gov.uk/publications/planningandbuilding/pps25floodrisk

GLA: *The London Housing Strategy: Draft for Public Consultation.* May 2009. http://www.london.gov.uk/mayor/housing/strategy/docs/london-housing-strategy09.pdf

GLA: *Sustainable Design and Construction: Supplementary Planning Guidance.* May 2006. http://www.london.gov.uk/mayor/strategies/sds/docs/spg-sustainable-design.pdf

GLA: *The London Plan: Spatial Development Strategy for Greater London.* February 2004. http://www.london.gov.uk/mayor/strategies/sds/london_plan/lon_plan_all.pdf

GLA: *Planning for Equality and Diversity in London: Draft Supplementary Planning Guidance.* December 2006. http://www.london.gov.uk/mayor/strategies/sds/docs/spg-planning-for-equality2.pdf

GLA: *Connecting with London's Nature: The Mayor's Biodiversity Strategy.* July 2002. http://www.london.gov.uk/mayor/strategies/biodiversity/docs/strat_full.pdf

GLA: *Green Light to Clean Power: The Mayor's Energy Strategy.* February 2004. http://www.london.gov.uk/mayor/strategies/energy/docs/energy_strategy04.pdf

GLA: *Housing: The London Plan Supplementary Planning Guidance.* November 2005. http://www.london.gov.uk/mayor/strategies/sds/docs/spg-housing.pdf

**Security**
ACPO: *Secured by Design – New Homes.* June 2004 (version 1).http://www.securedbydesign.com/pdfs/SBD-principles.pdf

Office of the Deputy Prime Minister: *Safer Places: The Planning System and Crime Prevention.* February 2004. http://www.communities.gov.uk/documents/planningandbuilding/pdf/147627.pdf

Office of the Deputy Prime Minister: *The Fire Prevention Handbook.* August 2005. http://www.firekills.gov.uk/handbook/pdf/handbook-english.pdf

**Site appraisal/development potential**
CABE and English Heritage: *Guidance on Tall Buildings.* March 2003. http://www.english-heritage.org.uk/upload/pdf/Guid_tall_build.pdf

English Partnerships: *The Brownfield Guide: A Practitioner's Guide to Land Reuse in England.* (Six parts and six annexes.) 2006. http://www.englishpartnerships.co.uk/docdownload.aspx?doc=Cover%20intro_0.pdf&pid=64241OphaK9K2AAJhl5lwMwRzZ4YhYXY

NIHE (Northern Ireland Housing Executive) Higher Density Design for Quality and Low Maintenance. http://www.nihe.gov.uk

Office of the Deputy Prime Minister: *Housing Land Availability Assessments: Identifying Appropriate Land for Housing Development: Draft Practice Guidance*. December 2005. http://www.communities.gov.uk/documents/planningandbuilding/pdf/143075.pdf

Office of the Deputy Prime Minister: Housing Market Assessments: Draft Practice Guidance. December 2005. http://www.communities.gov.uk/documents/planningandbuilding/pdf/142889.pdf

## Space standards (Parker Morris)

GLA: *Housing Space Standards*. August 2006. http://www.london.gov.uk/mayor/planning/docs/space-standards.pdf

Ministry of Housing and Local Government: *Homes for Today & Tomorrow* (the Parker Morris report).HMSO. 1961, 1964, 1969.

Ministry of Housing and Local Government: *Space in the Home*. (Design Bulletin no. 6) 1965 (extract)

## Urban design/external environment

Building for Life/CABE: *Accommodating the Car*. (Building for Life Newsletter 02/06) http://www.cabe.org.uk/files/building-for-life-newsletter-issue-6.pdf

Building for Life/CABE: *Better Neighbourhoods: Making Higher Densities Work*. March 2005. http://www.cabe.org.uk/files/better-neighbourhoods.pdf

Building for Life/CABE: *Evaluating Housing Proposals Step by Step*. March 2008. http://www.cabe.org.uk/files/evaluating-housing-proposals-step-by-step.pdf

CABE: *Better Places to Live by Design: A Companion Guide to PPG3*. September 2001.

CABE: *Creating Successful Masterplans: A Guide for Clients*. March 2004, new edition April 2008. http://www.cabe.org.uk/files/creating-successful-masterplans.pdf

CABE: *Decent Parks? Decent Behaviour?* May 2005. http://www.cabe.org.uk/files/decent-parks-decent-behaviour.pdf

CABE: *Design Re-viewed* [sic] *Urban Housing: Lessons Learnt from Projects Reviewed by CABE's Expert Design Panel*. July 2004. http://www.cabe.org.uk/files/design-review-ed-urban-housing.pdf

CABE. *Green Space Strategies: A Good Practice Guide*. May 2004. http://www.cabe.org.uk/files/green-space-strategies.pdf

CABE: *Involving Young People in the Design and Care of Urban Spaces: What Would You Do With This Space?* May 2004. http://www.cabe.org.uk/files/what-would-you-do-with-this-space.pdf

CABE: *It's Our Space: A Guide for Community Groups Working to Improve Public Space*. February 2007. http://www.cabe.org.uk/files/Its-our-space.pdf

CABE: *Paved With Gold: The Real Value of Good Street Design*. June 2007. http://www.cabe.org.uk/files/paved-with-gold.pdf

CABE: *Start With the Park: Creating Sustainable Urban Green Spaces in Areas of Housing Growth and Renewal*. July 2005. http://www.cabe.org.uk/files/start-with-the-park.pdf

CABE: *This Way to Better Streets: 10 Case Studies on Improving Street Design*. July 2007. http://www.cabe.org.uk/files/this-way-to-better-streets.pdf

CABE: *What Its Like to Live There: The View of Residents on the Design of New Housing*. November 2005. http://www.cabe.org.uk/files/what-its-like-to-live-there.pdf

DCLG: *Manual for Streets*. March 2007. http://www.communities.gov.uk/documents/planningandbuilding/pdf/322449.pdf

Design for Homes: *Perceptions of Privacy and High Density*. 2003.

English Partnerships: *Car Parking: What Works Where?* 2006. http://www.englishpartnerships.co.uk/publications.htm#bestpractice

English Partnerships and Housing Corporation: *Delivering Quality Places: Urban Design Compendium 2*. September 2007. http://www.urbandesigncompendium.co.uk/public/documents/UDC2FULL.pdf

Frith, M., Harrison, S.: *Decent Homes, Decent Spaces: Improving the Green Spaces for Social Housing*. c. 2005 http://www.neighbourhoodsgreen.org.uk/ng/_ui/dhds.pdf

GLA: *Providing for Children and Young People's Play and Informal Recreation. Draft Supplementary Planning Guidance*. October 2006. http://www.london.gov.uk/mayor/strategies/sds/docs/spg-children-recreation.pdf

Housing Corporation: *The Williams Report: Quality First: The Commission on the Design of Affordable Housing in the Thames Gateway*. http://www.housingcorp.gov.uk/upload/pdf/Thames_Gateway_final.pdf

Institute of Highways Engineers: *Home Zone Design Guidelines*. June 2002. http://www.ihie.org.uk/gateway/home-zones/home-zones/

Llewellyn-Davies for English Partnerships: *The Urban Design Compendium*. Second edition 2007. http://www.urbandesigncompendium.co.uk/OrderACopy.aspx

London Housing Federation: *Think Big: Delivering Family Homes for Londoners*. n.d. http://www.housing.org.uk/Uploads/File/London%20Housing%20Federation/Publications/Final%204pp%20summary.pdf

National Housing Federation: *No Parking: Making Low or Zero Parking Work on Higher Density Housing Schemes*. March 2006. http://www.eukn.org/binaries/greatbritain/bulk/research/2006/12/no-parking.pdf

# Index

# acknowledgments

**Levitt Bernstein**
Simon Aitken
Dave Burrough
Jo McCafferty
Andy Jobling
Julia Park
Sofie Pelsmakers
Jackie Wood

**Design for Homes**
David Birkbeck
Ivan Lazarevic

**Photographers who have kindly donated their work**
Nicholas Champkins
David Churchill
Peter Cook
Tim Crocker
Nick Dawe
Nick Hufton
Katsuhisa Kida
Benedict Luxmoore
John MacLean
Joanna Shaw
Gillian O' Sullivan
Tom Scott
Galit Seligmann
Morley von Sternberg
Charlotte Wood

**Architectural practices who have kindly contributed their work**
Cartwright Pickard
Chetwoods
Edward Cullinan
Rolf Disch
FCB Studios
Hawkins\Brown
HTA architects
Festico + Whiles
Maccreanor Lavington
Metropolitan Workshop
Monahan Blythen Hopkins
Munkenbeck and Marshall
Pollard Thomas Edwards
Proctor and Matthews
PRP
Rogers Stirk Harbour
Rolfe Judd
ShedKM
Sheppard Robson
ZEDfactory

**Structural engineering advice**
Edge Structures

**Manufacturers**
Envac AB

**Managing and recycling waste**
Robin Murray

**Hockerton Housing Project**
Bill Bolton
HHP Trading Limited

The Authors and Publishers would like to recognise and thank Design for Homes for all the support they have provided for this publication.

Design for Homes is a research company set up in 2000 to improve design, planning and construction which invests its profits in spreading awareness of what works best, such as by sponsoring David Levitt's book.

Part of the organisation's work is to investigate trade-offs between consumer preferences and professional imperatives. This has shaped research such as 'Perceptions of Privacy and Density in Higher Density Housing' as well as 'Car Parking: What works where', a toolkit looking at more than 100 treatments published with English Partnerships.

Design for Homes created the Building for Life assessment tool in 2002, now a core tool for the public sector to assess housing proposals. It was part of a team which created a similar tool for Ireland which became a statutory instrument in 2008.

The organization set up the swingacat.info website with the developer Gentoo making recommendations to householders on plan form and size of home for their families. It also published the 'Recommendations for living at Superdensity' report in partnership with four architectural practices whose work is featured in this book.

Design for Homes manages England's Housing Design Awards. It has made films of the best winners which are streamed from its website.

The organization is an expert on low-carbon strategies for housebuilding, working with partners such as the Zero Carbon Hub to find solutions and organizing study visits to see viable models in UK and northern Europe. Go to www.designforhomes.org for more details.